MARY WHITALL THOMAS

A
QUAKER CHILDHOOD

BY

HELEN THOMAS FLEXNER

What is your substance, whereof are you made,
That millions of strange shadows on you tend?

SHAKESPEARE, Sonnet LIII.

NEW HAVEN · YALE UNIVERSITY PRESS
1940

COPYRIGHT, 1940, BY HELEN THOMAS FLEXNER

PRINTED IN THE UNITED STATES OF AMERICA

TO SIMON FLEXNER

PREFACE

THE people in this book are described as they appeared to the author. The truth I have endeavored to present is the truth of my own impressions, feelings, and judgments during the seventeen years from 1871 to 1888 when I lived at home as the youngest daughter of a large family. I make no other claim for accuracy in this picture of a long-vanished world when belief in Progress under the guiding hand of Providence was the foundation stone of thinking and optimism the dominant mood.

My parents were typical of the last quarter of the nineteenth century, though they were somewhat separated from their contemporaries by being members of the orthodox branch of the Society of Friends. Quakers thought of themselves as a peculiar people with a definite mission in the world and my parents, while scrupulously doing their duty to the Friends Meeting in Baltimore, also took part in many outside benevolent activities.

Already as a small girl and throughout my childhood and youth I lived in the midst of great numbers of people. My older brothers and sisters, six of them, were dominant over me, petting me, teasing me, or disregarding me. Relatives of my parents' generation, grave, terrifying personalities, came and went in the house. Coworkers of my father and mother in some

good cause, religious, moral, or educational, appeared for conferences, staying sometimes as guests for weeks. So many people and so many crusades would have completely bewildered and overwhelmed me had it not been for my mother. Though my father was vivid to me and important, it was my mother who watched over me day by day and whose love was my refuge. Thus I grew up carefully protected and surrounded by people, but none the less subject to shattering influences and isolated in my own world, alone with myself like all human beings.

My memories of what I experienced, hoped for, and dreamed during these seventeen years of my life have been difficult to disentangle and interpret. Two main themes have seemed to me of paramount interest, the dilemma of a child with many older brothers and sisters, and, more significant still, the fate of my mother. She lived on for me after her death, always present in my imagination, until at last the impulse to tell her story and mine could no longer be resisted.

CONTENTS

ILLUSTRATIONS

A QUAKER CHILDHOOD

I

EARLY ENCHANTMENT

I AM seated in the rain-darkened hall on the top step of a long flight of stairs down which I dare not venture, watching for my mother to come home. For a very long time I have kept my eyes fixed on the dark street door under an oblong of grayness far off at the end of the vista, watching, watching for it to open and let my mother in. Though I catch my breath every now and then with a faint sob, I struggle hard to control my anguish. Suddenly an instant of terrible brightness shows the long handrail, the table, the sofa in the hall below, the hatrack, the frame of the window, the dark, square door, heavy, motionless, closed. Then darkness in a crash of sound. I scream wildly for my mother. From his room near by my father appears and gathers his little daughter up in his arms. I stifle my sobs against his shoulder while he assures me that my mother is safe. She will be at home very soon. God is watching over her. This is my earliest memory.

Moments of complete peace when I was a tiny child I also remember. My mother's soft embrace enfolding me, the nursery fire, my father's voice singing of trust in God, his figure looming vaguely opposite in the light from the flaming logs. Of my

1

little brother in my father's arms I am just faintly aware. My mother has rocked me into a state of enchanted oblivion.

My mother, my father, and God, fear and love for them—nothing else remains of the first four years of my life.

The next picture that presents itself has an impersonal quality, as though I were outside of it, a mere observer. I see a little girl standing before her mother in a bright, warm room and I hear a shrill childish voice whisper, "Get thee behind me, Satan." The child glances furtively over her shoulder. Only a broad band of sunlight in which the dust motes dance is visible at her back. Reassured, she looks up into her mother's face and repeats in louder, firmer tones, "Get thee behind me, Satan! Get thee behind me!" then throws herself sobbing into her mother's arms.

That trembling, excited child, so external to me now, was once myself, I know by some strange inner certainty. And the magic phrase I repeated was given me by my mother to control a passionate temper. But, alas! Satan thus frequently addressed was as real a person to me as any other. Even in the sunny, well-inhabited nursery where he was invisible, his presence behind my back made being virtuous far from a comfortable state. Outside the nursery with the shadowy solitude of the great house all about her a little girl might come upon him in some awful shape around any corner. The huge, dark closet in a back wing past which I was often forced to go was his favorite lurking place during the daytime. It was full of black-

ness, deep and impenetrable. Whether the door was shut or open, I raced by as fast as I could along the empty passage way to escape a sudden snatching of long arms. At nighttime Satan grew very bold. The whole house was haunted by his presence. Every empty room, even my mother's, was full of him, so that when I was forced to go upstairs after dark on some errand I begged my mother to send her voice with me. While the magic refrain, "I am here! I am here!" sounded in my ears, however faint and distant up the long stairway, I was not afraid.

All the forces that threatened my safety and my virtue were embodied for me in the person of Satan. Sometimes I caught a glimpse of him, shining eyes peeping from a shadow, outline of a dark form lurking; more often he was a presence felt but not seen. Immensely powerful as he was, this evil spirit was controlled by my mother and my father. In some mysterious way God helped them, I knew. He was outside, far away in heaven, for, unlike Satan, God had no dwelling place in our house. I prayed to him morning and evening, and I believed that he heard me. Still, when I had finished my prayers, the face into which I looked up was my mother's or my father's face. When my parents were at hand, it was they who helped me. If danger threatened me in their absence, I cried out passionately to God. But I could not have faith in Him for long; unless quickly rescued, I gave myself up for lost and sobbed in uncontrollable terror, as on one occasion I remember when in a crowd I was unable to find my mother.

3

Counted by the calendar, Satan's presence in our house must have been brief. I have no memories by which I can fix the date of his disappearance. What drove him out also remains a mystery. I am no longer afraid of him, that is all I know.

No one about me could have suspected the dark terror in which I lived. I believed in Satan as easily and on the same terms as I believed in every other person and thing in my world. He was an ever-present enemy against whom my mother often warned me. How could I understand that the name "Satan" was a symbol for her? Sometimes I could not see him, it is true, but sometimes there he was before my eyes, that was his particular power. I lived in the isolation of a younger child in a large family, the members of which came and went in the house for reasons not understood by me. My little brother, a year and a half my junior and delicate from birth, absorbed all the nursery attention that was left over after our baby sister, the tenth and last child in the family, had been cared for. Unless I was either naughty or ill no one had time to bother much about me.

All through the summer when from being five I became six years old, Dora was ill. Suddenly one morning I was told by my father that God had taken Dora to be an angel with Him in heaven. She was dead. Sent in to see my mother at last, I eagerly opened the door behind which she had been hidden from me for days. Though it was bright daylight in the hall, my mother's room was dark. At the far end I saw her bending over a pillow on her knees, but not until I had crept to her

side did she raise her eyes. Her grief-stricken face
transfixed me. I had perceived in a flash as I
entered that there was a motionless figure on the
pillow she held; its little white face with closed
eyes looked like a doll's face. I thought only of
my mother. She kissed me in silence and her
silence conveyed her grief to me with overwhelm-
ing force.

Later in the day when I was playing in the cool
shadow of the house, I watched a strange man
carry in through the side door a queer box, small
and narrow and shiningly white. Instantly I knew
its purpose. My baby sister was to be shut up in
that shining white box, and this was what it meant
to be dead. Horror seized me. And throughout my
childhood I continued to shudder before death
whenever I saw its trappings—a little white coffin
in an undertaker's window, a mound of green grass
on a hilltop with a white marble stone at foot and
head. To jump over the small heaped-up mound
of Dora's grave as my little brother in his high
spirit sometimes did when my mother took us with
her to visit it seemed to me an intolerable outrage.
My mind faltered before it. Once when I heard my
elders saying that my Great-Uncle Galloway Ches-
ton had died in the very bed where his wife also
had died years before, I broke in to ask, "Did he
die in the same sheets?" and then fled from the
room pursued by the horror of my question. For
many years when I woke suddenly in the night the
chill of those sheets shivered through me.

More peaceful memories center about the figure
of our family nurse whose sole charge Frank and I

became after Dora's death. Her face was very old and wrinkled. It was surmounted by iron-gray hair, parted and smoothed down on each side. Above the back of her head as I looked up at her, braids of a rich brown color showed—beautiful braids. Frank and I played together in the sunny nursery while she sewed. I can see her sitting in a low chair with her back to the window, one hand thrust into a stocking and a workbasket beside her. When we quarreled or were too noisy perhaps, she rapped one or the other of us sharply on the head with her thimble. We took care to keep within reach and waited with thrills of excitement for her sudden rap. The quiet smile that gleams on her face tells me that she knew how delicious to us was her part in our games. Memories of her out of doors I have none. Always she is in the house, appearing in some downstairs room to carry us off, buttoning up our clothes while we twist about impatiently, curling Frank's soft brown hair over his own little comb—how I admired the result!— or brushing my own wild red mop into smooth, hollow tubes over the long, varnished curling stick kept for that purpose. I was proud of my curls though I hated to stand still while they were being created. Always Nurse was gentle and kind even though I sometimes shed tears over the evening tangles.

When she left us, a year, perhaps, after Dora's death, or it may be only a few months, the responsibility of caring for Frank as well as for myself rested upon me. The first period of my life had merged into the second.

6

The meeting house of the Society of Friends, though a long way down the street and reached by horsecar, seemed almost a part of our house. Following my mother up the aisle on the women's side under the high windows, Frank and I were left by her on the front bench while she went past us up the gallery steps to her place facing the congregation. Above her on the men's side of the gallery benches sat my father at the head of the meeting. The big room, evenly lighted by a row of tall, blank windows high in the wall to right and left, was intensely quiet with the silence of many people. To sit alone with Frank on the front bench involved an awful responsibility even though my mother was there just above us. I constantly turned my eyes to her face while I tried to keep my small brother still and to sit very still myself during the long hour until, by shaking hands with the friend next him, my father broke up meeting.

Always my father preached. His voice rose and fell in an exciting way; his gestures were odd and interesting to watch. Usually Grandmother Thomas, just above my mother at the head of the meeting on the women's side, kneeling down, chanted a prayer. Her face, closed eyes, and pleading mouth, outlined by the stiff Quaker bonnet, was visible above the gallery rail. The rise and fall of her voice moved me strangely. Sometimes in the midst of the intense stillness my mother rose to her feet. Then I sat up very straight and listened intently, trying to understand the meaning of her words. She spoke of God's love for his children,

7

of the peace trust in God brings the soul, of salvation through Jesus Christ our Lord, but my imagination traveled no further than my mother. And the voice that told me next morning what dress to put on in answer to my daily question—"Mother, what shall I wear today?"—was the very same voice that had thrilled through me in the sacred quietness.

Even at this early age I hated to see my mother busy with household cares. The belief that I could relieve her of one duty at least by watching over Frank increased for me the pleasure of having him dependent on me. Now the baby of the family, Frank was petted by everyone. In particular he was idolized by my father, who used often to say that the diet of bananas and Apollinaris water devised by him had saved Frank's life during his dangerous illness. Thus the double tenderness of parent and physician, for my father was by profession a doctor, centered on the delicate little boy, who had only to ask for what he wanted to get it immediately. When still very young he had procured for us our new nursery carpet after much excited plotting upstairs. Frank was coached by our nurse in just what to say and when to say it, and she was jubilant over the outcome of her scheme. I have no direct memory of this incident. What remains in my mind is my delight in Nurse's successful plot, whenever I heard her tell the story. Frank's seat at table was next my father's and many were the delicious morsels transferred to his plate. A slice of white bread covered with carefully chosen bits of shad meat from which even the

DR. JAMES CAREY THOMAS

tiniest bone had been removed remains for me one of the greatest of life's unattainable goods. Still, in spite of this wistful image, I believe that I was not at any time jealous of Frank. It was natural that my father should cherish so charming and delicate a little creature. Moreover he was my own particular charge, and a little girl far down in the family acquired dignity from having so important a responsibility.

One summer's afternoon my little brother and I were playing near a group of our elders who were seated out of the sun under a canopy of trees. Some toy we wanted had been left in the nursery. Walking gravely over the grass to stand in front of my mother, I said, "Mother, will thee please take care of Frankie for me while I go into the house? I won't be long." My mother promised gravely that she would do as I asked, but an elder brother who was present by chance repeated my words in jeering tones, shouting with laughter. I had to hear the story told and retold many times, and once during some discussion of plans Bond, or perhaps it was Harry, said, "Since Nellie won't be here to manage, I suppose we shall have to ask Mother to do the best she can for us." Then my mother intervened, and from that moment the matter ceased to be a favorite joke with my brothers. But for a long time I continued to brood over my outraged dignity. Since I had not intended to put myself in my mother's place but merely to report to her that I was leaving the charge she had given me, I could not see why doing my duty should have made me ridiculous. I felt bitterly that

9

the boys were unjust as well as cruel in teasing me.

"Gather the flowers of pleasure in the fields of duty" was one of the homely precepts constantly repeated to us by my mother, who had learned them from her own father. In this instance the flower in duty's path had turned out to be a thistle that pricked sharply. "Stand up to the rack, fodder or no fodder" was another of my grandfather's sayings that proved misleading, since an empty fodder rack has a way of remaining empty. Still in spite of many disappointments I went on invoking these ancestral charms, in the hope, I suppose, that they might help.

I was without doubt a very good little girl. No promptings to say my prayers morning and evening were ever needed; I enjoyed going to meeting and to Sunday School; I always knew the Bible lesson. With enthusiasm I gave my pennies to the poor and signed the temperance pledge. Side by side with my little brother I delighted to march in the children's "Band of Hope" about the informal, low-ceilinged basement room of the meeting house which was entered not by the high stone steps and imposing great doors of the main room, but by a small door on a side street. Frank as well as I, initiated by my father, had taken the pledge necessary for joining, and I felt an exhilarating sense of virtue in renouncing intoxicating liquor, though I had never seen anyone drink it, much less tasted it myself. When my mother's mother, who lived in Philadelphia, was expected for a visit it was hardly necessary to remind me that Frank and I must behave very quietly. But we were both

warned often and with emphasis not to mention the piano we had seen covered over and pushed from its place in our sitting room back into a dark corner behind the sofa. This concealment, which amazed me, was explained to us as an act of consideration for Grandmother Whitall, who followed the strict Philadelphia Quaker tradition in regard to the sinfulness of music and would be distressed to find a piano in her daughter's house. I was thrilled by sharing a secret of this sort with my parents. For years the sight of our piano reigning again in its place gave me a stab of pride.

Besides my mother's family many other people were entertained in our house. I could not distinguish between them. The talk seemed always to turn on religious questions. Lingering near my mother I was often present at earnest discussions, and even as quite a little girl I began to ponder what was said. To my amazement I discovered that my mother and father differed on certain points. I took my mother's side the more passionately because visiting friends as a rule upheld my father. God was all powerful, loving, and just, so far there was general agreement. God was like my parents. Slowly I began to comprehend that he was believed also to be very terrible, cruel, and unjust, punishing forever the sins of his children who had died. My mother protested against the doctrine of eternal punishment. How I admired her when I heard her accused of the heresy called "restitution"! I paid close attention to every attack on her. Restitution meant, I found, that if you died without believing in the name of Christ, you would suffer

11

punishment for a long time in hell, but that at last even if you were a heathen and had never heard of Christ, you would get to heaven through Christ's sacrifice on the cross. This final act of mercy was denied by my father, and I heard him urge my mother not to preach so harmful a doctrine. To me even my mother's doctrine seemed horribly cruel. I could not believe that God would hand over to the devil any one of his children for punishment. How could my mother, who was herself incapable of cruelty, believe such a thing of God? I remember brooding over this question on many occasions which are associated in my mind with the big front parlor where visitors were entertained, yet I never thought of asking my mother to help me answer it. To express in words a conflict of emotions that seemed to be a criticism of her would have required a great deal of encouragement from my mother as well as more time than she ever had to spend alone with me.

Though I prayed to God morning and evening to forgive my sins for Jesus Christ's sake, I believe I had no real feeling of guilt before Him. I cannot remember rejoicing in His forgiveness or His approval. My prayers, in so far as they meant anything to me, served as charms against threatened dangers, Satan in particular. It was my mother's approval that I desired. I longed to please her so earnestly that doing what she told me was a joy. If by inadvertence I displeased her, then indeed I was sorry. I could not be happy until I had been forgiven by my mother.

With the Bible stories I was thoroughly familiar

of course, but no pictures helped out my childish imagination since images of sacred things were considered to be in the nature of idolatry by Quakers at that time. Used as I was to scriptural language and lover of long words like many children, there was still much I could not understand in my father's daily reading aloud from the Bible after breakfast. On the other hand our edition of *Pilgrim's Progress* was illustrated by marvelous pictures. I delighted above all in Christian losing his load of sins, the great bundle falling from his back and the ecstatic uplifting of his hands. I still enjoy thinking of them. Then there were the lions, terrible roaring beasts that barred the way just in front of him. They made me shiver with terror. How could Christian ever get by them? The picture over the page, showing these monsters held back by stout chains when they leapt fiercely out at him, was a great relief. Dramatizing the story, I used to make for myself and for my little brother bundles out of wooden blocks tied up in a towel and hang them over his shoulders and my own to represent our sins. Only for me the bending down and groaning under their weight was quite as much fun as suddenly to drop them with a clatter and stand up straight and free. As for the lions, I never attempted to face them.

In Santa Claus, who appeared once a year at the foot of our Christmas tree, I believed without question. Long before Christmas day actually arrived Frank's and my excitement began. We wandered about the house, opening the doors of closets, peeping under sofas and chairs, fingering pack-

ages, for we expected a present from every member of the family. Thus, one December afternoon we found hidden behind the books on a remote shelf a mysterious chariot with four horses made of gilt paper. This treasure we visited daily. Great was our amazement when a chariot exactly like it was presented to Frank on Christmas morning as having been brought from the North Pole the night before by Santa Claus in his reindeer sledge. We said not a word, but at the first opportunity rushed off to the bookshelf. Our treasure had disappeared. A strange coincidence that seemed; I shrank from the obvious conclusion.

The very next year our Christmas celebration was unusually splendid in honor of guests. The big folding doors between the front and back parlors remained closed for a whole day. When at last they were thrown open there at the foot of the glistening tree stood Santa Claus himself. Thrilled that we should be so honored, I gazed with keen excitement at the great Christmas fairy and between the white border of the red cap he wore and the long white beard I clearly saw the brows and eyes of my father. "It isn't Santa Claus at all," I cried out. "It's Father, it's Father." One of my elder sisters tried to quiet me, to stop the scene, but I would not be still. "Take off thy beard, Father; take it off, please." Jumping up and down in excitement I began to sob and stopped only when my father, wig and beard discarded, took me up in his arms.

Frank was greatly displeased by my discovery. He urged me over and over again to ask no ques-

tions about the Easter rabbit who laid the red, blue, and purple eggs in a straw nest for which we always hunted on Easter morning. We might discover, he pointed out, that rabbits do not lay eggs. The indifference to knowledge shown by my little brother shocked me profoundly, though I tried to make allowances for his youth. I never once suspected what seems probable to me now—that Frank had already questioned my father and learned the facts. A conservative by nature, he must have instantly grasped the advantages of a fiction that gave him pleasure. Though I did what he asked and kept my mouth shut, for me the thrill had gone out of the Easter rabbit.

"Little pitchers have long ears," this saying, thrown at us as a defense, we had taken as a challenge. Without going so far as to listen at keyholes, Frank and I often participated in family discussions at which we were not visibly present. Thus, when the extraordinary precautions practiced before Christmas were relaxed, I learned from a discussion between my parents that my mother had not approved the Santa Claus deception. She had merely refrained from interfering with my father, who delighted to give us pleasure, and the older children who felt that they themselves had suffered from too much austerity. It was a relief to me to have my mother's perfect truthfulness vindicated, though I had guessed her role from the first. Also perhaps the shock of my disillusionment was softened by pride in having made a discovery for myself and by a pleasant feeling of superiority over my little brother.

15

II

BROTHERS AND SISTERS

IN my position as eighth child and youngest daughter of the family I was molded by influences from its various members that were individual to me. Not only were my brothers and sisters different from the brothers and sisters of Carey, to take the extreme of separation, but my very parents were different from hers, transformed by the fifteen years that intervened between us. When in my childhood Carey and I looked together at my mother, perhaps we saw the same features, eyes and hair of the same color, the same bodily form, who shall say? The love we felt for her might conceivably have proved equal in quantity had an instrument to measure it existed; in quality surely our emotions, dyed by our conscious and unconscious memories, molded by the desires and purposes of our two personalities varied in a thousand ways. Even Frank and I, so near in age and at the bottom of the family, harbored memories a stranger might with difficulty recognize as referring to the same individuals.

Experience seems to dissolve away and become illusion in the light of this reflection. The persons that form and re-form before my imagination are cloud shapes and yet something controls and determines the shifting outlines of each. Belief in the existence of a single personality underlying

such varying manifestations in experience seems
an act of faith. Associated with my mother and my
little brother in my earliest memories is always
my father. I cannot picture him as he was at that
time. Upon what, then, was founded my conviction twenty years later that the form lying silent
and cold in death before me was the bodily presence I had known in my childhood? I cannot say.
Through all the changes of passing years my father
has been for me and continues to be my father.

The joy of surprise and adventure and morning
sunlight glorifies my first separate memory of him.
Waked very early and dressed in haste, I am now
seated at his side in the light carriage he always
drove himself. We are going far into the country to
visit one of his patients. My father points out to
me the different trees, names the birds singing
their morning songs; together we enjoy the flickering light and shade, the flash of dewdrops in the
thick grass. When we reach our destination I am
left to run about under the trees by myself for a
long time while my father attends to his duties. As
I am becoming tired and a little lonely, he appears. When I get back home again my brother is
just eating his breakfast. My delight in the trees
and flowers and birds must have pleased my father,
for I have a distinct impression that he took me
on such expeditions more often than he took
Frank. Indeed the only occasions upon which I
remember being alone with my father when I was
a little girl are in his light carriage, rolling along
behind his fast mare, Annie. My early love of the
country, fostered by him, was a bond between us.

Sympathy with my father to the extent of sharing with him this particular pleasure, I felt, but I appear to have had no other sense of his personality apart from his relation to me or to Frank or to my mother. My love for him was quite unlike my love for her, over whose feelings and thoughts I continually brooded.

On a still different plane are my childish impressions of my older brothers and sisters. They appear as no more than vague figures associated with some personal emotion they excited in me but did not share. The first trace I find in my consciousness of my eldest sister, Carey, is a mere bodily sensation—a warm, deep feeling of someone who seems to be Carey sitting beside me telling me stories, while I lie curled up in bed with the shadows of sleep all about me. Only the comfort of a protecting presence and a soothing voice in the darkness remains, but Carey herself has assured me that it really was she who sat beside me night after night. She thought it best to begin my education by telling me legends from Greek mythology. Anticipated gullet satisfaction is the nail that fixes my next memory of her. She is bending down toward Frank and me, two small figures side by side in front of her, and handing back for us to drink the bottle of dark licorice concoction we had just sold her for a five-cent piece. Only in a hieroglyphic sense can this memory be called a picture, but I can still see vividly before my eyes the long stretch of her study rug, edged with tangled fringes to be straightened out for three pennies. Bright light streams over my left shoul-

der, Frank's bunched-up figure crouches beside me, the red-and-white fringe pulls at my fingers, my muscles ache. Behind me, seated at her desk near a window absorbed in a book, I am aware of my sister, the source of our reward. When our work was done she used to let us admire, but not touch, the porcelain and ivory animals that paraded on her mantel shelf. A pair of green and gold Chinese dragons were my favorites. I can still see their lovely color and strange shape.

This must, I suppose, be a memory from the interval of two years Carey spent at home after finishing her course at college. All during my childhood she was now in the house and now away for long periods. When she graduated from Cornell at twenty I was still a tiny child of five, aware of her only as the wonderful big sister who had appeared as by a miracle to do delightful things for Frank and me. I well remember the reading lessons she gave me. I used to search through the house, my primer under my arm, in the hope of finding her with a few minutes free to devote to my instruction. By that time my father had already taught me my letters and taken me through *The Black Cat Book* while he shaved in the morning. It was his custom to begin the education of his children one after the other while he stood before his high shaving table with its small, round mirror and leather strop hanging at one side. On the other side nearest the window was a bundle of shaving paper attached by a gay red ribbon. The sharpening of my father's razor always preceded the lesson. During this ceremony his little pupil

of the year danced up and down at his side studying the picture at the top of the page, getting ready to read the big, black letters underneath as soon as he began to remove from his face its lather of soap with sure strokes of his glittering razor that left queer-shaped patches under his nose and about his ears. Before my turn came I had been present so often while my next older sister was being instructed that I could repeat by heart "The black cat sat on the mat" and most of the other sentences explaining the pictures. Thus I graduated from my father's instruction without having learned anything much and with an alarming reputation for cleverness. "Give her mind a rest," my father decreed. "She is too easily stimulated and excited for her strength. Let her wait for Frank," or words to that effect. Thus, as Carey was too busy really to teach me, I remained illiterate for a long time.

The pair of white horses with floating tails and manes, bright and slender creatures that sometimes stopped in front of our house, was there because of my eldest sister. Frank and I often stood at the window looking down at them. Hitched to some sort of carriage they must have been, and watched over by a coachman, but I see them standing side by side without harness, free as if pausing to rest in the Arabian Desert about which Carey had told me. They had once belonged to the Sultan of Turkey, I knew, and their presence in our street meant that my sister had a friend with her upstairs in her study. About this Miss Garrett floated a mist of romance. She herself had traveled with her parents in the country from which the white horses came.

She wore marvelous hats with long ostrich plumes and the softest of furs which my fingers longed to stroke. She always spoke to Frank and me very gently and kindly, but still it was just as well for us not to run about during her visits, making a disturbance; so we stood quietly side by side at the window gazing down upon the horses for a very long time.

To my eldest brother, John, I owe a sensation of terror that has remained in my nerves for nearly fifty years—an instinctive intuition of sex, perhaps. Arriving home for a college vacation he snatched me up as I rushed into the front hall to greet him, perched me high on his shoulder and capered off with me up the stairs. Flinging my arms about his neck, I pressed my cheek tightly against his. It felt hairy and rough. He had let his whiskers grow. The terror of that moment cannot be expressed. When at last he put me down trembling with rage and excitement I declared I would cut off his whiskers with mother's scissors. He said he would defend himself; I insisted I would steal into his room when he was asleep and quickly cut them off. All of this was quoted in the family as a great joke. Just why, I cannot tell. Perhaps my vehemence had caused a laugh in the first place or perhaps envy of John's masculine decorations had spurred on the other boys to keep the story alive. The shining eyes in their smooth young faces were fixed derisively on John, not on me; he was the butt of the story. Even I could see that his constant crowing over his whiskers got on Harry's and Bond's nerves.

21

All three of my big brothers made a pet of the little sister eight years younger than the youngest of them. Without doubt they must have caressed me more often than they teased me, though I remember the teasing with far greater vividness. My habit of leaning up against one or other whenever possible earned for me the name of "Lena Lana," which excited in me feelings of mingled pleasure and shame. I cannot distinguish John from Harry or Bond in these memories. What remains is my own emotion which has little reference to the particular brother who caused it.

Much information beyond my experience was supplied me by family folklore. With eager interest I treasured up every scrap of information I heard. Thus I learned that my eldest brother, John, as a small boy used to scream so terribly that the neighbors called him the gorilla. Once when he had got completely beyond control, my mother had exclaimed to my grandmother Whitall, who was standing by, "We must do something to stop that child's screams." My grandmother had replied, "We cannot kill him; we shall have to bear him." The strange word "gorilla" made John seem to me somehow different from the rest of us. Also I felt resentment against him for giving my poor mother so much trouble.

My eldest sister, as well as John, had been difficult to manage as a child. She began by playing the tyrant, and refused to go to sleep unless my mother leaned over her crib so that she could stroke the soft eyebrow above her until overcome by drowsiness. The story of how Aunt Hannah

22

had come on from Philadelphia expressly for the purpose of rescuing her younger sister from this intolerable slavery was amusing. She sent my mother out of the house for the evening and when Carey cried, it was Aunt Hannah who appeared. "Thee can scream thyself black in the face, thy mother will not hear thee," she said in a stern tone, bending down over the crib. Then into the little mouth that gaped with astonishment she thrust a lollipop. "There, suck that. It will comfort thee," she said, still in the same firm voice, and left the room. Not another sound was heard from Carey.

This particular tale of my eldest sister's childhood was a favorite with me. My eyes fixed on my mother's smiling face as I listened, I savored the sweetness of Aunt Hannah's lollipop in slow swallows. But the accident that happened to Carey when she was still a small girl excited unrelieved terror. Through the negligence of the cook in leaving her alone in the kitchen to watch a pot, she had set her little skirt on fire and had allowed herself to burn almost to death before she had run for help to my mother, who was ill with a headache. The picture of a little girl burning made shudders run up and down my spine. I might some day catch fire myself. If I did ever burst into flame I would burn to ashes rather than frighten my mother.

Desperately ill for many months, Carey endured awful agonies. My mother nursed her day and night, suffering almost as much as the child. At last the little invalid began to get well, could listen

to reading, could even be taken on the train to visit my grandparents, lying in a basket so big that the covers need not press on her wounds. I loved to hear every detail of her recovery. Even when she was convalescent my mother attended to all her business in the sick room. Among others the egg man came there one day to bargain with her, leaving his basket of eggs in the hall outside. I laughed uproariously over the story of how my mother, hearing a noise, had opened the door and caught John and Harry in the act of plumping the basket of eggs violently up and down, breaking every one of them. The smashing of the eggs—delightful to imagine in itself—had made Carey laugh for the first time in many months. My mother's pleasure in telling us this anecdote added to my own joy. The cleverness and love of learning for which Carey was famous in the family she owed to my mother's having given so much time to her during her long illness. I often heard my father state this fact and I believed it devoutly.

Frank and I spent many happy hours listening to my mother's recitals of our elders' mischievous pranks and absurd sayings. They took the place for us of the modern comic strip. John, sent on an errand to the cellar, came back empty handed to declare that he had found it "awful dark and 'scusting dirty"—an excuse that seemed to us exquisitely funny, though it made us shiver. Once my mother had arrived at home to find the boys fighting each other with potatoes in the front hall, while important ladies waited to see her in the parlor. To them she had made neither excuse nor

comment, which seemed somehow very noble on my mother's part. She used herself to laugh at her dismay when she discovered a small boy perched on the narrow mantel-shelf in the place of a cherished China vase lying in pieces on the floor. "Take joyfully the spoiling of thy goods" was a text she often had occasion to cite. Freshly made jam, however cunningly hidden away, disappeared as by miracle; sugar constantly crunched under foot on the pantry floor. It all sounded marvelous to Frank and me who were held in check by a more experienced discipline. Even the broken collarbones, the cuts and bruises and wounds due to falling from roofs or getting stuck on spikes or hit by bats, all long since happily grown together and healed, enchanted us. Once the three boys had failed to come back from a morning swim, though the sun was setting. To quiet her growing anxiety, my mother had sewed on the machine hour after hour through the long afternoon. At last little Grace crept to her side. "Mother," she said in an urgent, small voice, "if Bonnie is drowned can I have his silver cup?" At that moment the culprits were heard returning. Their only excuse was that they had forgotten time, but they were suffering agonies from sunburn. No other punishment was needed. In this I rejoiced.

Indeed it was hard for me to imagine either of my parents with the uplifted slipper or rod of tradition, which I was told they had wielded. By the time Frank and I were born they had long since abandoned punishment as a means of training up their children in the way they should go. To take

its place they had devised the method of guiding by praise. My brother Bond, the fourth child of the family, got the full benefit of their first enthusiasm for this idea. "Bonnie is a wise boy," they would say when he was naughty. "Bonnie never gets angry," even though he might be screaming with rage at the moment. However violently he pushed away his plate at breakfast my father or my mother would say to him, "Bonnie knows that it is good for him to eat oatmeal. Bonnie is a wise boy," until he swallowed the stuff he hated chanting between the spoonfuls, "Bonnie is a wise boy."

These tales, even though stamped with my mother's approval, did not endear Bond to me. I enjoyed much more the story I heard Harry tell about him.

"One day when Bond had been particularly insufferable I threw him down on the pavement and sat on him. 'Now promise to behave,' I said to him as I pommeled him. 'I won't let thee up till thee promises me to behave.' He struggled and struggled, but couldn't shake me off, I was so much bigger and stronger. At last, 'If thee'll let me go, I'll promise to behave,' he panted, and like a fool I let go of him. Up he jumped quick as lightning, scampered off, and shouted back over his shoulder as he vanished around the corner of the house, 'Behave bad! I'll behave bad.'" Harry ended his story with a delighted laugh over Bond's triumph.

The hero of this tale seemed to me far more like the lively brother I knew than the "wise boy" my mother held up to me as an example. How-

ever, Bond was still very well pleased with himself. I did not wonder at all that Harry had once sat on him, though they were now such devoted companions.

For Harry I must early have felt a special affection. I remember well his devotion to the skye terrier someone had given him. This unfortunate animal, whose name comes back to me as "Mihylax," whatever that stands for, had developed incurable fits, and was to be shot. I watched my brother, a tall lad of sixteen, perhaps, far removed from me in age, go slowly off by himself into the garden with his head down to mourn for his pet. Personally I did not like the dog, whose horrid long hair always felt damp when I tried to pat him, but I was so dreadfully sorry for Harry that I can still see him walking past me with bowed head through the garden door. I believe this to be the first feeling of disinterested sympathy I ever had for anyone except my mother.

The only one of the four boys with whom I had any real association in my early childhood was my younger brother Frank. My early memories almost always include him. For many years he and I did everything together: got up and went to bed, dressed and undressed together; played together; said our prayers and performed our small daily duties together; enjoyed the same toys and the same food; had the same friends. In fact we formed as it were a single entity. If either of us had a request to make neither ever said, "May *I* do this or have that?" Always it was *us* that we called ourselves. "Please, Mother, give *us* a penny," never

me; or "May *us* go for a walk before supper?" The whole family acquired the habit of using *us* as a corporate name for subject as well as object of the verb, totally disregarding grammar. On the street we walked with our arms about each other's shoulders, a quaint little pair that was smiled on and no doubt protected by the neighbors. We were never interfered with or offended, except once when a tall youth swung his long leg over our heads as he passed by us. This outrage to our dignity we resented instantly and never forgot.

Since I was the elder by more than a year the responsibility for us both rested on my shoulders. Frank was not only part of me, he was the most important part. My mother had entrusted him to my care and I would have faced any danger to myself to protect him. Sympathy of a kind for him I surely had, but my activities in his behalf prevented my thinking of my little brother as an independent being with feelings of his own that I might possibly fail to understand.

Of the two sisters immediately older than I, Grace and Margaret, only Grace caught my imagination. I remember wonderful stories about her independence and her beauty told Frank and me by our nurse in the early days before she left us. Grace, Nurse boasted, had escaped from her into the world outside the nursery as soon as she was tall enough to reach the knob of the door—the very knob there before our eyes that we were unable to turn. Her beauty as a little girl had been dazzling. People used to stop on the streets to exclaim over her long, bright colored hair, her dark

28

eyes, and her straight, small figure. "Her manners were something beautiful. A perfect little lady she was!" In Nurse's voice a note of pride vibrated. I was exceedingly impressed. Thus Grace became a heroine to me in my childhood, though I can recollect no personal incident that includes her until she emerges for me as a young lady surrounded by admirers of the other sex.

Of Margaret, however, I have many vivid memories, mostly I fear of the envious sort. She was my immediate superior in age, sufficiently near for me to measure myself up against her, but much as I longed to do some of the things she did, it was the lovely pink and blue bows of ribbon with which her white dresses were tied up and adorned that excited my envy. When I begged for ribbons like Margaret's my mother explained to me that brown ribbons were more suitable for me, because of my red hair. Margaret's dark hair required bright colors to set it off. Then Margaret's eyes were blue-gray while mine were brown. My ribbons matched my eyes, my mother pointed out. For a little girl with red hair and brown eyes only brown ribbons were appropriate. This was a law of good taste, my mother said, which was, I felt, as much as to say a law of God. I accepted it once for all without another word, but my eyes remained fixed on Margaret's pink and blue bows with a feeling of rancor.

Many annoyances due to our time relation fell without doubt to Margaret's lot as well as to mine. She had, I believe, no occasion to pay much attention to Frank and me, but we were there under

fect from morning until night. She was constantly
having to shout back at us, "Now, children, don't
come always tagging after me"—an insult that
wounded our feelings without deterring us. Above
all we were anxious to join her and her two inseparable friends when they climbed up the ladder
into the front attic where they remained often for
hours. Her stories of the horrible monster who
inhabited it, designed to frighten us away I suppose, kept us lingering in the hall below, fearful
and fascinated, until they reappeared to show their
blackened hands and faces as proof of thrilling
adventures. Later when I became familiar with
the attic myself I accused Margaret, or Daisy as
we called her, of deception, but she explained with
an air of triumphant condescension that the bogey
she had described to us was merely her name for
the dust and darkness. Silenced, I pondered this
explanation in my own mind. It was true in a
sense, I could not deny that; I admired Margaret's
cleverness, but all the while I felt that she had lied
to us "on purpose," and her refusal to acknowledge anything but perfect truthfulness rankled.
Still, even my own secret thoughts of her had to
wear the mask of affection. Of course I was devoted
to Margaret. That I should fail to love any one of
my brothers and sisters was unthinkable.

Both our parents, my father quite as much as my
mother, insisted on kindness and consideration in
the family circle. They would not listen to our
complaints and criticisms of each other, and quar-
reling in their presence was not tolerated. On this
point my father was exceedingly firm, requiring

in particular consideration from the boys for their sisters. When they failed in it even the older boys were sent away from the table at mealtimes. My mother, leaving such punishments largely to my father, exerted herself in her own way to control our youthful carpings. "Whatsoever things are good, whatsoever things are pleasant, think on these things," she would often say to us, quoting the Bible, and I remember the very tone of voice in which she used to quote the apostle John's admonition to the Romans, "Little children, love one another."

III

TWO SIDES OF THE HOUSE

Strange people passed in and out of our house all day long. This coming and going of people was part of my world. Many of the frequent visitors were relatives of my father's, I knew, but even relatives made little impression upon me. The memory of Grandmother Thomas praying in meeting with uplifted face and pleading mouth which I have already recorded is the only distinct image of any one of my father's people that remains from my early childhood.

However, I had learned certain things about them from my mother. My father's sister and his four brothers were not, I found, his whole sister and his whole brothers with the same father and mother, like Frank and me and all of us, they were only a half sister and half brothers. This astonishing state of things had come about because my father's mother had died when he was a baby and his father had married again. But stranger still, my Aunt Mary Thomas and my four Thomas uncles were not the children of the Grandmother Thomas I knew. Their mother, like my father's mother, had died long ago and my Grandfather Thomas had married a third wife before he himself had died. So Grandmother Thomas was not really anyone's mother or grandmother! She was not really any relation to us at all. It did not seem

right, somehow, to call her "Mother" as my father did, or "Grandmother" as I did myself.

When I understood the state of things in my father's family I was gravely shocked by it. I disapproved of my grandfather's many marriages and said so plainly in words it sometimes amused my mother to repeat. Still she impressed on me that my Grandfather Thomas had been a very good and religious man, a powerful preacher as well as a distinguished physician. It was to him, my mother said, that she herself owed her own complete and final consecration to God, from which there could never be any turning back. Until she had married and come under Grandfather Thomas' influence she had been a vain and selfish young woman, in spite of her pious upbringing, she assured me. I believed what my mother told me, of course, but still I could not forgive my grandfather his three wives. I hated to be reminded of him. His name aroused in me, I suppose, a half-conscious dread lest my own mother might die, and my father put some other woman in her place, following Grandfather Thomas' awful example. Perhaps it was a secret fear of this sort that prevented my ever feeling close to my father's people, or perhaps I have merely forgotten early attachments that were not reinforced by later experience, for I have no affectionate memories of them. I must have once "loved" them I suppose—at least my Aunt Mary, who was very kind to Frank and me.

My father's commanding position in his own family could not escape my observation even as a

small child. His sister and his brothers showed their respect for him by addressing him always as "Brother James," not just James, as would have been natural. They consulted him constantly and deferred to his opinion, as did also his aunts and his stepmother. My mother explained to me that he had been brought up separately from the second family by his father's three sisters. One of these aunts had died before I was born, but the two survivors were awe-inspiring old ladies in Quaker dress. They had great influence with my father, whom they adored. Since they had both married late in life and were both childless it was natural, my mother said, that they should look on my father as if he were their son. On his side my father repaid their early care of him and their love with dutiful devotion. Nor did he forget his own mother.

The names of my brothers and sisters in which as a child I took passionate interest helped to fix these facts in my mind. My eldest sister was called after my father's mother, "Martha Carey," as was proper in the sad circumstances. John, the next child, had my Grandfather Whitall's name. Then my father felt that the eldest of the aunts who had brought him up should be honored in the name of the third child. As he happened to be a boy, "Henrietta" became "Henry" for his benefit. So it went on, each new child being assigned to honor one or the other side of the family. Greatly interested, I counted my older brothers and sisters up on my fingers, not forgetting the baby brother, James, who had died long before and was now an

angel in heaven with Dora. My mother explained to me that by the time I was born she and my father had felt free to choose any name for me they liked, and how it happened that Frank, though younger than I, had a family name. While he was still a baby the eldest Whitall grandson, Frank Pearsall Smith, had died tragically on his eighteenth birthday. This clever, handsome boy, who was the adored son of my mother's sister, Aunt Hannah, was also Carey's best-beloved and most intimate cousin. Unable to resist Carey's heart-broken pleading, my mother consented to name the new baby after him. Of the ten children in the family only Dora and I had been given "fancy names" as I said.

I was very proud of the fact that my name had been chosen just for me, that it was my very own and not the name of some relative, but my satisfaction received a severe shock when Carey explained how it had come to me.

"I named thee after the most famous woman who ever lived," she said to me one day when I was still quite a small girl. "Thee ought to be thankful to me."

"Tell me about her, Carey," I begged.

All eager interest, I settled myself to listen, but when I understood from my sister's story that my namesake, Helen of Troy, had run away from her husband and had caused a terrible war that lasted ten years before she would go back home again, I was horrified.

In a passion of tears I flung myself down on the floor. "How could thee name me after such a

35

wicked woman, Carey?" I wailed. "I'll have to be like her, now thee has given me her name! I can't change my name!"

"Nonsense, child! Don't be a little goose. Thee needn't worry. Thee'll never be like Helen of Troy." My sister laughed, but at the same time she seemed utterly disgusted with me.

I raced off to my mother. "Mother, why did thee let Carey name me after that wicked woman?" I said, sobbing. "I'll have to be wicked, too, like Helen of Troy."

My mother wiped away the tears that rolled down my face, while she explained to me that Helen of Troy had nothing to do with my name. She had selected it herself from a list she and Carey had jotted down together.

"I chose Helen for thee," she said, "because it went well with Whitall. Helen Whitall Thomas would sound well, I thought, when it was read out in Meeting. Thee sees I hope thee will grow up to be a useful member of the Society of Friends, perhaps even a preacher. Thee might be sent to London Yearly Meeting with a Letter of Recommendation from Baltimore Yearly Meeting." My mother smiled at me. "Think how lovely thy name would sound read out in London Meeting House!"

So what Carey had told me was not true! Everything was all right. My mother never failed to make things right for me. My pleasure in my name was now greater than ever, for I knew very well what important occasions Yearly Meetings were.

Every autumn our house was crowded with delegates to Baltimore Yearly Meeting who came from

all over Maryland and also from other states, even from England. During the days it lasted Frank and I were greatly excited by the bustle and hurry that reigned. We watched the guests when we could from various points of vantage. Most of them were strangers to us but we knew two old gentlemen who occupied the same room in the back wing year after year. They were farmers from the country district near Baltimore and never failed to send my mother some gift at Christmas, a bag of buckwheat flour, a tub of sausages or scrapple, barrels of apples. In any group we could pick out these benefactors and say to them very politely as instructed, "Thank thee for thy nice Christmas gift, Zachariah McNaul," "Thank thee, Ezra Calkins," remembering the strange names without being prompted.

We particularly enjoyed the feast that was held every evening in our dining room. To share in it we had to steal down the back stairs, slip out through the kitchen door into the garden and climb up the grape arbor with infinite precautions to keep out of the light that shone here and there in oblong patches from the dining-room windows. Perched in a safe place we watched the guests about the long table eat the delicacies set before them. If anyone used the back of his hand for a napkin or a knife for a fork we stuffed our hands into our mouths to keep from laughing. Such lapses, which occurred also at breakfast when we were openly present, we delighted to cite later in excuse for our own bad manners and we listened with complete lack of conviction to our parents'

explanation that country ways differed from city ways. When the varicolored molds of ice cream were at last carried in through the swinging pantry door Frank and I climbed carefully down the arbor again and were back in the kitchen in time to get our share. We ate it very slowly, taking a little bit on the end of the spoon and concentrating on the different flavors, chocolate, strawberry, and pistachio, while the colored servants passing to and fro on their duties stopped for a minute to watch us with delighted smiles.

The more serious side of Yearly Meeting was seen by Frank and me only when we went as usual to the Sunday morning meeting for worship. The meeting house was crowded, every bench seemed full and the atmosphere of solemnity was intense. My father occupied his usual place and broke up meeting by shaking hands with the friend next him, but I had to search for my mother among the visiting Friends on the women's side of the gallery. Sometimes at home my mother allowed me to stand near her when there was an informal gathering in our front parlor and it was then that I heard the discussions of doctrine over which I puzzled my head so painfully.

Though I clung to my mother whenever I could, I did try day by day not to bother her or interfere with her religious duties, for I felt their great importance. On the other hand when I was ill I claimed her entire attention, as did every member of her family. In retrospect all my childish illnesses are illuminated by her presence. The sight of her near me warming up a spoonful of oil over

a hissing gas jet to pour in my ear eased many a sharp stab of pain for me, and the long illness from which I suffered in early childhood remains in my mind chiefly as the occasion of certain delightful adventures with my mother—watching her eat her dinner from a tray by my bedside and suddenly, once, jump up with a crash of dishes to escape a tiny mouse I saw whisking off. She laughed over her folly as gaily as I did and always afterwards scattered crumbs for "our four-footed friend" who turned up at dinnertime day after day. A streetcar ride with her marks my recovery. Together we shared the fun of concealing my shaved head from our fellow passengers by the row of my curls she had kept and sewed around the front of my bonnet. Though the ladies on the seat opposite stared hard at us both, they could not guess that my head was completely bare under its brown velvet covering. Meeting my eyes my mother smiled at me gaily, and I felt that she enjoyed fooling the ladies as much as I did.

In this particular illness my father also figures, lying on the bed beside me and singing to me songs that miraculously had in them the name by which he always called me, "Nellie Bly Shut Her Eye," "Nellie Was a Lady," and other Southern melodies. He provided ice cream for me the very first time I said I'd like some. My father's belief that plain ice cream could not hurt sick children once they were well enough to ask for it was very popular with his children.

Even when we were all in good health my mother must have had difficulty in doing any work

outside her own home, but she managed it some-how. I now know that she helped herself out with Frank and me by putting us in the infant class at the Friends Academy, the school maintained by Baltimore Meeting for their children, in the man-agement of which my mother was a leading spirit. Not the faintest memory remains in my mind of attending this class but records show that my little brother and I were among its pupils when he was five and I six years old. I imagine my mother tak-ing us with her down to the schoolhouse, leaving us in our classroom, and then going on herself to the board room for a committee meeting or a consulta-tion with the principal. Her work for the meeting was never interrupted for long. As soon as possible after the seclusion made necessary by the birth of a child or some severe illness or contagion in the family, she resumed her religious duties.

If my mother ever had anything in the nature of a holiday it must have been during visits to her parents. Living in a different town, she kept in touch with them by frequent letters as well as by mutual visiting, and every summer she took her increasing flock of children to spend a month or two at her father's country house in New Jersey, "The Cedars." Her brother and one of her sisters had houses of their own near by, and Aunt Han-nah, her oldest sister and dearest friend, was usu-ally a visitor at The Cedars, like my mother, ac-companied by her children. Indeed my grand-father had built a special house on his place for Aunt Hannah's family. It was of wood, long and low, with a veranda running the whole length of

MY MOTHER AND THE OLDER CHILDREN

it, onto which the bedrooms opened, and it was called "The Barracks." I remember well how it looked, though no image remains of the big house where we stayed.

Even as a child I felt nearer to my Whitall relatives than to my father's people whom I saw so much more often. My mother's family was like ours. Grandfather and Grandmother Whitall were my mother's own father and mother, her sisters and her brother were her very own. I loved to hear stories about them, and I found her father's adventure particularly exciting. He was the son of a Quaker farmer in New Jersey, but had gone to sea as a common sailor when he was a young man for some reason I have forgotten or never understood. Holding strongly to the Quaker principles in which he had been brought up, he neither drank nor swore nor played cards. None the less he was liked and respected by both the crew and the officers of his ship and was rapidly promoted. Soon he had hopes of being made first officer, but at just that time a deep conviction of sin came upon him because of his laxity in maintaining his religious principles. He felt that it was his duty to bear unmistakable testimony by assuming the Quaker dress, a black swallow-tailed coat with a high collar, topped by a broadbrimmed hat. The head of the line of ships on which he served was not a devout man, much less a Quaker, so when a summons to the company office came my grandfather was thrown into great perturbation of spirit. All chances of further promotion would be destroyed, he might even lose his present position as second

41

mate, if he were to appear before his chief in Quaker plain clothes. But how could he reconcile it with his conscience to resume worldly clothes for the sake of worldly advantage? My grandfather's struggle was severe. In the end right won: he wore his Quaker coat to the interview and was given command of a ship! There was something vaguely comic for me in the picture evoked of a young man dressed in the Quaker coat and hat I had seen worn only by old gentlemen; still I admired my grandfather's courage and his virtue, and I rejoiced in his reward.

When he married he left the sea to enter on a business career, but his first venture proved disastrous. Due to the folly of his partner, or worse, my mother hinted, my grandfather found himself laden with debts. Though a settlement was made by part payments to the creditors, my grandfather regarded himself as morally bound to return the sum originally due to the very last penny. In my mother's childhood the economy practiced by her parents was exceedingly strict, she said. One day when she was helping herself largely to butter her father remonstrated.

"Does thee realize, Mary," he asked her, "that a pound of butter costs fifty cents?"

"It's worth it!" my mother replied, spreading a thick layer on her bread.

"Wasn't Grandfather angry with thee, Mother?" I asked. "Didn't he punish thee?"

"Grandfather was never angry," my mother replied, and then added, "When I thought the matter over by myself I was ashamed of my selfishness and never wasted butter again."

The need for economy was, however, finally done away with by the success of my grandfather's second business venture, a glass manufactory which prospered increasingly. He was able to retire early with a comfortable fortune and leave his business to enrich his son and his sons-in-law, Aunt Hannah's and Aunt Sarah's husbands. My father, being a doctor, was deprived of this opportunity to grow rich; still he and my mother received generous help from her father and brother at more than one crisis of their affairs. The Whitall family was in spirit truly patriarchal.

On New Year's Day a reunion always took place at my grandparents' Philadelphia house. Every member of the family group attended, if to do so was in any way possible. In the course of years certain customs had grown up giving the New Year's Feast the character almost of a ritual. The youngest grandchild capable of standing alone tottered down the center of the dinner table and the baby in arms was brought in to be admired and welcomed by the assembled family. My grandfather recited a rhymed chronicle of the last year's events, composed by him and containing gently humorous references to everyone from my grandmother down to the youngest grandchild. Prayers of thanksgiving to the Divine Father ended the ceremony.

Grandfather Whitall was not a preacher as Grandfather Thomas had been. He made no journeys to London Yearly Meeting as a delegate from his own meeting. None the less religion was the center of his life. He took his due part in the activities of the Philadelphia Society of Friends,

but the great influence he exerted was private and personal. He was a Quaker mystic, my mother said, which meant, she explained to me, that he lived in close communion with God. Every morning and evening he spent an hour by himself in meditation. It was in these quiet hours that he heard God's voice.

So when I came suddenly upon my grandfather one day seated motionless in his armchair with closed eyes I knew he was not asleep. He was talking with God. I stopped short where I was and stood very still. Perhaps if I listened intently enough I might hear God's voice speaking to my grandfather. But the room remained quiet, not even the faintest whisper reached my ears. After a long time my grandfather opened his eyes, saw me, and smiled at me gently. These moments of intense listening for God's voice in the room with my grandfather are among the most vivid memories of my early childhood. He died when I was six years old.

One other picture of him remains in my mind. He has arrived at The Cedars from town in his closed carriage drawn by two black horses and is stepping out of the carriage into a group of children clamoring to know what treat he has brought them. I seem to see a great bunch of bananas lifted from the back seat by the coachman and my grandfather breaking off a curly banana for each child; but I believe all these details are reconstructions from stories I was told and from bunches of bananas I saw hanging outside of fruit shops. The element of personal emotion is entirely lack-

ing. That my grandfather, though so indulgent as a rule, was also a strict disciplinarian, I knew. The boys stood in awe of him. Once my brother Harry, while eating a large preserved peach in the Cedars' pantry, which was forbidden territory, suddenly saw my Grandfather Whitall watching him from the doorway. So great was Harry's fright that he swallowed the huge peach, stone and all, in one gulp. My grandfather, describing the scene, used to say that Harry's throat had swelled like the throat of a boa constrictor, but the act of disobedience was not condoned. The story was told as a warning.

Of my mother's mother I must have been very fond, since I searched the fields about The Cedars for her favorite flower, the lacy wild white carrot, to make bouquets to give her. Roadsides white with these blossoms always bring Grandmother Whitall's name to my mind, accompanied, however, only by the vague image of a little girl bending down to pick a flower. An aura of devotion surrounds her in my mind. She was adored by her husband and children. She was loving and wise and sympathetic; everyone went to her with his troubles. All this I knew, but there were no thrilling incidents, no amusing stories about her to stamp themselves on a child's mind. My mother's hiding our piano, as I have described, before a visit from Grandmother Whitall impressed her Quaker strictness on me, but is a memory of my mother rather than of my grandmother.

Around my mother's eldest sister, Aunt Hannah, legends clustered. As a child I delighted to hear

about her exploits, and somehow the elderly aunt I knew fitted the stories. She possessed a passionate vitality that made her seem capable of anything. During part of my early childhood she was abroad with her family having marvelous adventures of a religious nature among the English aristocracy, but if I heard of them I was too young to understand what they were all about. She returned to America in time to join the patriarchal group at The Cedars during the last years of my grandparents' lives, and it was then, probably during the very last summer, that she began to take notice of me. I used to run down by myself from the big house to The Barracks where the Pearsall Smiths lived and I have a vivid impression of Aunt Hannah coming out through one of the doors that opened on the long veranda to greet me. In a way she adopted me, calling me "little Hannah" after herself, perhaps because of my passionate childish piety. She must have seen that I was bothered by fears and sensitive feelings, and no doubt the stories I remember were told me with the purpose of helping me over my troubles.

When she was a small girl Aunt Hannah hated the sunbonnet her mother tied under her chin every morning before she started off to school, and one day, unable to bear the hideous thing on her head another minute, she tore open the strings, snatched the bonnet off, and began kicking it in front of her through the dust of the road. When she got to the bridge over a stream she had to cross Aunt Hannah gave the sunbonnet a terrible kick, and raised her eyes to see how far it would go.

There at the end of the bridge stood the Devil, grinning at her and beckoning her to follow him. She was so terribly frightened that she picked up the sunbonnet and put it on her head all covered with dust as it was. At that very instant the Devil disappeared. Aunt Hannah never again refused to wear her sunbonnet though she hated it always with an undying hatred.

At the end of this story my aunt used to explain to me that she had not really seen the Devil at all. She had just imagined him because she knew that by being so naughty she was following her own evil desires and not listening to the voice of her Heavenly Father.

Stories about my mother delighted me above all others. I kept asking Aunt Hannah about her.

"Thy mother was a very determined child," she assured me. "Thee must know that she was dreadfully jealous of Tim, the cat, whom thy Aunt Sarah and I adored. Once when we three happened to be left all alone in the house, Sally and I determined to prevent her for once from disturbing Tim who lay purring loudly in the chair he preferred. We told thy mother that the stool was just the right size for her and ordered her to sit on it. Thy grandfather's chair belonged by rights to me as the eldest, and Sally of course had thy grandmother's chair; the stool was left for thy mother. 'What about the other chair?' thy mother asked. 'I have a better right to a comfortable chair than the cat,' she declared and began walking over to it to chase Tim out.

"We caught hold of her, forced her down on the

47

stool, and held her there. She struggled at first, but when she found she could not possibly get free she sat still and said quite quietly, "If you don't drive that horrid old cat out of my chair and let me sit in it, I will scream until the neighbors come.'"

"Did the neighbors hear her and really come, Aunt Hannah?" I asked. "And what did they say?"

"We knew thy mother too well to risk it. When she opened her mouth to scream we let her go, and poor Timothy had to lie on the rug."

Aunt Hannah and I laughed many times over this story which I loved to hear repeated.

The reason she paid so much attention to me at this particular period was partly, I suspect, to take me off my mother's hands by amusing me herself. After Dora's birth my mother did not regain her strength for a long time. The arrival of her last three children within a period of five years had been too great a strain even for her vigorous health. I feel sure that Aunt Hannah, who had so often before come to the assistance of her youngest sister, was doing so now, though at the time I had of course no suspicion of this.

Aunt Hannah herself had had five children but the death of her oldest son, Carey's chum, for whom Frank had been named, left only four Pearsall Smith cousins, no one of whom was near Frank and me in age. That she protected the interest of her own children with fierce energy was well known at The Cedars. Barring this she was indulgent to all her nephews and nieces, for she loved children and young people. Taking the small girl

I then was "under her wing" as she herself would have said, could have been no hardship for her.

I must have played with my cousins at The Cedars, I suppose. I remember the swing under tall trees in which I was tossed up almost to the skies; I remember the secret hiding place in the center of a thick clump of box trees, through the branches of which we pushed our way; and I remember the terror of seeing my little brother Frank seize hold of the tail of one of the big black carriage horses in an effort to swing back and forth between its legs; but I do not remember a single one of my cousins. Only two were suitable playmates for Frank and me, both boys, sons of Uncle James and Aunt Sarah. Frank no doubt deserted me for them. I must have wandered about a good deal by myself. Once I got lost all alone in my grandfather's great cornfield. Without noticing the way I was going I wandered on and on between the cornstalks that rose high above my head, their sharp leaves shining and their tassels waving against the blue sky. When at last I grew tired I had not the faintest idea how to get out of the field. It was huge, I knew. I might wander about in it for hours. I might miss my dinner and my supper too. Blindly I dashed first this way and then that, trying to find my direction, and at last stood still, utterly exhausted. Then it flashed into my mind that my mother had told me I could always get out of the cornfield by walking straight ahead along a single row. Immediately I chose my row, followed it on and on and by good luck came out in sight of the house.

The older cousins paid no attention to the little children. They paired off among themselves, according to age, driving the light wagon, riding the pony, swimming in the pond, playing games together, but toward the end of the summer a great hunt was organized in which all the grandchildren, young and old, took part. The game, I remember, was played on a still clear evening when darkness was beginning to fall.

A small band of the swiftest cousins remained as hunters near the corncrib, empty now before the harvest, while the others scattered like animals to hide behind trees off over the lawn and fields within certain bounds. After an allotted interval the hunters sounded their cry and started in pursuit. Anyone caught was shut in the corncrib but could be set free if another of the hunted crept up unseen and pulled the pin from the door. I was instantly captured and imprisoned. For a long time I waited alone in the corncrib watching with intense excitement through its open slats dim figures dart about in the twilight across clear spaces between shadowy trees, but, alas! no one of them darted to my rescue. The shouts that I heard, now distant, now near at hand, filled me with terror and hope. At last other prisoners were brought in and the picture fades.

IV

EUROPEAN SURPRISES

AFTER more than twenty-five years of married life, my parents were planning to go off alone together on a religious mission—the only kind of holiday that would have seemed possible to them. They had been appointed delegates, my mother together with my father, by Baltimore Yearly Meeting to visit the London Yearly Meeting of the Society of Friends. Later they were to travel for a few weeks on the Continent before returning home. My sister Carey and her friend, Miss Gwinn, who was studying with her at the University of Leipzig, were to join them during the summer vacation.

Money for the journey was forthcoming now that my mother had inherited her share of Grandfather Whitall's fortune. Before this, with so many children to feed, clothe, and educate, my parents had constantly fallen into debt. My father's inherited fortune was small and he gave hardly more than half time to his practice of medicine. Some of his patients failed to pay their bills and to some he never sent a bill. It was fortunate for us that we did not depend wholly on my father's income, that through the medium of my mother's family the Lord did provide, according to the promise in the Bible—trips abroad, bicycles for the boys, pretty clothes for the girls, as well as our daily bread.

In addition to being a preacher and a physician my father was also trustee of a number of educational institutions, sat on the managing boards of several hospitals, and acted as president of more than one charitable society—all unpaid but time-consuming jobs. No wonder we were often forced to wait midday dinner for more than an hour before he appeared, weary but always able to enjoy his food. Clearly my father needed a rest: small girl as I then was, even I could see that. However, not until I read my sister Carey's letters after her death did I learn that he was threatened with a serious physical breakdown at this time. It appears in these letters that my parents had long cherished the hope of making a pilgrimage together to the Holy Land, but this had now to be abandoned as too strenuous for my father's health. Since the journey to England on which they had decided was necessitated by my father's health and also fulfilled a religious obligation it must have been with clear consciences that my parents planned to leave their children for four long months.

But, alas! they had counted without me. When it was explained to me gently and with due regard for my feelings that, along with Frank and Margaret and Grace, I was to be left behind in the care of my father's aunt and his sister, I would have absolutely none of it. My first outbreak was expected and discounted. But I continued to mourn and to grieve. Nothing could reconcile me to being separated from my mother. I neither slept nor ate. Fearing the effects on my health of such despair, my parents were not long in deciding to

take Frank and me with them. So two children of eight and nine years were to share their journey. This theft of my mother's holiday seems to me by all odds the worst act of piracy I ever committed. She was to have no other chance of escape from family cares.

When Carey learned that Frank and I were not to be left at home, she protested vehemently.

"About Europe," she wrote my mother from Leipzig, "Frank and Nell do seem a difficulty. I do not see how you can possibly take them with you. We have not seen one child in all our travels."

Letters went back and forth across the Atlantic, but my sister's protests were useless. One sunny morning early in the following May Frank and I stood safely beside our parents, waving good-by to Harry from the deck of the steamer that was taking us to England.

On the voyage I was prostrated by seasickness, a dead weight on my mother's hands, though Frank ran about the boat in the best of spirits. During our stay in London, where our parents were busy from morning to night, they engaged a governess to look after us. Frank and I had long been used to independence and prided ourselves upon it, but we saw that London with its crowds of people and carriages was no place for us to wander about in by ourselves, and so we accepted an attendant without protest. Miss Adams took us to the park and the zoo, played games with us in the late afternoons, and kept us company at meals. She sang lovely songs to us, she was young and pretty; we were both fascinated by her. Only once

while we were in London did we really bother our parents, and then I was to blame. I begged them to take us with them to hear their Letters of Recommendation read out in London Meeting House.

My father vetoed the suggestion. "Business meetings are no place for children," he said. "I thought we engaged Miss Adams just to save us from such difficulties."

My mother meditated on this for a moment while I watched her with anxious eyes. By now I had learned not to interfere on such occasions but to leave things to my mother. She understood the reason for my request and I felt sure she would somehow persuade my father to grant it.

"Why couldn't Miss Adams take the children up to the back gallery?" she asked. "They have to go for a walk in any case, and up there they would not be noticed."

My father shook his head, refusing for some time, but finally yielded on condition that Frank and I would be perfectly quiet and not attract the least attention. We promised faithfully to be good.

Thus in due time I found myself hanging over the gallery rail, together with my little brother, looking down on a hall no larger than our meeting house at home and arranged in the same way but darker and somehow more impressive. Somewhere among the English people that filled it were my parents.

"Look, Frank, there's Mother!" I whispered. "Right over there. And there's Father at the end of the bench opposite."

Not finding anything to interest me as the meeting proceeded, I soon stopped trying to listen. When the familiar names, "James Carey Thomas," "Mary Whitall Thomas," sounded out, I knew that I should hear them. But time went on and on, Frank grew restless, and finally Miss Adams whispered to me that we must go, she could not keep him quiet any longer. She had to remind me of my promise to my father before I would consent to tiptoe along the gallery behind her and Frank, down the creaking stairs out into the street, dreadfully disappointed.

When we left London and Miss Adams behind us to travel about England, paying visits here and there to English friends, Frank and I were back again on my mother's hands. My efforts to help her with the packing and such things were not successful and I began to realize that taking "us" along was not such a simple matter for my parents as it had seemed to me back at home in Baltimore. So when my mother told me that Frank and I were to be left alone for a few weeks with Carey in Leipzig while she and my father made a rapid tour through Italy, I made no objection. It was very kind of my sister, my mother explained, to look after us, busy as she was with her studies at the University. My father and she could not take us with them to Italy. Without Carey they would have had to give up the trip. She trusted me to be very good and to obey my sister, and several times she cautioned me that Frank and I must try our best not to annoy or in any way disturb Miss Gwinn.

All this I remember my mother's saying to me, but she did not tell me that she had practically forced Carey to take charge of Frank and me. Several of my sister's letters to my mother written during June, 1881, when we were already in England, set forth the difficulties of having two small children with her in Leipzig. She would have to give us her bedroom and sleep on a sofa in her study, which would be very disturbing, though she did not really mind that. But the walls were thin, everything could be heard through them, the children would disturb Mamie's reading. Then there was no one to look after Frank and me, take us for walks or amuse us. It would be far better to leave us in England. She hoped my mother would find some way of doing this. However, if there were no possibility of making other arrangements for Frank and me, Carey would do her best, she said, to persuade Mamie to put up with us.

My sister had set her heart on her parents seeing Italy, above all Venice and Rome. "I cannot imagine the gates of pearl and the streets of gold much more wonderful," she wrote them. In the end she got Miss Gwinn's consent only by promising to spend an extra week with her in Paris after we had sailed home in September.

The last of this series of my sisters letters reassures my mother as follows:

"Thee knows that if I devoted myself to the children for a year or five years I would then feel I had not done half enough to express my gratitude to you for the benefits, above and beyond

your duties as parents, which you have bestowed upon me."

With a few exceptions all Carey's letters from abroad are addressed to my mother. In one of them she says, "Tell Father I want to write to him but my pen always begins *Dearest Mother.*"

On the way to Leipzig my parents stopped off at Minden, where, by some chance I have never understood, a small circle of German Quakers was settled. Seeing my father preach through an interpreter who stood beside him and interrupted him at intervals, I found exciting. All too soon we reached Leipzig, and in no time at all after that Frank and I were established in the flat Carey and Miss Gwinn occupied, and my parents had gone off to Italy, leaving us alone with my sister.

Frank and I created a sensation, as Carey put it, when we first appeared on the streets with her and Miss Gwinn. Several times young men stopped short on the pavement to watch us all go by together—University students, my sister said they were. She denounced this rudeness, but somehow seemed more amused than annoyed by their staring.

"It's a good thing the children are no younger!" I heard her say to Miss Gwinn with a laugh.

I wondered what difference our ages could possibly make to the students but did not ask my sister about it. I was now too old to be always asking questions like a baby and moreover my sister had told me not to interrupt when she and Miss Gwinn were talking together.

Busy from morning till night with her lectures

and her studying, Carey never had more than a few moments to devote to us at home, and when she took us out walking Miss Gwinn always made one of the party. Here in Leipzig Carey seemed very different from the gay, indulgent sister who had told Frank and me stories and given us pennies for little services in Baltimore two years before. She saw that we had everything we needed and kept track of what we did; she was kind and gentle in her dealings with us, but somehow she seemed to have become unapproachable, almost a stranger. Without feeling exactly afraid of her, I stood greatly in awe of my sister. None the less almost at once I found myself forced to oppose her.

On the first Sunday after our arrival she told me to get ready to go with her and Miss Gwinn to an out-of-door concert in the Rosenthal.

"Today is Sunday, Carey," I objected. "Thee must have forgotten it's Sunday."

"Of course it's Sunday!" she replied gaily. "Does thee think I have time to go to concerts on week days?"

"But, Carey, it is a sin to go to a concert on Sunday. Mother would not like us to do it." I spoke with earnest solemnity.

My sister looked at me thoughtfully for a minute. I half expected her to give up going herself now that I had reminded her of my mother's wishes.

"Did not Mother tell thee that thee was to obey me?" she asked me at last. "I wish thee to go to the concert. If it's a sin, it is my sin, not thine. Run get thy hat and come along!"

Could I accept this? I wanted to desperately, but my conscience forbade.

"Frank and I cannot go, Carey," I repeated. "Mother would never let us go. I want to obey thee, but I can't go to a concert on Sunday. Please don't ask me to do what Mother would disapprove of." I struggled hard to keep back the tears that rose to my eyes.

"Don't cry, child! If thee insists thee can stay at home by thyself. Frank will go with us. He likes running about in the park."

Frank, however, decided to stay with me. The prospect of a long afternoon alone with Carey and Miss Gwinn obviously did not attract him.

The next Sunday a compromise was effected. I consented to go to the Rosenthal and walk about with Frank near enough to the music stand for my sister to see us, but far enough away not to count as attending the concert. I agreed to this so as not to make trouble, but I felt that it was not right. The question of Sunday morning breakfast also was settled without much difficulty. On week days we went to the near-by hotel for breakfast as well as for dinner and supper, but on Sundays my sister slept late and dashed across the street to buy what was necessary for breakfast from a little shop like a hole cut in the wall of the high building opposite. Frank and I watched her bargaining with the old German woman who looked out over the tiny wooden counter below the hole. When I objected to eating food bought on the Sabbath Carey provided milk and bread

on Saturday for Frank's and my Sunday breakfasts.

The real struggle arose over dressing Frank up in my clothes and passing him off as a girl at the Bade Anstalt so that he could get a bath. There was no one to take him during the hours reserved for men and boys. He had to go with Carey or not at all. Her little flat contained no bathroom of course, and the water for washing had to be carried up by the caretaker. A weekly visit to the Bade Anstalt was highly desirable. When I objected that Frank's masquerading as a girl would be acting a lie, Carey's face suddenly lost its look of gay energy and grew very stern and the voice in which she spoke to me was vehement.

"I cannot be bothered with thy foolishness any longer," she said. "Thee has got to give in this time. Thee is a very self-willed, disobedient little girl, setting thyself up against me in this way. It's outrageous and I won't have it! What Frank does is not thy business. He wants to go to the bath, doesn't thee, Frank?"

Though I looked at my little brother pleadingly, he declared for my sister. It would be a joke to dress up in my clothes, he said, and began prancing about the room in comic imitation of me, laughing at me all the while.

Since no principle was involved in my going to the Bade Anstalt, I was obliged to accompany the others, but I did so with a burning heart, feeling that I was taking part in a deliberate deception.

For a time I brooded over the difficulties of my position. Carey had called me disobedient. She

would complain of me to my mother, I felt sure, and my mother would be distressed that Carey had been bothered. But she would understand and approve of my conduct. She would be pleased with me for refusing to do what she had taught me was wrong. My mother and Carey did not always agree. I knew that not only from the different accounts they had given me of how I came to be called "Helen" but also from discussions I had once or twice heard between them. So I was certain that my mother would uphold me, and having settled this point in my mind I stopped worrying. My sister for her part never referred to the struggle between us. She continued to treat me as kindly as before.

The days passed slowly for Frank and me. I was put to it to keep my little brother amused, but the situation was even harder for him. I at least had a job to direct my energy, while Frank's impulses were constantly thwarted. "Please, Frank, don't make so much noise, thee'll disturb Carey and Miss Gwinn," I was always admonishing him. I felt sorry for the poor boy, but I had to keep my promise to my mother. When the weather permitted we spent the mornings in the town gardens, which were gay with flowering trees my father would have loved. Yellow laburnums and pink hawthorn trees grew about the shining surface of the pond where swans majestically sailed. Frank could run about in the gardens and make as much noise as he pleased. We played games together and fed the swans under the watchful eye of the policeman on duty. By my sister's orders we did not at-

tempt to play with the other children. She had spoken to the policeman about us, she said, rather damping Frank's ardor until they made friends by nods and smiles. This kindly German never interfered with us, that I remember. On rainy days Carey allowed us to play in her study, since our room was so tiny. We had to be very quiet, as Miss Gwinn was almost always in her room, which opened out of Carey's. Often the two young women shut themselves up away from us in Miss Gwinn's room, closing the door between and talking in such low tones that Frank and I could not hear even the sound of their voices. We observed how carefully they kept the door shut and resented it.

One morning when Carey came back from the University she threw her books down on her desk and hurried past into Miss Gwinn's room without noticing Frank and me playing dominoes at the small corner table. Wide-eyed with amazement I stared after her through the door she had left open.

"I knew it would happen," I heard her say in a voice quite unlike her usual voice. "The outrageous behavior of those Russian women has ended by closing the German universities to women, even Leipzig." Coming to a stop still in my line of vision, my sister raised both hands above her head and dropped them again as she did when she was excited. "Professor Curtius has just been telling me about it. He is sure he can get a special permit from the Minister of Education for us to go on attending lectures. Still even Professor Curtius may fail. To think that just be-

cause those Russians can't behave themselves, all my work for two years may be wasted!" Carey's voice sounded more excited than I had ever heard it.

In our corner Frank and I sat motionless as two frightened mice, but Miss Gwinn, though she could not see us from her sofa, was none the less aware of us listening there in the next room.

"Do close the door, Carey!" my sharp ears caught her murmur and that ended the conversation for us.

I had, however, heard enough to excite my curiosity. What could the Russian women have done? I seized the first opportunity to ask my sister.

I could hardly believe it when she told me that every one of the Russian students was married. My sister explained to me that no woman could leave Russia unless she had her husband or one of her parents with her. Many of them married complete strangers just to get across the borders of their own country. As soon as they were safe in Germany husband and wife separated, each going his or her own way. The women as well as the men did just what they liked. This outrageous behavior had caused a great scandal, discrediting all the women students at German universities.

"It is dreadfully wrong of them, dreadfully unfair to other women," Carey said, seeming to forget me as she talked on. "Unless women stand together they can accomplish nothing. Women must learn to be loyal."

My sister's earnestness impressed me greatly. I

hated the Russians for making so much trouble but, my curiosity satisfied to the limits of my understanding—to live away from one's husband was a deadly sin in my eyes—I soon ceased to think about them.

Frank did not like Miss Gwinn and avoided her as much as possible. I on the other hand soon began to feel strongly attracted to her. Her very appearance fascinated me. Tall and exceedingly slender with crinkly black hair and pale skin, she was quite different from anyone I knew. The Thomas family all had hair that gleamed in the light. We were inclined to be short and sturdy and were energetic and quick in our movements, not languid like Miss Gwinn. We laughed aloud gaily, whereas she hardly ever laughed at all and then only very softly. The slow smile that often curved her lips puzzled and fascinated me. I did not quite know what it expressed. Since she attended few university lectures, she spent her days in her room. Always when I got a glimpse of her she was curled up on the sofa there, absorbed in a book that seemed somehow too heavy for her thin white hand to hold. Once she explained to me that she was reading many different languages, Greek, Spanish, French, as well as English, and she showed me a book printed in each one, permitting me to turn over the pages for myself. I looked on her as a marvel of learning and my awed admiration must have pleased her, since sometimes after our supper when Frank was safely tucked in bed she invited me to draw my chair close to her sofa while she read poetry aloud to me, Swinburne's poems

only, as I remember. I never tired of sitting still for however long a time listening to the sound of her voice.

Swinburne's rhythms lulled me into a state of enchantment. Conveying to me no definite pictures, no clear ideas, they opened up vague, vast vistas to my imagination on a beat of recurrent melody. The three poems my mother was in the habit of chanting to her children had produced something of the same magic effect, though weakened by too great definiteness. "The Ballad of Lord Lovell," delightfully gay and amusing, made me laugh always; Elizabeth Barrett Browning's "A Child's Grave at Florence" brought tears to my eyes, for I well understood that my mother's beautiful voice had become so sad when she repeated it because she was thinking of Dora; the story of "The Romance of the Swan's Nest" ("Little Ellie," we called it) I could easily follow, though the significance of its frustrated dreaming escaped my conscious intelligence. It was my favorite. Swinburne's poetry was far more exciting and mysterious. By the time we all left Leipzig together and journeyed to Switzerland to join my parents I had learned "The Garden of Proserpine" by heart and could also repeat many lines from Swinburne's other poems.

My delight in seeing my mother again was boundless. I flung myself into her outstretched arms, completely happy and at peace. But after this first meeting was over I found myself still in a way separated from her, for Carey absorbed her attention. I did not resent this, since the im-

portance of my sister to my mother had always been a basic fact of my life. Now she and Carey had been separated from each other for a long time and had many things to talk over. If I were patient the opportunity would soon come for me to tell my mother all about my difficulties in Leipzig. I could afford to wait since I was sure my mother would be on my side.

My sister, however, upset everything for me, forestalling me by telling my mother in my presence the story of the Bade Anstalt, making a kind of joke of it. While she enlarged on what she called my silly scruples I stood by, watching my mother's face with increasing consternation. She did not seem in the least shocked by Carey's passing Frank off as a girl. On the contrary she praised my sister's cleverness in managing a bath for him and she laughed over Frank's mimicking of me when he was dressed up in my clothes.

At last I collected myself sufficiently to break in. "Please, Mother, listen to me. Carey hasn't told thee about wanting us to go to concerts with her on Sunday afternoon." I spoke with confidence, sure that my mother would disapprove such a disregard of the Sabbath.

My mother's face lost its smile. She was silent for a moment, then said to me gravely, "Thee must not forget that taking care of Frank and thee was very hard for Carey. She had to do what she could in the circumstances. Thy duty was to obey her and not to make things more difficult for her by objecting. It was not thy business to judge."

I stood by my mother's chair speechless with

66

amazement. Never could any human being have been less prepared for a disaster than I was for my mother's condemnation.

She drew me to her and kissed me gently, no doubt reading my protest in my face. "I know thee did what thee thought was right," she comforted me, and let me run off to hide the tears with which I was struggling.

"Poor child!" I heard my sister exclaim as I was closing the door. "She takes everything too literally."

At the family hotel where we stayed in Geneva *vin ordinaire* was supplied for luncheon and dinner. Black bottles stood up and down the long table, making it look very strange. Frank's curiosity was great when he saw our fellow guests pour a mysterious red fluid out of these bottles into their glasses. A bottle without a cork stood right in front of his own plate. It contained wine, my father told him. He could not drink wine because of the temperance pledge he had taken.

"What does wine taste like, Father?" he asked. "Please let me have a sip. Just a sip wouldn't hurt."

My father explained with great care the nature of a pledge to my little brother, who seemed satisfied. But with the persistence of a favorite child he returned to the charge. At every meal he teased for just a taste.

Finally my father said to him, in a tone of irritation he seldom used when speaking to Frank, "Do stop thy begging. Thee would not like it at all, I assure thee." Then, seeing Frank's mouth

67

open to protest once more, he hurriedly went on, "It might not be a bad thing for thee to learn now what horrid sour stuff wine is. I'll give thee a little to teach thee a lesson."

With consternation I watched my father pour a small quantity of the bright red wine out of Frank's bottle into his glass. When my little brother lifted the glass to his mouth and I perceived that he was actually going to break his pledge I burst into tears.

My father turned to my mother and said in a tone of utter exasperation, "Do quiet that child, Mary. The children are a dreadful nuisance! I can't stand being bothered in this way. I begged thee to leave them at home where they belong."

Unable to quiet my sobbing, my mother led me out of the dining room up to my own little bedroom. While she dried my tears she talked to me very severely, blaming me for my lack of self-control, big girl that I was. The public exhibition I had made of myself had disgraced my father and her. She had expected better behavior from me, she said.

"I will try to be better, Mother," I promised, struggling to control my sobs. "I'm terribly sorry. But what will happen to Frank, Mother? He has broken his pledge." At the thought of my little brother's deadly sin my tears gushed out again.

My mother took no notice of my question, perhaps she hadn't really heard it. She gave me a drink of water, bathed my hot face, covered me up on my bed and when I was a little quieter she left me, telling me to lie there without getting up un-

til she came back. After my violent weeping I fell asleep and must have slept for hours, since the room was dark when I opened my eyes to find my mother standing beside me.

Never once after that did anyone speak to me of the scene I had made in the dining room. It was just as though it had never happened. I did not dare speak about it myself, even to my mother. I felt that I had disgraced myself so terribly that it could not be mentioned. My mother never tolerated our making scenes, above all in public. I had been very wrong to burst out crying, that I acknowledged to myself humbly. But I was right about the temperance pledge. And I was right about Sunday, too, and acting a lie. Why had my mother countenanced my father's giving Frank wine to drink? Why had she laughed at me with Carey and scolded me? Why had she failed to support me when I was only following the principles she herself had taught me? What could be the reason? Was it possible that my mother did not really mean what she said to be taken seriously? These questions repeated themselves over and over in my mind during the days of our being stormbound in Geneva.

Days of bewilderment they were for me as I mooned about the big hotel rooms. My mother seemed to be always occupied with Carey and Miss Gwinn. Frank had deserted me to attach himself to my father. Too unhappy to join them, I felt deserted by everyone, alone and utterly discouraged.

But at last the skies cleared and we started on

our tour through Switzerland. The rapid succession of new experiences diverted my mind. I could not help being amused; everything interested me. Thus the enigmas that had haunted me were thrust down unsolved into the depths of consciousness.

A party of six, we traveled by public horse diligences or, when these were not available, by private carriage. The start in the mornings was thrilling. The luggage had to be stowed away, our places chosen. In the cold air Frank and I ran about while we waited. And every day we were given bundles of religious tracts to scatter among the swarms of children who begged for pennies behind our carriage. The bits of paper we threw out fluttered in the wind; the children snatched at them, running and leaping, then lagged in the road to examine their treasure. Sometimes a shout of disappointment reached our ears; small fists were raised and shaken at us. I was bothered by this demonstration, but my recent experiences did not encourage me to protest. I could not help finding it amusing to throw out the tracts and I suppose I must have believed they would do the children good in the end. Our supply never failed, for my parents had brought with them from England a great quantity in different languages—blue tracts for Italian, white for German, pale yellow for French. In them, I understood, the gospel message was set forth with suitable simplicity. To distribute them was, my parents said, the only way they had to help people whose languages they could not speak and whose religion was mistaken.

In a Catholic country there were many things that astonished me. The roadside crucifixes, the shrines to the Virgin set in village walls, the people crossing themselves with holy water and kneeling in churches all seemed very strange to me, and were all explained by my parents as manifestations of dark superstition. But it was only the wooden crucifixes along the road in the country that made a deep impression on me. I could not bear to look at Christ's suffering, bloodstained face, his bleeding side, his hands and feet nailed to the rough cross, pitilessly revealed under the open sky. With this horror I associate the horror of goiter-swollen throats in the Rhone Valley where many of the inhabitants were idiots, I was told, because of the water they had to drink. Years later, hearing of the iodine cure for these people, I felt as if some hidden malady in my own body had been healed.

The comedy of our journey was supplied by my mother's wedding ring. As a Quaker she had never worn a ring of any sort. When we were about to leave England for continental countries and stay in hotels among real foreigners—the English were our own people—her unencircled finger loomed large for my father. What would Frenchmen, Germans, Italians think?—that question disturbed his peace of mind. I heard it discussed, understanding only that to wear a wedding ring was the custom for married women in the strange countries we were about to visit. Concerning the awful implications of its absence I knew nothing, of course. Though she protested, my mother yielded to my

father's anxious insistence. A gold circle was purchased and stuck on the third finger of her left hand. But she was always taking it off, leaving it about, and several times forgot it entirely on the dressing table of her hotel room. Letters had to be sent back to recover the lost emblem; one or two, perhaps more, new rings had hurriedly to be supplied. Finally we all watched to see that it was in place. "Mother, where is thy ring? Has thee lost it again?" I remember the fun of asking her this question in a shocked tone of voice. She laughed gaily and appeared to regard the whole matter as a kind of joke. I suspect her of enjoying the opportunity to tease my father.

My father loved pictures, and I was his companion when he visited the galleries of Belgium and Holland after Carey and Miss Gwinn had returned to their studies in Leipzig. Of all the pictures I saw on this first European journey I remember only one. Hung quite low by a doorway on the right-hand side, a small canvas of the Devil in a red cart pulled me up short as, following my father, I was about to pass through. Later in Antwerp and at The Hague I hunted for this picture, hoping to discover why it alone had remained vivid for me. I did not then suspect the obvious reason.

On the ship going home, my mother spent much time with two Cowley fathers who were among the passengers. Strange figures they seemed to me in their coarse brown robes tied about the waist with cords. Indeed, to my untutored observation, they looked exactly like the monks I had seen in France, but my mother assured me they were Protestants

and Englishmen. Their religion was mystical like hers, and like her they were dedicated to a life of strict Christian sincerity. I accepted what my mother said, though I knew that my father disapproved of the Cowley fathers as tending toward Roman Catholicism.

Grace and Margaret welcomed us home with enthusiasm. They had not enjoyed the supervision of my father's aunt, our formidable Great-Aunt Julia Valentine, and his half sister, our Aunt Mary. Grace complained bitterly of the trials she had lived through, as I well remember. A mirror that had fallen from the wall of her room and been smashed to bits on the day of our departure figured in her story as an ill-omened beginning, well justified by the event. She had been subjected to regulations and penalties unsuited to her status as a young lady. She had submitted for her parents' sake, she explained, but the months of our absence had been exceedingly unpleasant months for her.

Now reunited, the family settled back into its accustomed ways, profoundly relieved that so long a separation had passed without misfortune. Both my father and my mother offered fervent thanks to God at our family prayers for His great goodness to us.

V

OBSTINATE QUESTIONINGS

WHATEVER the deeper psychological effects of our journey may have been, Frank and I returned to Baltimore superficially much the same little boy and girl who had left it. In my little brother's case the long months of traveling about Europe could only have intensified the melancholy and depression which in maturity he declared were the dominant moods of his childhood, but of which I was at the time largely unconscious. No one, I believe, took Frank's occasional fits of depression seriously. The year before our journey he had been found late one afternoon seated on the top step of the long stairway leading down into the front hall, and had been heard to say over and over to himself, "Nobody loves me in my own house." I remember well that this complaint, far from arousing sympathy for Frank, caused general amusement, since he was my father's special pet, whose least wish was always granted. Again, Frank's insisting that he hated Paris and wanted to leave it because the horses there "looked so sad" was considered strange, but nobody, not even my mother, suspected that he was transferring his own dominant emotion to the many horses with hanging heads in those clattering foreign streets.

No doubt Frank behaved so quietly because he was sunk in the listlessness of utter boredom. There was nothing to interest and amuse a small boy on such a journey as ours. What the effect on him of breaking his pledge and taking his first drink may have been I can only conjecture. My guess is that it was not very great. At his age and with his practical temperament I should suppose that both taking and breaking the temperance pledge were no more than a game to him. He was never much impressed by the seriousness with which I questioned things, and the various fusses I made were highly inconvenient for him. No doubt in his own boyish way he thought me as foolish as did my eldest sister.

I am unable in my own case also to estimate accurately the change made in me by my experiences abroad, though I know that they affected me profoundly. The responsibility for both Frank and myself that rested on me by giving me a definite occupation kept me alert, and no doubt sharpened my impressions. In every new situation that arose I had to decide what behavior my parents would approve. Sure at first that I knew just what was right, later after my disgrace in Leipzig and Geneva, I became anxious and uncertain. I could no longer automatically apply the rules I had lived by before. For some reason I did not understand, my parents had suddenly ceased to uphold them.

I had long been aware of a certain capriciousness in my father. He sometimes lost his temper and scolded us with unreasonable severity. Still, his

75

solid figure and large-featured, smooth-shaven face with its kind eyes looking very dark under gray hair represented for me rocklike safety. I never doubted for a moment that he knew what was right and would not willingly himself depart from it. Thus his encouraging Frank to break the pledge so solemnly made gave me a severe shock; but my mother's upholding first Carey and then my father disturbed me far more, since I had never until that time known her to fall short in any way of the standards she had taught me. Consciously to criticize my mother was beyond my powers; what she did must be right, but I no longer knew what would please her. The joy had gone out of being good.

It was fortunate for me that I had picked up a love of poetry to fill the void left by the gradual fading away of religious emotion; fortunate above all that I had in my head bits of verse to repeat over and over to myself instead of the customary texts from the Bible. Uncertain and given to brooding by temperament from early childhood, I had relied on the hypnotic effect of half-under-stood Biblical phrases to help me through my inner difficulties. Since I could not always be running to my mother with my fears and my hurt feelings I had dealt with them myself by repeating texts from the Bible over and over in my mind. I now slid easily into repeating lines of poetry for purposes of incantation. Thus Swinburne's "Garden of Proserpine," which I had learned by heart in Leipzig, gave me comfort when I most needed it.

Almost any one of the verses could be crooned

until I was at peace, but the last verse was best
of all:

> *Then star nor sun shall waken,*
>   *Nor any change of light;*
> *Nor sound of water shaken*
>   *Nor any sound or sight;*
> *Nor wintry leaves nor vernal*
> *Nor days nor things diurnal;*
> *Only the sleep eternal*
>   *In an eternal night.*

I quite failed to understand that it was a hymn
to death I chanted. Swinburne's sonorous nega-
tions inspired in me only a mood of peaceful
brooding, vaguely illumined by a pale goddess and
a garden murmuring with the sound of waters
and the whisper of soft sighing. I was unconscious
that a change in my deepest feelings had taken
place, and my behavior remained much the same.
I said my prayers morning and evening, I went to
meeting, I tried to do my duty; only the fact that
during those first months after our return from
Europe I took comfort in such melancholy images
revealed the profound spiritual shock I had received.

Meanwhile, together with the love of poetry I
had acquired in Leipzig a respect for learning. My
sister's joy in her work pervaded the atmosphere.
She was on fire with enthusiasm. Miss Gwinn too
was very happy reading her books all day long. For
the first time I got a sense of interests that were
not inspired by religious motives. But occasionally
even my sister was discouraged, I learned from
what she and Miss Gwinn said to each other. Carey

was preparing herself for a career as thoroughly as if she were a man, in spite of the fact that when she returned home she might find no suitable career open to her. Very few good positions were ever offered to women, they agreed. This difficulty bothered Carey. Preoccupied as I was in Leipzig by my own troubles, I paid little attention to my sister's anxieties. None the less they made an impression on me, and later I remembered certain pronouncements of hers that at the time I was hardly aware of hearing. Thus already in my eleventh year I had begun to perceive the possible disadvantages of being born a girl.

At home when I was a small child there had been little to suggest to me the restriction placed upon women in the outside world. Our family sitting room was presided over by a large steel engraving of Elizabeth Fry in Quaker cap and flowing Quaker dress. When I joined the family group around the fire after supper there she hung, an imposing figure on the wall above me. We all honored her because she had visited the cruel British prisons of her day and reformed them. According to Quaker theory women were the equals of men, the two sexes facing each other "with level-fronting eyelids," a phrase I often heard. And in practice twice a week at the Sunday and Thursday morning meetings for worship I saw my mother sit opposite, even though a little below, my father in the raised gallery for ministers and elders. On the one occasion when I attended a joint business session of the Men's and Women's Monthly Meeting, as I pushed open the door at the far end of

the room I saw my mother and my father seated side by side in solitary state before a long table littered with papers. They performed respectively the duties of clerk of the men's and clerk of the women's meeting. I remember the sharp stab of pride I felt as I stood in the doorway to look at my parents.

My mother's personal prestige was such that everyone who came to the house paid tribute to her in one way or another, and the admiration of which she was the object separated her from ordinary people. That she could be considered in any way inferior was an idea which did not occur to me. Still, long before I was aware that she was subject to restrictions because of her sex, I must have had under my eyes many evidences of the fact that I failed to see. Max Beerbohm's cartoon of Rossetti being introduced to John Stuart Mill shows better than any words, perhaps, the state of mind that blinded me to all such intimations, absurd as it may seem to compare a little girl's feelings for her mother to the adoration of a painter and poet for a beautiful woman.

Mill is in the act of presenting to the artist his book *On the Subjection of Women*. Rossetti in his studio stands under the picture of the woman the torment of whose beauty he had spent his life in assuaging by painting her image. His hands make no motion to receive the gift. Can women be subjected by men? He knows there is no possibility of it. When I came upon this cartoon while turning over the pages of Beerbohm's book in London long years after my mother had died, emotion

surged up in me. Rossetti's figure held my attention though one glance had sufficed to stamp forever on my memory the entrancement of his face and attitude, his utter incomprehension. No more easily could I have regarded the glorious creature who was my mother as being in need of emancipation.

When I search among childish impressions for facts significant of my mother's real position, I find only a few and those of the homeliest sort. First there is the scheme to get a new nursery carpet, which I have already described. It was my father's consent, not my mother's, that had to be obtained. This I obviously accepted without question as entirely proper. Then on several occasions I heard my father complain to my mother of the expense involved in employing a protégée of hers to help with the cleaning—an old woman and, as he thought, not worth the wages paid her. My mother's answer to these remonstrances was to keep Mrs. Webster, who needed help, out of my father's sight—as I well remember, since I was cautioned not to speak of her in his presence. I should have understood from this that my father had control of the family pocketbook, and probably did understand, though I thought nothing of it. Before I was old enough to have any real knowledge of the power of money, my grandmother Whitall's death had put my mother in possession of her inheritance, freeing her from a sense of economic dependence. I did notice that my father showed a greater sense of being in the right when he criticized my mother, her preaching in particular, than she showed in

her comments to him. But she was in every way gentler and less easily excited than my father. Visiting friends agreed more often with him than with her, asking his opinion rather than hers. I merely thought them stupid. I heard her regret her lack of education, since at sixteen she had finished the course at the best girls' school in Philadelphia, and there was no woman's college then in existence to which she could go. After her marriage my father had begun to teach her Latin, which she passionately desired to learn, but Carey's birth put a stop to that. My mother's powerlessness to get the education she desired was a signpost I should have paused to consider, but I speeded by, no doubt because my mother seemed perfectly well educated to me.

One scene that I remember did arouse passionate indignation in me. My father objected to a friend of my mother's because she was *a divorced woman*. My mother pointed out that her friend had been compelled to get a divorce because of flagrant misconduct on the part of her husband, that no smallest blame could rest on her.

In a strangely changed voice my father laid down the law, leaning forward in his armchair to face my mother. "Understand this, Mary. I will not permit any divorced woman whatever to enter the doors of my house. I do not care what her husband may have done. How can thee know that she was not to blame in the first place? Women often drive their husbands into temptation."

"Why does Father look so fierce?" I asked myself in amazement, and then suddenly I saw that

81

my mother's face was gleaming with tears in the lamplight.

"Thee is hard and unjust, James," she said. "Men are very cruel to women. I cannot understand how thee can be so unjust."

"Father, look! Mother is crying. Thee has made Mother cry!" Indignantly I drew his attention to what he must himself clearly have seen. My father's answer was to send me out of the room.

How I came to witness such a scene between my parents as a small child I do not know. Probably it arose with sudden violence in the course of ordinary conversation. It has remained vivid in my memory, and even now, though in the fourth decade of the twentieth century it seems quaint even to me, none the less it still moves me to indignation, not any longer against my father, who was no doubt powerless to escape the ideas of his period, but against the age-old unfairness to women of the order of things.

So by early emotion was the soil of my mind prepared for passionate interest in righting the wrongs of society to my mother's sex and my own. The memory of some indignity suffered by her mother is the reason many a woman of my generation carried on the fight for women with an intensity that seems to their children and grandchildren, girls as well as boys, absurdly exaggerated, quite comic in fact. One suffrage leader I know was as a child bewildered and outraged by discovering that the ignorant day laborers on their Ohio farm all went to the polls to cast their votes, but that her mother, far more intelligent and efficient

than any of them, was denied this privilege merely because she was a woman. Another waited with her mother in the carriage outside the voting booth while their illiterate black coachman made his choice of a president to rule over them. Indignation for what is felt to be a flagrant injustice to ourselves or to someone we love arouses passionate zeal even in mild-minded people. Many men to their honor became crusaders for the cause of women because of their mothers, or because of their wives, like, for instance, John Stuart Mill. When a sense of injustice to one's own self is added to a man's more impersonal motive, the tempation to go to unreasonable extremes becomes greater. People so moved find a sense of humor quite beside the point.

Carey herself had been forced to fight for the privilege of receiving an education, not only against the general social prejudice but against my father's veto. Conventional both by temperament and training, my father accepted the ideas of the group into which he had been born. Like nearly all Quakers, he was proud of Quaker principles and traditions without feeling any great necessity to test the one against the other afresh in changed social conditions. His grandfather had not counted the cost of freeing the slaves brought him by a Southern wife—that was incumbent on every Quaker of his period who came into the possession of slaves. During the Civil War my father himself —though a passionate abolitionist and supporter of the Union—had automatically refused to join the army medical corps. The equality of the sexes

was as much a matter of principle with Quakers as pacifism, but it did not operate as effectively for reasons perhaps not difficult to understand. Their noncoöperation with government forced Quakers to live a life apart, forming as it were a state within a state, persecuted at first, tolerated later. As time went on the men gradually began to take a man's part in government. John Bright in England was a power in parliament, though not without suffering severe criticism from his fellow Quakers. Living more and more coöperatively with the communities in which they were settled, Quakers had to make some sort of practical terms with the prevalent customs and in so doing were influenced by them. This was specially the case with the men, whose activities took them outside the family and the religious group.

In the seventeenth century the founders of The Society of Friends had valued inspiration in both men and women far more than education, of which few possessed very much. However, they soon began to set up special schools for the training of their children. It is fair, I think, to assume that in these early schools a sincere effort was made to educate the girls as thoroughly as the boys. But in the course of time, along the Atlantic seaboard of the United States, at least, this original equality of the sexes in education was lost. A settled life in one community had brought prosperity to many Quaker families. They had become landed proprietors of a sort or successful merchants and manufacturers, and they began in their schools and colleges to follow the general rule of the people

about them in giving greater educational advantages to their sons than to their daughters. My father himself, and all three of his half brothers, had received a college education, but neither my mother nor his sister had enjoyed a like advantage. Thus he was dreadfully shocked by Carey's determination after she left school to continue her studies at a non-Quaker, coeducational college where she felt she could get the best training. He set his face against it and a severe struggle ensued between my father on the one hand and Carey, supported by my mother, on the other. Since I was a child three years old and still in the nursery when this battle raged, I possess no knowledge of it at first hand, but none the less from hearsay and contemporary letters I have formed a vivid idea of the way in which it was fought.

My father's objections to Carey's going to Cornell University were threefold—social, domestic, and religious. It would be disadvantageous to her first because she would there be thrown with all sorts of people and would probably fall in love and insist upon marrying some unsuitable fellow student or professor. If she escaped this danger, which seemed highly improbable to my father, years of study would unfit her for happiness in domestic life where women's true happiness lies; and most terrible danger of all, her religious faith might be undermined, destroyed even, in a non-Quaker, all-too-probably free thinking atmosphere. Driven from one position, my father took up another and finally entrenched himself behind the impregnable bulwark of expense. He could not

afford to send Carey to college. Such an outlay for four years was not to be thought of, he said. Carey assured him she would cut down the four years' course to two years. She was sure she would be able to do it. The expense even for two years was more than my father felt he could meet. Though it was true that he utterly disapproved, his disapproval could not be considered the deciding factor, he declared. He simply did not have the money to do as Carey and my mother desired. Further discussion was useless.

From the beginning the odds were in my father's favor. The whole community was back of him, an invisible but strong support, and the members of his own family in the midst of whom we lived day by day sympathized with him and pitied him openly. Overburdened as he already was with the support of eight children, including Frank who was then the baby, how could he agree to further unnecessary outlay?

"Poor Brother James," I can imagine Great-Aunt Julia or Aunt Mary or Uncle John exclaiming with sad headshakes. "Carey asks altogether too much of her father."

Had the education of a son been in question, my father's family, highly conservative and sufficiently well-to-do, would have felt differently about the expense. A daughter was another matter in their eyes. Carey and my mother appeared to be beaten. My mother, however, still had a weapon in reserve.

"Nothing is left for us but tears," she told Carey. "I have used every argument I can think of in talk-

ing with thy father. Reason will not move him. Now we will see whether he can stand out against our weeping. We shall both have to cry day and night, thee as well as I."

Carey was ready even for that. So together and separately they wept and they wept. My father pled with them, lost his temper, called them unfair, shut himself up, stayed away from home, all to no purpose. They accepted his reproaches in silence and in silence continued to weep whenever he appeared. Worried and distressed beyond endurance by their red eyes and wet faces, my father surrendered at last.

"Since nothing else will satisfy thee," he said to my mother, "I will somehow find the necessary money, almost impossible as that will be. But," he added, turning to Carey, as she herself recounted the story, "only for two years. After two years thee will have to return home whether thee has been able to get thy degree or not."

"I told my father not to worry about my degree. I would attend to that myself. No one believed I could do four years' work in two. I had to cover the freshman and sophomore years while I was attending junior and senior classes. Often I worked all night long. In the winter when my room grew terribly cold at night I took my books down to the cellar and sat in front of the furnace. By opening the furnace door and crouching down near it on the janitor's chair I managed to get a glow on my page bright enough for reading. I had to keep watch for the janitor, who was a lazy fellow and often slept late. Only by using every moment

was I able to get my degree in the time allowed me by my father."

It was in some such words that Carey used to tell the story of her going to college. I was almost grown up before its various incidents, learned now and then by chance, fitted themselves for me into a complete narrative. The knowledge of past events in our family was taken for granted. The younger children were seldom told anything, other than a few amusing anecdotes. We learned only what circumstances or some particular interest of our own brought to our attention. Sometimes information that was common knowledge to my elder brothers and sisters came to me with a disconcerting shock of surprise. When my curiosity was aroused, I had to go about learning the facts discreetly to avoid a rebuff, but in the course of time I became fairly skilled in this, having found out by experience that people enjoy talking of themselves.

I greatly admired the energy and intelligence displayed by my sister in getting a college education, while my father's utter helplessness against the unquenchable weeping of his wife and daughter produced a comic effect that somewhat mitigated my condemnation of his behavior. But my mother was the real heroine for me. It was she, and she alone, who had won the battle by her amazing steadfastness and ingenuity. I thought above all of my mother. The knowledge that she had been forced to employ a method so alien to her noble courage was dreadfully painful to me. Without suffering that indignity she should have been able to give her talented eldest daughter, on whose

career her heart was set, the education she herself had longed for and been denied by destiny. That my father, loving her as I knew he did, should have forced streams of tears from my mother's eyes was a terrible proof of the power exerted by prejudice on the men of his generation.

Perhaps it may be thought that my mother's tears were in fact not very bitter tears, that, being accustomed to her position as a Victorian woman, she did not suffer from the sensitive pride since developed in many women. She may even have enjoyed weeping as a successful strategy in an exciting battle with my father. I never put any such comforting interpretation on her tears, and am still unable to do so. I remember too well the expression of composed sadness that habitually settled on her face when she ceased to smile or to speak. Although she was always cheerful in action, I knew even as a small girl that my mother was fundamentally sad at heart. This profoundly intuitive knowledge aroused my passionate devotion. I was continually on the alert to help her in any way I could, and I grieved that I was able to do so little for her. Spoiled child as I certainly was up to my twelfth or thirteenth year, I was never impertinent or consciously disobedient to my mother.

VI

INCIDENT AT BREAKFAST

THE beginning of Frank's and my formal education had been long delayed, but now, back in Baltimore once more, we were at last sent as regular pupils to "The Friends Academy." We landed both together in the lowest class, thanks to my father's fear of overtaxing our brains. At first I was a bit abashed to find myself with younger children, though I knew I had been held back not because of any personal defect but *on principle*, which was in itself a kind of distinction. Then, too, it seemed natural for Frank and me to be together, so I accepted the situation without loss of self-respect. Probably I failed to realize that my ignorance was really disgraceful for a child of ten. I wrote badly and could read only the simplest things without help. A story or a poem I had once heard read aloud I could make out again; but a new page daunted me. Quite obviously I belonged in the lowest grade.

Most of my classes I have completely forgotten, but the delight I felt in tracing the outlines of classical heads has never faded from my memory. Their regular profiles seemed to me entrancingly beautiful; and they were *Greek*. I felt somehow exalted by their being Greek, so much had Carey already impressed the splendor of Greece on my imagination. Frank hated drawing and was soon

FRANK AND HELEN AS "US"

excused by the teacher. In the informal, flexible grouping of the lower grade he and I were gradually separated, whether in the natural course of things or by design, I do not know. The quaint combination called "us" was not recognized by our teachers.

Once even in this carefully controlled lot of children the unfortunate color of my hair got me into trouble. When the whole grade was assembled one day for a test we were asked the meaning of the word "auburn." Silence fell; then a boy in the front row shot up his hand. "Auburn," he proclaimed, "is a red color two shades darker than Nellie's hair." The eyes of all, boys and girls alike, turned to look at me as a shout of laughter resounded in which even the teacher joined. I was dreadfully humiliated. This scene and the wild excitement of swinging at the end of the line when we played crack the whip in the schoolyard are still vivid to me. Besides these memories here recorded nothing remains of the long stretch of days that made up my first year at school. Incidentally, at the end of it I had not yet learned to read to myself with pleasure.

At home my tenacious verbal memory and a certain sharpness of comment concealed to some extent, I believe, the backward state of my education. My mother at least was proud of my knowing so much poetry by heart; and my ability to recite from beginning to end Swinburne's "Garden of Proserpine," pronouncing the long words correctly, seemed to her a remarkable feat for a child of my age. It was part of her policy to encourage

any special ability shown by her children, so no doubt she felt it was for my good to display my accomplishment in public.

One afternoon when her committee of ladies had finished its business my mother sent for me. Dressed by her orders in the green velvet frock she had bought for me in England, my hollow round curls falling in shining neatness over my fine lace collar, I stood before the circle of bonnets in the familiar front parlor, shy but proud. As I repeated verse after verse of my remarkable poem in the cadenced voice that hypnotized me, I watched from under lowered eyelids the faces of my mother's friends, and I saw the looks of admiration with which my appearance had been greeted change slowly to looks of bewilderment and then to grave disapproval. Though the momentum of habit sufficed to carry me through to the last word, I was dreadfully abashed. A glance at my mother's face revealed her still smiling, proud and delighted, unconscious of the impression I had made. Even the faint praise with which one of the ladies broke the silence that fell when I had finished appeared to satisfy my mother.

"Yes, she has a wonderful memory," I heard my mother begin, but I could bear no more. I rushed from the room without asking permission or saying good-by to anyone.

Never again did I allow myself to be dressed up and lured down to the parlor to make a fool of myself.

My mother's greatest self-indulgence, the only one, in fact, I ever observed in her, was providing

pretty clothes for her children. I well remember the eagerness she showed when engaged in selecting English costumes for Frank and me in a London shop. Frank was much admired in his little black velvet suit with its red tie that set off his dark eyes and curly dark hair, and my green velvet frock was considered very becoming to me. Perhaps my mother's pleasure in displaying my English costume to her friends may have played a part in the scene I have described. However that may be, it is a fact that she liked to see her children, her sons as well as her daughters, well dressed, following in this, I feel sure, the example of her own mother.

My first experience of what clothes can do for one had, as it happened, been provided me by Grandmother Whitall. When I was still a very little girl she gave me for Christmas a small tippet and muff of ermine, the fur set aside for kings and queens, I was told. This tippet and muff were the pride of my childhood. My neck encircled by the regal collar, and holding in my hands the regal muff, I walked out of our front door, no longer myself but a princess. I trod the pavement with stately steps, bowing graciously to the crowds of subjects that thronged the empty streets.

Soon after her marriage my mother had renounced all finery for herself, but in her girlhood she had loved pretty clothes. One evidence of her former finery still remained packed away in a big pasteboard box on the top shelf of her closet upstairs. Sometimes when we begged her she would take down the box and unfold before our de-

lighted eyes the lovely dress of white satin she had worn as a bride. The kerchief and ruffles and full-gathered skirt were trimmed with folds of the crinkled Chinese crêpe of those days, imported in clipper ships. Once white as snow these folds of crêpe had turned with time to a bright canary yellow, producing a gay effect when we beheld them. We stood around my mother in a circle and exclaimed over the size of the bodice, impossibly tiny as it seemed to us. Then I always ran off to my father's table to examine the miniature of her before her marriage. Thus I delighted to worship my mother as a young girl with golden-brown ringlets and a rose in her bosom.

Except for a white house dress which she brought home from England, I never saw my mother wear any other color than black, but I loved her dresses. Always cut according to the same pattern, a long princess overdress buttoned close from the throat almost to the knees, then flaring to reveal the skirt, they were made of excellent stuffs, of softest cashmere, of heavy silk or fine velvet for ceremonious occasions. They felt deliciously soft to my stroking hand. At her throat she wore a full white ruching or a bit of folded net, fastened by a shining black enamel brooch in the very center of which was a tiny pearl. This was absolutely the only jewel my mother possessed. Her street mantles were of black silk, but for winter doubled with gray squirrel skin. I never saw her in the regulation Quaker poke bonnet she had adopted after her "conversion" by my father's father, for she soon abandoned it, disliking the attention it attracted

on the streets. The bonnet I knew was small and made of black silk, with strings but no trimming. You did not really notice it since it left visible the hair above her smooth forehead and her level eyebrows. The gaze of all beholders was attracted to my mother's face. Its harmonious proportions and quiet coloring, soft golden-brown hair, gray eyes not conspicuously large, and faintly red, composed lips, seemed somehow to have a spiritual quality. In repose her expression was sad, but when she spoke my mother's face quickly took on a look of gay animation. She used to smile with her eyes alone, drawing my heart out of my bosom.

Sometimes the cost of our clothes seemed to bother her. Certainly I heard her more than once defend herself against the charge of extravagance in that respect by maintaining her right to spend part of her own income on her children. I never heard any suggestion that her care for our appearance might have a worldly influence on us. Perhaps that battle had been fought before I was old enough to know about it. My sisters may have rebelled against wearing plain, peculiar clothes and forced concessions that in my time were accepted as a matter of course.

It is also true that regard for external appearances formed a part of Quaker tradition. The decent neatness required of Quaker women from the first had become elegance, as the way of dressing originally adopted from the plain people of seventeenth-century England, and kept unchanged as a matter of principle, went out of fashion. The simplest costume of Charles II's day seemed orna-

mental in the nineteenth century. The long, un-broken lines of the full skirts gave them grace and distinction. Often they were made of silk that had been especially dyed the approved shade, a lovely soft gray or a deep, lusterless plum color. The kerchiefs and caps were of finest muslin or net and had always to be perfectly fresh. Indeed, to appear as was proper, a strict Quaker lady of the old school needed the attentions of a special maid and often had them, though little was said of the matter. My mother's mother, my father's stepmother, and the aunts who had taken him in charge after his own mother's death were beautifully dressed old ladies, majestic in their fine simplicity. I admired their stately appearance and was greatly overawed by it. On the street their "plain bonnets," large and ugly in shape, spoiled the effect, but in the house they were a delight to behold. Even as a small child I saw very few men who still wore the distinctive Quaker costume, but these few were impressive on the street as well as in the house. Their wide-brimmed hats, their swallow-tailed coats with high, straight collars gave them an air of ceremonious dignity. The costume of both sexes must have been troublesome, since every article had to be specially made according to the ordained pattern.

My mother's clothes were easy to procure and really simple. Being black and conforming sufficiently to the prevailing mode, they attracted no attention. They were, however, not beautiful, and worn by a plain woman, they would have seemed gloomy. That they were a trial to my beauty-loving father I well understood. Still, since my

mother had adopted her way of dressing as a matter of principle, I felt she was right to disregard my father's protests. It was only by citing the example of Mrs. Gurney, whom we had visited in England, that he persuaded her to get the white dress which gave him so much pleasure. If an eminent English Quaker lady like Mrs. Gurney thought a white dress permissible at home, my father argued, it could not be unsuitable for my mother. Disliking, perhaps, to set herself up against Mrs. Gurney and no doubt glad to please my father, she made this one concession.

My father's devotion to her showed itself in many ways. It was her beauty that had first attracted him when, as her brother's most intimate friend at Haverford College, he had visited my grandfather's house in Philadelphia. He had insisted on marrying her at once, although she was only seventeen years old. Stories of his ardent courtship, of my grandmother's protests that her daughter was too young for marriage, and of my father's promising even to do the housekeeping himself until she was able to manage, were favorite stories with me. I felt that my mother had been the most beautiful young girl who ever existed and was now the most beautiful person in the whole world. I have little doubt that in this I was only echoing my father's opinion.

Once a bachelor friend of long standing who, late in middle age, had married a young wife, boasted to my father of the pleasure he found in having a lovely woman as a companion. "I have lived for many years with a beautiful woman,"

was my father's reply, reported to us with keen satisfaction in his quick rebuke of his friend's presumption. For days after this incident I held up my head with pride.

When we came downstairs in the morning the letters always lay in a pile on the breakfast table by my father's plate. He sorted them out and handed them to the rest of us seated up and down the table, according to their addresses. Usually he gave my mother her letters without comment, but one morning I heard him say to her sharply, "Here is another letter for thee from David Uptigraff." Amazed by the tone of his voice, I stopped eating my hominy and looked at my father.

His face was red and he kept his eyes fixed fiercely on my mother's face while he continued, "That is the fourth letter thee has received from him since we came back from the conference in Chicago. If David Uptigraff wishes to continue his discussion of restitution he can continue it with me. I shall write and tell him so, unless thee prefers to do it thyself."

Never before had I heard my father speak in such a tone to my mother or look at her so fiercely.

The voice in which she answered him was, however, perfectly quiet and gentle. "I have already told David Uptigraff that no purpose can be served by continuing our correspondence. This letter requires no answer, I am sure. We will read it together after breakfast."

The funny name David Uptigraff, repeated so often, stuck in my mind and perhaps accounts for my remembering this scene with particular clear-

ness, but I was also amazed by the fuss my father made over so simple a matter as a letter.

It never occurred to me that he could be jealous of David Uptigraff. I had no smallest suspicion that he constantly stood on guard over my mother against the admiration of other men. Even Carey, with fifteen years' advantage over me, did not suspect during his lifetime any such feelings on my father's part. She was amazed by the evidence of it she found in my parents' papers after both their deaths. Looking over a box of letters my mother had preserved, she and Harry came upon a remarkable declaration of love made to my mother by Cousin Josiah Page in the course of explaining why he had discontinued his frequent visits to our house. My father, he said, had perceived that she was taking the place in his heart left vacant by his own wife's death years before, and had advised him to absent himself. "I want thee to know, Mary, before our relations become purely formal, that I am deeply devoted to thee. This devotion will continue to the day of my death."

Such is my sister's description of the letter she and Harry destroyed under the first impulse of their shocked surprise.

Though my mother thought of herself as God's servant in the world, she must have been aware all her life long that she was a beautiful woman. Her face had the quiet harmony of line and color in which beauty dwells. It was lovely with the loveliness of Titian's goddess in "Sacred and Profane Love," as the Borghese picture is called. Love's perfect naked body, her honey-colored hair, the

small steady flame of the lamp she holds, the long, level clouds in the pale yet bright sky behind her were later to express for me in visible symbols the effect produced by my mother's presence. She would have been horrified by the comparison, but she well knew that the small categories of ordinary human judgment did not apply to her.

Devotion was always being thrust upon her; to ward it off abroad and meet its demands at home was an ever-present problem. Her children constantly claimed her attention, asking for some service from her or merely hanging around her out of pure affection. She attended to our needs always, but did not encourage our demonstrations. I remember hearing her say many times over that she would like as well to gaze up the chimney as sit looking into anyone's eyes. As to holding our hands, she would rather hold a brick than a hand. The ridiculous comparison mitigated the rebuff for whoever was bothering her at the moment. "I love you, my children, but I do not love your faults," she often told us, and we knew that she spoke the truth, since for all her gentleness and gaiety, she was an austere judge.

VII

FRIENDSHIP AND SEPARATION

An upper window of our house looked out over our garden across a narrow alleyway to the garden of the house back of us. After school and on Saturdays I often watched from this window a fair-haired little girl play in her garden, sometimes alone, sometimes with her brothers. I watched her with such close attention that before ever we spoke a word to each other I felt that Peggie White and I were friends.

In the wall of the alleyway that separated Peggie's domain and mine there was a big iron hook to which my father's coachman, old black Horace, used to tie up the horses, one after the other, when he washed and curried them. Frank and I still enjoyed standing in this alley to watch him at work, and one day our neighbor and her brother joined us there. They had heard the stamping of the big carriage horses over their garden wall, they told us. When Horace led his charges with shining coats and combed manes and tails back to their stalls, Peggie White and George followed along with us, and from that moment the doors which had been shut between our two families stood open. Peggie and I played together at home, but Frank ran out on the streets with the White boys.

At this time, before the house was enlarged, our garden was a fascinating place for children. A

wooden grape arbor arched up to the second story over the brick walk that bordered the grass where a magnolia tree grew with flowering shrubs—Hyrus Japonica, syringa, and forsythia. Along the fence bloomed a row of flowers, my father's special delight. The Whites' garden, paved with gray flagstones except for a flower bed or two, was more properly a yard, but the great attraction on our side was really our stable and carriage house with its big hayloft above. Outside against the wall of the stable where the brick walk turned at right angles to reach a back door into the street, stood a low wooden trough in which Horace mixed the mash of bran and oats for the horses' afternoon feeding. Peggie White and I, standing side by side, loved to watch him pour water into this mash through the black hose worn gray in spots here and there and leaking a little, and then stir it up with his pitchfork. Horace was a short, stocky man, almost as broad as he was tall. His face was very black; when he spoke, which was seldom, his voice sounded deep and rumbling. While we trusted him completely, we did not attempt to converse with him. He was like an attendant spirit clothed in uncouth shape; his impenetrable, faithful stupidity gave him a kind of fairy-tale mystery.

We experienced many a thrill while exploring the hayloft together when the boys were not there to push us too near the holes that yawned above the horses' haycribs. Once a year a ratcatcher came to clear the stable of rats with his ferrets, terrible, fierce little creatures, yellowish in color with red eyes and hardly bigger than their darting victims,

who squeaked a high piercing squeak when caught by the neck and shaken to death. From the raised back porch outside the kitchen I had seen the beginning of one of these hunts, but as soon as the rats began to dart out of the stable pursued by the ferrets and then to squeal, struggle, and lie about limp on the bricks, I rushed away. Not all Frank's jeering and teasing could make me watch another rat hunt. I had seen him dash about the yard in wild excitement, shouting like a little fiend, and felt no desire to emulate his courage. To be called a coward and a *girl* was much preferable to hearing the rats squeak when the ferrets pounced on them.

As my younger brother became healthy, his real nature asserted itself. He was a lively, high-spirited, self-confident boy, full of physical magnetism. He loved having a good time and instinctively justified what gave him pleasure. His annoyance as a small child when I tore the mask from Santa Claus's face and his zeal in rushing to the defense of the Easter rabbit were early indications of his temper of mind, while I, enjoying the good things life provided, always desired the added gratification of getting my pleasure, as much as might be, without self-deception. To the day of his death, when my brother and I discussed the world together there arose between us the old fundamental opposition. Experience had enlarged our problem for us both, without essentially changing it. I had learned, theoretically at least, that one must choose between privilege and justice—no Easter rabbit, no blue and purple eggs; while Frank on his side had perceived the danger

of doubting, even in his own mind, the divine right of property. We were always extremely fond of each other, but from the moment when he pushed open the garden gate to range abroad and I stayed behind in the home enclosure we spent, on the whole, little time together. It surprises me that I should not remember suffering any pain in the course of my separation from Frank as a child. For him it could, by the nature of things, be only a release, but it seems to me that some regrets on my part would have been natural. The fact is that I remember none.

I did not feel responsible, though I was distressed of course, when my younger brother came running home one afternoon bleeding profusely from a cut in his chin. My mother, who seemed always at hand when needed, washed out the wound and plastered it up, cautioning Frank as she worked over him not to chase again after wagons with anything protruding out at the back, steel rails or anything else, but she did not scold him. She expected us to look after ourselves and took our small accidents calmly. She allowed us to climb all over the roofs of our house, though they were on three different levels and by no means easy of access, but she cautioned us in regard to the dangers. "Never forget while you are climbing up that you must climb down again," I remember her saying. "Look about well to see that you won't get stranded. Only foolish people attempt impossible things." Whether as a result of her maxims or because we were strong, active children, very few accidents happened in the family

and not one of them proved serious. My father suffered far more from nervousness about us than my mother, but even he avoided interfering. All he asked was to be kept in ignorance of our exploits until they were over.

After Frank had accomplished it, I cherished the ambition to make "the grand climb" across the roofs of the house to the very front where, by leaning out over the edge, you could look down at the streetcars crawling along Madison Avenue far below. The climb started by scrambling up the wooden grape arbor to the roof of the low back extension, an easy first stage even for a small child. Frank and I had long been familiar with it. The next stage was more difficult. You had to stand on a tool chest and cling by the rain pipe to hoist yourself onto the roof of the main back wing. Then you could walk triumphantly upright past the kitchen chimney and the dining-room chimney to the place where the wall of the front wing confronted you with its roof high above. This, too, I had done many times, but as yet I had got no farther. Now at last I stood examining the wall of the front wing with the firm intention of scaling it. Frank and his new friend, George White, stood on either side of me explaining just where I must put first my right foot and then my left foot, pointing out the projections to which I must cling with my hands.

"It looks hard from down here, but it's really awfully easy," Frank said. "I'll show thee how easy it is."

As I examined the widely separated window

ledges and the frail projecting rain gutter all desire to trust myself to them evaporated. When Frank started on his demonstration I turned tail and fled back along the roof, dodging around the chimneys, and scrambled down again into the garden where Peggy White was anxiously awaiting my return. She hated climbing, heights made her dizzy, she said, so she had refused to go up with us.

In the house the boys still sometimes joined Peggie and me for lively games. We played hide-and-seek in the upper stories and turned somersaults over a couch conveniently placed between our parents' bedroom and the guest room. The game was to see who could make the dash around including the somersault the greatest number of times without stopping to rest. Then there was the pantomime game called "Kissing the Pope's Toe." There could be no variation in the roles, whoever played them. The Pope always sat in the same high armchair, gorgeously draped in my father's purple dressing gown, his bare foot stretched out on a footstool, and on his head he poised a large pillow to represent the triple crown. The penitent, wrapped in a gray blanket, crept toward him and as he kissed the Pope's toe the Holy Father murmured, "Bless you, my child, bless you!" and nodded his head three times without displacing the pillow if possible. Its inevitable fall was greeted with shouts of triumphant laughter.

This game was clearly traditional, since we could not have invented it, but who taught us its ritual I do not now remember. It may possibly have

been current in the White family, which was low-church Episcopalian and so anti-Catholic, or one of my older brothers or sisters may have initiated us. That my mother knew nothing of our games I am convinced. She would not have tolerated our making a mock of what other people held sacred nor would she have permitted the abuse of her guest-room furniture. Probably we never played them when she was at home. Our more boisterous pleasures were apt to be cut short by indignant elders with a prejudice against noise, and we no doubt made our plans with the spontaneous dexterity in avoiding prohibitions that all children seem to possess. On rainy days we resorted to "Parchesi" or "Old Maid," but the boys soon grew tired of sitting still around a table.

During this year and for several years after our return from Europe my mother had little time to devote to me. She was busy from morning until night, often out of the house but often, too, receiving visitors at home or writing at her own particular table in the crowded back parlor. She was the president of nine societies, according to the family boast. Imperfect as was the comprehension I had of their various purposes, I was convinced that each and every one was immensely important. I did not expect my mother to pay attention to me, and when she did, it was like receiving a gift from heaven. A drive alone with her, an hour in front of the fire talking or repeating poetry made me happy for weeks. Her aloofness transformed my love for her into a kind of adoration.

When people asked my mother, as they some-

times did, how she was able to accomplish so much, she always gave the same answer. "I never do myself what anyone else can do for me; I never walk when I can ride and I never pay social calls." All this was true, but if summoned to give help or spiritual comfort she would put on her bonnet and go off without delay. Her quickness of decision and energy were amazing; they made shopping with her a bewildering experience for her youngest daughter. Much as I loved being with her, I remember dreading our seasonal outfitting expeditions. Before I understood which one of the hats I had been trying on pleased my mother, off she had gone down the aisle between the heaped-up counters and out of the shop door. I was forced to run as quickly as I could to catch sight of her before she disappeared between the swinging doors of our next shop. Once indeed I lost her entirely; she was obliged to hurry back and hunt before she found me standing on the street gazing about me in bewilderment. Though she did not reproach me by a single word, I felt the disgrace of my incompetence.

It must have been at this time that my mother felt it her duty to attend sessions of the Magistrate's Court before which women were tried. The only other woman in the courtroom, she sustained and supported the defendant by her presence and bore silent witness before the judge that he was responsible to the feminine half of the community even though it possessed no political power. To insult my mother proved impossible even for the kind of men my imagination summons up as fre-

quenting such a court; in her presence they were invariably polite. Dressed in the simple, nunlike costume she habitually wore, she sat day after day on a courtroom bench and followed the proceedings with watchful, intelligent eyes. I like to think that her presence there on that bench may have mitigated the lot of a few unfortunate girls and women. What my mother then saw of the special laws for her sex aroused her indignation. She agitated for a change and was able to bring about some improvement in the criminal laws of the State of Maryland which at that time discriminated against women with shocking unfairness. Preoccupied with such things, it is not surprising that my mother hurried through the business of supplying her children with hats and shoes, or that she left us to follow our daily routine by ourselves, once she had arranged it for us. Since I was free to appeal to her for advice or help at any moment, I never felt that I was neglected.

I could, however, count on an hour or two with my father at least once a week. He enjoyed having a child on the seat beside him when he drove himself about in the afternoon to pay his professional calls. I was always eager to go. Often, too, I went with him when he visited the open-air market on Saturday afternoons to which the farmers came from the surrounding countryside. My father seldom failed to find time for this expedition. It was easy for him to drive downtown in his carriage to the market after his day's work was done, and he greatly enjoyed exercising his well-known skill to choose delicacies for his family. But usually it was

late before he arrived. The gas flares were already blazing. Black Horace, short and broad, a huge basket over his arm, followed my father. The lights, flickering in the wind that blew through the unwalled shed, cast strange shadows. As he passed along my father was solicited from every side by his name. "I have a fine fat pair of ducks for you this week, Dr. Thomas. I have been saving them for you," or "Dr. Thomas, the asparagus is just as you like it today, green and tender," or "Our sausage meat has turned out wonderful, Doctor. Just you try it!" While he felt the breast of a chicken or admired the tender green row of peas in an opened pea pod, my father asked after the families of the stallkeepers. Sometimes he knew the names of the children. He had visited the farm perhaps to prescribe for one of them in a crisis of illness. Often he was forced to pause and give a bit of advice even when he purchased nothing, but his progress seemed very rapid to me, trying not to lose him. The movement of people, the strange flickering lights under the high market roof delighted and confused me. I wanted to linger and look, but on went my father, and Horace's basket filled up as by magic. All too soon we were outside again at the place where we had left the carriage. The basket, flowering on top with fresh lettuces, with cauliflowers, with boxes of strawberries, with cherries tumbling out of a paper bag, was stowed away in the front beside Horace. I sank back on the cushion close to my father, leaning against his shoulder in happy exhaustion.

One story told him at the market delighted my

father. A customer had asked the wife of a farmer, a Quakeress as it happened, to send the purchases he had made to the Reverend Thomas Masters at the Rectory of St. Stephen's. Abigail Hodgkins, to whom as to all Friends the hireling ministry of the Episcopal Church was anathema, gazed at him for a moment in silence. Perceiving by his round black hat and his round white collar that the Reverend Masters himself stood before her, she handed him over the counter her order book and pencil. "Will thee kindly write down the name and address here," she said. "Thee can reverend thyself. I do not feel called upon to do it for thee." We all laughed again and again at this story. For my part I felt that it was somehow a vindication of Quakerism.

My father was easy to approach; he seemed almost on a level with me. When I annoyed him he showed his annoyance frankly. He scolded me with the irritation of an equal so that I felt free to answer him back. I liked to do little services for him. When he settled down on his bed to rest after midday dinner I used to tuck the warm coverlid under his shoulders and give him a little pat before I left him. Then, if I were going out with him, I came in an hour to wake him and put the cuff links in his fresh shirt. We were such good friends that he even permitted me to tease him, seeming to enjoy his own follies, but my mother did not approve of this. Taking me aside, she reproved me gravely for impertinence to my father one day after I had been particularly witty at his expense and my brothers and sisters around the

dinner table had laughed. She spoke so seriously that I tried not to displease her again in this way. However, my father was well able to hold me in check whenever he desired. "Wisdom will die with thee, my dear child," he sometimes assured me in a suspiciously flattering voice, and when I grew excited and vehement, "Shake not thy gory locks at me," he would say with a twinkle in his brown eyes. The mere drawing down of the corners of his mouth was often enough to deflate me. Every now and then one of his children would annoy him beyond endurance and then he said the most devastating things, but if we reproached him with them when he was no longer angry, he more often than not repudiated his own words.

"I never said that, child. How can thee imagine that I would say such a thing?" he asked, shaking his gray head from side to side.

"But, Father, thee did say it," we insisted and called a witness, when one existed, to support the accusation.

"Well, perhaps I did," my father sometimes conceded. "I cannot remember every word I may let fall when you are making such a racket."

In any case we did not take his strictures seriously, though in the bottom of our hearts we knew they were often perfectly well deserved.

All during my childhood, until I had learned to read and forget myself in a book, I hated solitude, so when neither my parents nor my usual playmates were available I used to hunt about for one of my older brothers or sisters whom I could join.

During this winter I found my surest refuge in Harry.

Our family consisted day by day of my parents and Harry, Grace, Margaret, and me, three girls in a row with Frank at the tail end. Harry had returned home to attend the Johns Hopkins University after two years at Haverford, the Quaker college my father himself had attended and of which he was now a trustee. The reason for Harry's return I never knew. Perhaps expense had something to do with it, since Carey was in Europe and Bond already a freshman at Haverford. John alone of eight children was self-supporting, having been taken into the Whitall glass business by my mother's brother immediately after leaving college, as a measure of family justice. For whatever reason, at home Harry was studying at our university and, as it happened, much under the influence of Sidney Lanier, whose lectures he attended. He read a great deal of poetry, Tennyson chiefly, and Poe, as I remember, and he liked to read it aloud. I on my side liked to listen. Snuggled up against him in his big chair, I never grew tired of the sound of his voice even when the words had lost all meaning. I rarely had to push myself on him; often it was he who sought me out.

"Want to read poetry with me for a little while now, Helle?" he would ask when he came home in the late afternoons, the very time of day during which I felt most at a loss.

The favor shown me by my big brother flattered me greatly. I did not know that he was already in

love, and if I had known I could not have guessed that my presence made it easier perhaps for him to invoke the presence there by his side of his adored Zoe Carey. To such misunderstandings the young are continually exposed.

VIII

GRACE'S CHARMS

EVERY spring since my grandparents' death had closed The Cedars, my parents had faced the problem of finding a refuge for their family during the hot months of our Southern summer. This year we would have to stay away longer than usual because our house in Baltimore was to be enlarged. My parents were worried about the expense involved since every penny they could scrape together would be needed to pay for the alterations. Finally Aunt Hannah came to the rescue by lending them her house in the suburbs of Philadelphia for the whole summer.

The Pearsall Smiths' adventurous spirit was taking them off early to the New England coast and later into the Maine woods on a camping expedition with tents and guides, and Grace was accompanying them as she often did. Aunt Hannah herself delayed her departure for a few days after our arrival to settle us in, and during that brief interval my relationship to her underwent complete transformation.

It happened that Frank and I had the ill luck to break one of the Pearsall Smiths' croquet mallets while using them as crutches in a race about the garden. We were absorbed in fitting the splintered pieces of the handle together when Aunt Hannah suddenly appeared coming rapidly toward

us down the garden path. Without allowing us time for a word of excuse or apology, she began to berate us in unmeasured terms, standing over us on the garden path. As I looked up into her face that was white and stern with anger and listened to her vehement words that poured over me on and on, my heart hardened against my aunt. I lost all sense of guilt for misusing the croquet set as I knew we had done, and felt only that I was being outrageously treated. What was a croquet mallet to make such a fuss about, even if it did belong to Alys? Our breaking it was an accident, and accidents happen to everyone. Aunt Hannah was unjust and she was dreadfully violent. Feeling that I had never before known what she was really like I recoiled from her in dislike, and with the implacability of an outraged child I ceased from that moment to trust or to love the aunt who had been so good to me in my early childhood.

When my father could manage it he joined us in Germantown. He was camping out in our house with the cook to look after him, and he reported always on the progress the working men had made since his last visit. Frank and I were keenly interested since a new little room was being built for each one of us. We pestered my father with questions about them. "Were the windows in yet?" "Was the plaster on?" "Was it dry?" We longed to be on the spot with my father to watch our rooms come into existence.

This was a summer of anticipation for both Frank and me, an interval of waiting for changes to take place. Not only were we to have new rooms,

we were also to go to new and separate schools in the autumn. The Friends Academy had been forced by lack of pupils to discontinue its lower grades and new arrangements had already been made for us. Without hesitation our parents had decided on a well-established boys' school for Frank, but the problem of what to do with a girl had proved more difficult. The fashionable institution to which some years before Grace had persuaded my parents to transfer her had proved wholly unsatisfactory from the point of view of education. Grace herself was pleased with it, because she found there the kind of companions she desired and had not found at the narrowly sectarian Quaker academy. My parents did not consider for a moment the possibility of sending me to Miss Hall's with Grace, but the other girls' schools in our town seemed hardly better. Fortunately just at this time plans were announced for opening a new institution to provide a sound, sensible education for girls. After much discussion both Peggie White and I had been entered in it. When the day of Frank's and my returning to town finally came the opening of our schools was still two weeks ahead. Taking possession of our new rooms was the immediate excitement.

We understood very well what the alterations in the house were. The back wing had been built far out into the garden beyond the place where the grape arbor had stood and a sitting room for my mother had been contrived between the back parlor and the dining room. My father had assured us that the dining room was even larger than be-

fore, but I could not understand how this could be when most of my mother's room had been taken out of it. Above the garden end of this sitting room for my mother the two new little rooms for Frank and me had been built of exactly the same size and exactly the same shape immediately over each other. We were wild to see them. After a quick dash through my mother's room into the dining room we raced upstairs. Frank did not stop on my landing but went on up to inspect his own room. In a minute I heard his knock on my ceiling, which was his floor, and by prearrangement I ran to my window and put my head out, twisting my neck to get a view of his window immediately above. There he was leaning far out.

"Don't fall, Frank," I cried. "It's dangerous to lean so far out." But in his excitement he paid no attention.

"I've got a bed and a chair and a bureau and there's lots of room left," he called down to me.

"My room is really very big," I boasted. "I can have the large table."

We went on comparing notes, Frank looking down and I straining my neck to look up. Our rooms seemed perfect to us and we settled ourselves in them as it were for the rest of our lives.

But the very next afternoon my mother called me to her. "There is something I want to talk over with thee, Nellie," she said. "Sit down here by me and listen quietly while I explain to thee what it is."

Perceiving that my mother spoke very gravely, I thought that I must have displeased her in some

118

way, but I soon found that was not the trouble. She was preparing me for something, I could not make out just what. Then suddenly I understood. My own room was not really mine. Grace, just back from her summer with Aunt Hannah, claimed it for hers. Passionate protests rose to my lips. I managed to force them down, but I could not control my tears.

"It is hard for thee, I know," I heard my mother's gentle voice saying. "It is a great disappointment, but thee must try to understand Grace's side. As the oldest daughter at home she took it for granted that one of the single rooms was to be hers. She feels that by sharing a room with Margaret for so many years she has earned a room to herself. Thy father and I must be just not only to thee but also to Grace."

"Would I have to go in with Margaret, Mother?" I asked, seizing on the implication of her words. "I can't go in with Margaret, really I can't! She always finds fault with me and orders me about. Please, Mother, whatever happens, don't put me in the room with Margaret. Please, please!" I was sobbing violently by now.

My mother let me sob on unchecked for a moment. When I was a little calmer she said, still gently but very gravely, "Thee is too big a girl now, my dear daughter, to break out in this way. It is time that thee learned greater self-control. I want thee to try very hard. Thy father and I have indulged thee too much, I fear. The older children think that we spoil thee and Frank. You are the youngest of the family, which may be a bad thing

for you." My mother paused, then smiled at me and said, "Does thee not think thyself that thee has a little too much thy own way?"

"If thee wants me to do it, Mother, I will go into Margaret's room," I managed to speak almost calmly, then broke out again into a wail. "Margaret doesn't understand me, Mother. Thee knows thyself how she is always correcting me. She'll hate having me in her room. We can never be happy together, never, never." I forced myself to stop my outpouring of words and fixed imploring eyes on my mother's face.

She looked greatly distressed. "It is a hard decision to make," I heard her say in a low voice as if to herself. "Grace has the upstairs sitting room almost entirely for her own use. Perhaps if we let her furnish it as she likes and entertain her friends there, she will not care so much for the little room. It is really very small for a young lady."

I caught at the straw my mother unwittingly held out to me. "It's much too small for Grace, really it is. Where would she keep all her dresses? The room was meant for a little girl!"

"That is not for thee to decide." The grave shake of my mother's head as well as her words rebuked me. "I will talk the matter over once again with Grace and with thy father. If Grace insists on her right to the single room I feel we must give it to her. On thy side, thee must prepare thyself to accept thy father's and my decision quietly, whatever it may be. I trust thee not to make a fuss. Do not speak to Grace about the room, and remember!—no more tears and no more

pleading either to thy father or to me. Now go wash thy face in cold water. That will make thee feel better."

When my mother put anything up to me like that my whole effort was to obey her. Even alone in my little room while I lay awake thinking that I might never sleep there again, I wept only for a short time and stifled my sobs so that no one should hear them. I managed to go through the next morning without breaking down but as the afternoon wore on the pressure became very great. I took refuge in the garden, rocking back and forth in the new swing, crooning to myself, in an effort to control my despair. Words helped me always. I fitted words to my crooning.

> *She did not cry*
> *Though a tear dropped down from her soft,*
>   *dark eye.*

Repeating this over as I swung back and forth, I searched for a rhyme to carry it on.

> *She would not cry*
> *Though friends might die,*

With difficulty I found the next line,

> *And foes come raging o'er the land,*

then in a burst of inspiration, went on

> *And brothers, husbands go to fight*
> *The furious rebel band.*

Splendid! That was splendid, and it was enough. Still, was it quite right? "Husbands" wouldn't do.

I must change "husbands." But somehow in the end the line sounded so much better to me just as it had first come into my mind that I could not bring myself to change it.

Pleased to have made a poem, I chanted it over and over, still feeling desperately melancholy but calmed and assuaged.

When at last I returned to the house the first person I met was Grace.

"Where has thee been, child? I've been looking for thee everywhere," she said. "I want to tell thee that I have decided to give the little room to thee. Mother thinks it best not to put thee in with Margaret, and she's probably right. Thee is much too spoiled ever to get on with Margaret."

"Oh! Grace, that's awfully kind of thee. I'm so happy I can hardly believe it!" I cried all in one breath, then pulled myself up sharply. "I promised Mother to be good about giving up my room," I said earnestly, "Please take it, if thee really wants it. I won't make a fuss."

Grace laughed. "No," she said, "it's thine. Take it, but do try not to be so dreadfully spoiled."

Grace was an angel. After this she might laugh at me and say anything she pleased to me without my minding. I was overwhelmed by her goodness and my own happiness.

Arranging our possessions in our new little rooms proved a great delight for Frank and me. We constantly ran up and down the flight of stairs that separated us to inspect the changes we made and we consulted together, leaning out of our windows. Conversation conducted in this way had

CAREY

GRACE

MARGARET

HELEN

THE THOMAS SISTERS

amazing charm. We chattered on endlessly. Then on the day our schools opened this Indian summer of companionship between Frank and me ceased. "Us" went finally out of existence.

Peggie White and I were put in the same class at Miss Bond's school. I was mortified by this, since I was a full year older than Peggie and had at last become aware of what was proper for my age. I exerted myself with all my might to "catch up" as I said, and soon learned to read easily, mastering even the long words. By the end of the school year I was promoted to the class above Peggie and was also chosen from among the beginners in French to be "Heliotrope" in the French Flower Play that was the big feature of our closing exercises in June. I had to carry a large bunch of heliotrope and make a short speech in French—an overpowering excitement that deprived me of the power of sleep both before and after it.

The three Miss Bonds who ran the school were Southern ladies of excellent family. They all took part in the teaching, but the leading spirit was the second sister, Miss Christie, a remarkably clever young woman with decided ideas of her own. Though I had no classes with her during my first year I felt her power and stood greatly in awe of her. Her tall figure, the rapidity with which she approached, her eyes that seemed to shine the more brightly because they were half hidden between puckered lids, her emphatic voice, all intimidated me.

Peggie White and I were now inseparable companions. We began the day by walking down the

street together to school. Peggie's father brought her to our door every morning and waited to see her safely in the house. When I heard his ring I had often to leave untasted on my plate the pile of buckwheat cakes our cook browned to a turn. This annoyed my father, who loved good things himself and liked to see his children enjoy them. Peggie could wait a few minutes, he protested. She was too early in any case, she always came too early. But I knew it was we who were always late and dashed off in spite of him. Peggie and I played together in the afternoons, completely disregarding our brothers and completely disregarded by them. From the backs of our two houses we rigged up overhead communication by means of a basket and string, which sagged sadly because of the long distance; we made candy and ate it. We consumed so much candy in fact that I rapidly became the puffy-cheeked little wretch shown in photographs of this period. In short we did the things small girls not yet in their teens usually find amusing. Still all the while, much as I enjoyed our activities, I felt underneath that they were trivial and unimportant compared with the things my elders did. Watching what went on at home and listening to what was said still interested me more than anything else.

My imagination was now caught by Grace. Next after my mother I liked best to attach myself to her. Perhaps it was gratitude for her generosity in not taking my room that made me so devoted to Grace at this time, and perhaps she endured my hanging about her because she was conscious of

having already done me a favor, and one favor leads to another. I was her abject slave, ran all her errands, laughed at all her jokes, and admired her extravagantly. She permitted me sometimes to play at being her lady's maid, and I was ambitious above all to brush her beautiful bright hair that was so long it fell almost to the hem of her dress. One evening when she was seated in front of her dressing table I persuaded her at last to let me try. She sat still under my ministrations for a few moments, then just as I was getting the rhythm of the stroke she suddenly reached back her hand and took the brush from my fingers. "If thee showed any talent for it I would let thee brush my hair, but thee has no talent at all," she said, and I still can see before me the determined expression on her face reflected back to me by the mirror. Her decision was final, I perceived, and I never again asked for that particular privilege. She continued to let me watch her dress, get her frocks for her out of the big walnut wardrobe at the far end of the room, pick up what she dropped, and admire the final result of our combined efforts. Sometimes, seeing herself look unusually pale in the mirror, she would open a particular little drawer, take out a bit of scarlet ribbon, wet it in Eau de Cologne and rub it lightly on her face to produce a delicate pink flush that was extremely becoming. Of this proceeding I was warned to say nothing. Though I was frightfully proud of Grace's confidence in me, sometimes I could not help being a little shocked by the strange things she did. Prudence prevented my expressing any such feelings, and I

soon forgot my scruples in the delight of watching her.

The gay young girls with whom Grace had made friends at Miss Hall's school often came to visit her, and young men with banjos and tenor voices also began to appear at about this time. My sister entertained them in the upstairs sitting room that was now her own. She had pushed the piano against the end wall between the gas fixtures which she had adorned with pink globes. They cast a lovely soft glow when the light shone through them. Bright chintz curtains hung at the windows and the sofa had a slip cover to match them. Grace had begged of my mother the old-fashioned mahogany secretary and the round Chippendale sewing table my father had inherited. These pieces gave the room great distinction. Grace herself was pleased with it and for my part I thought it marvelous. I insinuated myself into the company she entertained there as often as I could. If I heard the sound of laughter or of music I would drop anything to creep in and listen.

Gilbert and Sullivan's operas were then the rage. Grace had somehow managed to get permission to go to see them, and like the other young people of the day, she was constantly singing songs from *The Mikado* and *Patience,* solos and choruses. Seated in my corner I delighted in the gay songs, but it was my sister's rendering of passionate, melancholy music that I most loved.

She possessed a contralto voice of beautiful quality, and if a note now and then came flat I never perceived it. Standing in a noble attitude beside

126

the piano, her music clasped firmly in one hand, the other hanging loose, her figure fitted into a tight Victorian costume, her small head proudly erect under its weight of shining hair, Grace sang with penetrating sadness:

> *Oh! that we two were sleeping*
> *Under the church yard sod.*

The tears that streamed down my face I could not restrain, but I took care that no sound from my corner should attract attention.

"Rocked in the Cradle of the Deep" also moved me profoundly. Later Henry the Fourth's invocation to sleep:

> *Wilt thou upon the high and giddy mast*
> *Seal up the ship-boy's eyes and rock his brains*
> *In cradle of the rude imperious surge—*

could do no more for me with its divine beauty than reproduce the sensation I then experienced.

Small wonder that I worshiped my sister Grace and used all my childish ingenuity to please her. At home she rarely forbade my joining her and her friends, but on the other hand she never took me out with her, nor did I expect her to do so. The fast black mare Aunt Hannah had given the family had been named "La Reine" by Grace and was considered by her to be her own particular property. About this there was lively dispute in the family. Did not my father feed and care for La Reine? Certainly he did. Therefore we argued that we all had a right to drive her in the jolly

two-wheeled open carriage of those days with the seats back to back, called a dogcart. Still Grace managed to keep a certain priority of claim. When she wanted to use the dogcart, the rest of us gave way. On bright afternoons she would start off looking wonderful on the front seat, her small hat pushed down over her eyes, the reins held in one hand and the long whip aslant in the other. A young man took his place by her side and another couple climbed up behind. Standing on our front doorstep, I watched the gay party until it disappeared around the corner and then slowly I turned back into the house.

The Christmas and Easter holidays brought Bond home from college to form part of our family circle for a while. When he was in the house I kept away from Grace, who adored him. She must have conveyed to me, though I have forgotten in just what way, that my company was no longer welcome. At mealtimes, of course, I saw them and one morning lingering over the breakfast table in our sunny dining room after my parents had left I heard an exciting discussion between Bond and Harry and Grace about a recent religious revival at Haverford College. Both Bond and his roommate Tom Worthington had fallen completely under the spell of the preacher who engineered it. Bond described how he had pleaded with his college friends in public and in private to repent and come to Christ. He and Tom had held meetings in their own room and had actually kneeled down in the studies of other men to offer up prayers for their salvation.

"How could I have done such a thing? How could I?" Bond repeated over and over, jumping up from his chair and pacing about the room. "I must have been crazy, crazy. That man made me go out of my mind. How can I face those fellows again? I had not even sense enough to leave Jim Bates alone." He clenched his fists at the thought.

Harry put his hand on Bond's shoulder. "Don't take it too hard, old man," he said. "People soon forget. It does not matter really. They'll like thee all the better for making a mistake or two. Remember that thee is the finest athlete at Haverford and Jim Bates knows it."

Bond went back to his seat. "If religion makes people do such things, it's dangerous. I have finished with religion for my whole life," he declared, but more quietly.

"It is revivals, not religion, that are dangerous, Bonnie," Grace broke in. "Thee knows Father does not approve of revivals for young people. Edward Merritt should never have been allowed to preach at Haverford."

Bond's buckwheat cakes had grown cold on his plate. Late in the morning though it was, Grace sent me to get a fresh supply. Willingly I went out through the swinging doors, down the passage way to the big kitchen, one whole side of which was filled by our huge stove. General messenger for the family and lover of cake as I was, I had long ago learned how to flatter the cook, a little wizened colored woman, tough and high tempered with the other servants. In spite of occasional grum-

129

bling she never refused any demand of mine, however unreasonable. I believe that she enjoyed spoiling us all, for she used to put her head out of the kitchen window and invite anyone who happened to be in the garden to taste the first rolls or cookies of a baking while they were still hot from the oven. She often handed out to us thick slices of bread covered with brown sugar or molasses. So on this particular morning she made no difficulty. Soon the hot buckwheat cakes appeared with a garnish of sizzling sausages, and Bond at last ate his breakfast.

Somewhat later during this same holiday, while wandering idly about the garden, I came upon Grace and Bond smoking cigarettes behind a screen of bushes. Bond immediately began to warn me to say nothing, but Grace only laughed and blew a whiff of smoke in my excited face as I pulled up short at the sight of them. She knew that I accepted everything she did without criticism and that I was to be trusted.

Margaret, however, was not so lenient a judge. She and Grace were certainly uncongenial at this time, which must have made sharing a room with Margaret harder for Grace than I had any idea of. Bond rather than Margaret had been Grace's intimate always, and as she blossomed into young ladyhood Harry's friends, grown men though they were, began to court her favor, while they still ignored Margaret. Thus the two sisters had been impelled away from each other. How often they disagreed behind the closed door of their room I do not know. It happened only occasionally that

Margaret was present when I danced attendance on Grace.

One Saturday morning Grace was kept in bed by a cold. Bored no doubt beyond endurance by my efforts to amuse her, she expressed a desire to smoke. She had no cigarettes, I was too young to be sent to the drugstore on that particular errand, so she asked Margaret to get a package for her as she went down the street.

Margaret turned slowly about from her own mirror in front of which she was adjusting her hat. "Smoking is wicked, Grace," she said in a tone of solemn reproach. "Thee knows very well it is wicked. Father has forbidden the boys to smoke. He never dreamed thee would do such a thing."

"All right then," Grace answered her crossly, "don't get the cigarettes. If thee wants to be so mean, it is thy own affair."   .

Great tears rolled down Margaret's face. She began to sob. "Do stop crying. Thee is not a baby any longer," Grace said in a scornful tone turning her head on the pillow to look out of the window away from Margaret's accusing eyes.

It seemed to me that Margaret was always weeping and I despised her for her tears. If anyone criticized or teased or shocked her in the least, instantly tears filled her eyes and rolled down her face right where she was, at the dinner table, in the parlor, anywhere at all. If my feelings were hurt I rushed off and wept, when I had to weep, all alone by myself in my own room.

Margaret was by no means a solitary child.

Though I did not admire her many other people did. She had her own group of intimates, the boys and girls of her class at the Friends Academy, members of our Meeting, sons and daughters of relatives or of close family friends. By them and by her teachers she was both admired and respected. She did well in her work and was a very pretty girl with a satin-smooth skin, soft dark hair, and gray eyes that took the color of her dress in a fascinating way, showing now blue, now green, now steel dark. I was no longer consciously tormented by my childish envy of Margaret's dresses and ribbons, so bright and gay compared with the dark colors imposed on me by my red hair, but I still had an undefined feeling of resentment against her. My praise of her pretty looks was not wholehearted. I remember circling about her, examining her clothes when she was dressed up for some picnic or party. "Thee looks lovely, Margaret, really thee does. That dress is awfully becoming," I would say, but I took no pleasure in Margaret's clothes or in Margaret herself. Her poise and competence always made me feel uncertain and incompetent. Harry's nickname for her, "The Duchess," somehow summed up her personality. She really was like a duchess. Grace was totally different. Sometimes to be sure she too mounted a pedestal, but more often she raced about amusing herself with things Margaret and I never dreamed of doing.

While I was well aware of my gay sister's difference from the rest of us, it seems not to have struck me as strange. Grace was Grace, that was all there was to it. Later I wondered how she persuaded my

parents to allow her so much freedom, above all how she got permission to go to Miss Hall's fashionable school for young ladies.

"How did thee ever get to Miss Hall's school, Grace?" I once asked her, when the passage of time had made us almost contemporaries. "Aunt Hannah must have helped thee to persuade Father and Mother, I suppose."

"Aunt Hannah had nothing to do with it," Grace repudiated my suggestion emphatically. "I managed the whole thing myself."

"But in what way did thee manage it?" I persisted. "Father may not have been hard to persuade, but Mother must have set her face firmly against it. I really should like to know how thee persuaded Mother."

"Mother made more difficulties than Father, thee is right there," my sister conceded. "I was forced to explain to Mother just how I felt. I made her see what a misfortune it was for me that she had neglected her social duties so entirely. When she married Father, he knew everyone in Baltimore, but Mother refused to pay social calls, and of course Father's old friends dropped him, all except the Quakers. I told Mother I felt I had a right to make friends with the children of Father's friends, and my only chance of meeting them was to go to the school they attended. Mother acknowledged the justice of what I said, and gave her consent."

I thought all this over for a minute. "Did not Mother feel badly when thee reproached her in that way?" I ventured to ask.

"She was not in the least upset. She said she could not do everything. With such a large family she had to neglect either social calls or the religious work which was her first duty. She had done what she thought right. She was willing I should go to Miss Hall's school if I believed that I could find the friends I wanted there. Since I was interested in them, she thought I might as well see for myself what worldly people were like."

I listened to my sister's explanation with amazement. She could not possibly have been more than fifteen years old when she changed schools, probably she was only fourteen. I found it hard to believe that she had spoken to my mother in the way she described when she was so young. True, I reflected, Grace had always been old for her years and she had held the position of eldest daughter at home during the long periods when Carey was away at boarding school and at college. My mother must have depended on her a great deal. Then her association with the older boys, especially Bond, had no doubt helped her to grow up quickly. Still, in spite of all these things I thought her arguing with my mother in the way and at the time she said highly remarkable.

I could not help suspecting that the conversation she reported was not one conversation, but rather a summary of arguments renewed again and again during several years. The early victory Grace won in the matter of her school involved her inevitably in further struggles. It gave her the chance to make the friends she desired, but did not give her freedom to share their amusements. She

was forbidden to dance with boys and she was forbidden to go to the theater. When she could persuade my parents that a show was entirely innocent, like Gilbert and Sullivan's operas for instance, she got permission to see it, but each such concession was considered a special favor, and the prohibition against dancing with boys was never relaxed in any way. A girl of my sister's spirit did not, I feel sure, submit without a struggle to such restrictions.

Grace was scrupulous in obeying the express commands of my parents. She never, I believe, did what they had forbidden her to do, though she may have disregarded other implied prohibitions as she certainly did that against smoking cigarettes. This could not have been easy for her. I once heard her describe her embarrassment when the mothers of her friends urged her to dance with their sons at informal parties.

"Surely Mrs. Thomas would not object to your waltzing with Bobbie. He is a very good boy. Mrs. Thomas would approve of Bobbie, I know," her kind hostess would say, no doubt distressed to see Grace continue on at the piano while the other young people whirled gaily about. Or it might be Dick or Alfred who was vouched for. But Grace always refused. She tried to make the ladies understand that dancing itself was what her parents objected to, not the particular partner. They shook their heads in bewilderment and one or two seemed even to feel offended. However, all her friends' mothers agreed in praising her loyalty to her own mother. Thus while she lost to a consider-

able extent her natural position among the friends she had chosen, she won the respect of their parents.

The older ladies talked to Grace more seriously, I fancy, than they did to other young girls. She was often forced to discuss her elder sister with them, since the curiosity aroused by Carey's strange behavior had by no means died down. Indeed the longer she and Mary Gwinn remained abroad the greater the scandal. Grace explained and defended her sister as well as she could, but sometimes the exasperation of having to parry so many attacks passed the limits of endurance.

One afternoon, returning home rather late, Grace came immediately from the front hall into my mother's sitting room, still with her hat and coat on.

"Why, why," she exclaimed to my mother, "did Carey have to cut up that mouse? If she wanted to see its internal organs, very well, but why did she have to talk about it? All Baltimore has heard the story and is shocked by her lack of modesty. I have to defend Carey at least once a week while she is enjoying herself off in Europe."

My mother had laid down her sewing. "Who has been talking against Carey now?" she asked.

"Sally Montgomery's mother it was today," Grace replied. "When she had finished asking me if the mouse story could really be true, she said she pitied thee for having such a strange daughter. I suspect she is afraid to let Sally associate with me because I am Carey's sister, though she keeps saying how different I am. I don't take Mrs. Mont-

gomery seriously, of course, she is so very old-fashioned. But I do wish Carey had never seen a mouse!"

Grace ended up with a laugh, her sense of humor asserting itself. I laughed too. Seated near my mother doing my lessons, I had heard every word Grace said. The mouse seemed to me very funny. My mother, however, neither laughed nor smiled.

"Mrs. Montgomery might find something better to do, I think, than abuse thy own sister to thee. Her opinion does not matter since she is quite incapable of understanding Carey, but it is unkind of her to attack thee."

Grace seemed surprised by the seriousness with which my mother took her story. She left the room looking sober herself.

In spite of knowing that Grace had certain annoyances to bear, that she felt herself restricted in certain ways, I never dreamed during the years when I danced attendance upon her that she could be seriously depressed or unhappy. She seemed gay and self-confident, always, to me. Young people came and went in the house, Harry's friends as well as her friends—I did not distinguish between them. Grace's life seemed to me full of pleasure and excitement and she herself was a dazzling heroine in my eyes.

IX

HAPHAZARD READING

THE art of reading to myself, once it was mastered, transformed life for me by giving me an independent occupation and amusement to which I could turn at any moment. At first I used my new skill to read over again the books that had been read aloud to me by members of my family, especially the "Elsie books." I could now devour chapter after chapter without having to stop just when I was most excited, if my mother, or whoever, was called away or grew tired. I could linger for as long as I liked over an exciting scene—Elsie falling in a faint from the piano stool where her father had ordered her to sit until she played the frivolous song he insisted upon her playing for him though it was Sunday, and Mr. Travilla rushing to pick Elsie up and hissing over his shoulder at the tyrant, "Dinsmore, you're a brute"—could anything be more thrilling! And when Elsie had grown older, somewhat but not too much older, the revelation that Mr. Travilla, her father's intimate friend, desired to make Elsie his wife was as delightful as it was amazing. Nothing could invite reperusal more often than this climax, along the road to which I had shed so many tears. My mother, who had more than once dried my eyes with her own handkerchief, deplored the effect of

the Elsie books on me and would have confiscated them, had not my eldest sister prevented.

In later life Carey often declared that she brought me up on the Elsie books, laughing over the incongruity of such a confession on her part. "I gave them to thee in the first place and persuaded Mother to read them to thee, so thee sees," she would say, rubbing it in, "I am responsible for corrupting thy literary tastes when thee was hardly more than an infant!"

However, my sister flattered herself. No one, I believe, could have prevented my reading the Elsie books, neither my mother nor Carey herself, had she wished to do so. Every small girl of the period delighted in Elsie's adventures, which embodied in such a fascinating way the current brand of sentimentality. At some time or other I would surely have got hold of them and I was no doubt fortunate in achieving them early and without the emphasis of a struggle, for I soon lost interest in Elsie —long before the series was completed, in fact. Elsie the widow had no smallest interest for me.

In surmounting the hazard of Lot and his daughters I was not so fortunate. When pious parents urged their children as a religious duty to read the Bible through from the first chapter of Genesis to the last sentence of Revelations they must have forgotten the terrible story of incest that lurked near the beginning of Genesis for them to come upon before their zeal had abated. Like many another child I was brought up short by this story. The first reading bewildered me just because the narrative was so simple and so clear. What those

eight verses of the Bible seemed to mean, they could not possibly mean. I read them over until I was convinced that Moab and Ammon were in fact the children of Lot and his two daughters. Horrifying as it was, I was forced to accept this as true, and in so doing I clearly perceived that there was some simple fact connected with the birth of children of which I was totally ignorant. I could not by any manner of means make out what it could be.

Sex was never discussed in our family. The word itself was much too shocking to be mentioned. Nursery experience had made me familiar as a tiny child with the physical differences between little boys and girls. I accepted it along with everything else and thought nothing of it. In the same spirit I accepted the current explanation that when a baby arrives the doctor brings it. My complete faith made me laugh Peggie White to scorn for believing that a stork and not the doctor brings the baby. There were no storks in Maryland, I pointed out. Peggie's belief was ridiculous, while mine was supported by evidence. But Peggie stood up for her side. How did I know, she asked, that storks do not fly about at night? Had I ever watched for them? Babies were born at night when we were asleep. Let me deny that, if I could. So we argued each for the truth of her own explanation, each profoundly convinced by her own argument.

Once I had asked my mother what kind of child "an illegitimate child" might be, having heard the term by chance. "A child whose parents are wicked

is called an illegitimate child," she had informed me and dropped the subject. Later I learned from some conversation or other that the mother of an illegitimate child was not the wife of its father. This seemed very queer to me—I could not puzzle it out since I knew that only married women had children. However, I did not like to bother my mother with further questions. Something in her manner of answering before put me off. Now the story in the Bible, which by definition could not be wrong, had settled certain things for me. It made no mention of either a stork or a doctor or of marriage. Obviously no one of them was necessary. I decided to find some older person who would explain to me the real truth about the birth of children.

The easiest thing to do was to sound out my sister Margaret. She enjoyed being appealed to, and was not likely to laugh at me. Of course she might not know herself, but there was no harm in trying. I decided to ask Margaret. So the very next afternoon at the time when she always studied her lessons I climbed the stairs to her room. I found her, as I expected, seated before her table hard at work over her books and I stood beside her while I explained my errand. She expressed surprise at my question, but answered it quite willingly. She had herself been informed by Grace of the facts I wanted to know, she told me, and went on to explain them with a youthful bluntness that gave me a shock. Was she quite sure that what she said was true, I asked? Yes, she was sure, because Grace, enlightened first by a gossiping girl at

141

school, had rushed in indignation for denial to my mother, and my mother had confirmed the truth of what the girl said, though she blamed her severely for discussing such matters. Had Margaret talked with my mother about them? I asked. No, she had not. Grace had told her that my mother had been terribly embarrassed when answering her questions. Margaret did not want to trouble my mother.

For my part I had no inclination to discuss the subject further. I never mentioned it to Grace nor did I speak of it again to Margaret. Least of all could I pass on my information to Peggie White, since that would be to do the very thing my mother so disapproved in Grace's friend. My mother's attitude had stamped the whole subject of the birth of children as not to be spoken about, as somehow shameful. Whenever it obtruded, I thrust it out of my mind. None the less, without being conscious of curiosity I noted sharply any chance bit of information that came my way and left it to fit automatically into the general pattern. I do not now remember in what way I learned that my mother had forced herself to forewarn her sons of the temptations with which they would be confronted in the world. This duty to the boys, which both my parents felt imperative, my father, I was told, refused to undertake. It could best be performed by the boy's mother, he said. Girls never thought of such things, nice girls that is. So I turned my mind away from them, and in time the information Margaret had given me ceased to haunt me.

Strange indeed it is to contemplate in these out-spoken days the puritan ideal of feminine chastity that prevailed in the last century. The emotional and intellectual atmosphere has changed so profoundly that we shall now probably never understand all the implications of that ideal. Was sex really regarded as shameful by the mothers of the huge families of those days? Or was there not rather perhaps a sense of sacred mystery in marriage, a kind of religious fervor veiling the physical that could not be discussed, above all with one's daughters, who were in their turn to perform the miracle? Strange cross impulses and inhibitions must have operated, that arose, we may suppose, from emotional depths to which neither reason nor common sense ever penetrated.

Fortunately for me, I was a busy child. My days were full of normal schoolgirl activities shared with a congenial friend and I delighted in reading. My father and my brothers I continued to love and admire as always. Had I been idle at this period, ill perhaps with time vacant for brooding, the shock I had received might have had far more serious consequences.

Peggie White, I believe, grew up without curiosity regarding sex. I cannot of course be sure of this. My own shrinking from the subject after Margaret had expounded it to me would probably have prevented Peggie from discussing it with me, had she felt the impulse to do so. Still, nothing in my memory suggests that sex was on her mind. By temperament Peggie was easygoing. She accepted things as they appeared on the surface,

never probing down for explanations or reasons. She was, however, by no means stupid, quick-witted rather. When I challenged an inconsistency or a flat contradiction, as I thought, she invariably put me off with some lively answer, as in the matter of the stork. She used her mind to defend the truths she had been taught, but always with good temper. Her family numbered among its ancestors several colonial clergymen of the Church of England and all the Whites, simple and friendly as they were, impressed me with their sense of knowing themselves established in the correct tradition. I enjoyed going to Peggie's house and often had dinner there. The Whites kept a weekly fast of a Friday, mortifying the flesh on lobsters and oysters and diamond-backed terrapin in a way that struck the Quaker in me as highly incongruous. But I made no comment. For a guest to criticize the food set before her would have been an unthinkable breach of good manners and also I particularly enjoyed the Friday dishes. The thought of the strange delicious food I ate as a little girl in the Whites' dining room still gives me pleasure.

As I grew older and more and more addicted to reading, the library in Peggie's house gradually replaced the dining room in my affections. It was lined from ceiling to floor with open bookcases. Mr. White's calf-bound law books filled rows and rows of the shelves, but above the leather sofa in one corner was a section devoted to stories, sets of novels, and many bound volumes of old magazines. Urged on by me, Peggie, whose father could deny her nothing, begged permission for me to

borrow books from these shelves. Mr. White stipu-
lated only that I should never take more than one
book at a time, should leave a note of it on his
desk, and return it before I carried off another
book. These conditions I scrupulously obeyed but
I sometimes spent hours on the convenient sofa
with a pile of bound *Harper's Weekly* or *Littell's
Living Age* on the floor beside me, turning over the
pages and stopping to read whatever caught my
fancy. I can imagine no more tempting amusement than this for a bookishly-inclined child.

The yellow maple-wood bookcases with glass
doors that stood in our back parlor, on the other
hand, did not tempt me. The doors were always
locked and though the keys stood in the locks,
there was something forbidding in having to turn
a key. Then people were continually passing by,
asking questions or making comments. Still, I examined the bookcases sufficiently to learn that they
contained only books on serious subjects, religious
books mostly, since my father's medical library was
in his office. On an upper shelf, however, I could
see a set of *English Poets* in uniform dark volumes,
and I climbed on a chair to look at them. The
front page of every volume was adorned by a
small picture of a young man in a high hat and a
young lady in a bonnet, driving along together in
a buggy. The inscription underneath informed
me that the books were a wedding present to my
parents from Uncle Robert and Aunt Hannah
Pearsall Smith. I was amused to find that the
young man and young lady were my father and
mother and the buggy a doctor's buggy, but pages

and pages of verse with not a picture to break their monotony daunted me, so I put the volumes back in their places unread, and did not disturb them again for many years.

The shelves on one wall of Grace's sitting room upstairs, on the other hand, were endlessly attractive. In addition to holding her own library they served as a general refuge for old books. Many volumes discarded by Carey when she left for Germany were stored there, and there one never-to-be-forgotten afternoon I found a book with a strange name stamped on its back in gold letters. *The Poems of Percy Bysshe Shelley,* I read aloud, making six syllables out of the name. What a marvelous name for a poet! In high excitement I hastened to open the book. Its pages had wide margins adorned by red lines which gave to the enclosed verses a strange distinction. I had never seen printing like this before, nor pictures like the illustrations the book contained. A slender lady with hair streaming in a torrent down her back and trailing after her on grass studded with flowers attracted me above all the rest. I had to know the story of that strange beautiful lady, so, standing where I was in front of the bookcase, I read "The Sensitive Plant" through from beginning to end, then with the book still open in my hand rushed along the passage way to my own little room and flung myself down on the bed in a passion of tears.

It is not difficult to understand why this poem of Shelley's moved the little girl I then was so profoundly. Without being aware of it I identified

myself with the Sensitive Plant. And the lady who tended the garden, "the wonder of her kind," who was she, who could she be for my imagination but my mother?

> *This fairest creature from earliest spring*
> *Thus moved thro' the garden ministering*
> *All the sweet season of summertide*
> *And ere the first leaf looked brown—she died.*

Discovering Shelley's poetry in this way by chance and unaided by anyone made me feel him my poet in some very special sense. I appropriated the volume I had found and gave it chief place beside the Bible in my own small bookrack, only dimly conscious that it had once belonged to Carey and of course totally unaware of its being a pirated American reprint of an English edition. I cherished it for years as my chiefest treasure, reading in it constantly and learning many passages by heart. To be a poet like Shelley seemed to me the greatest thing in the world. I longed passionately to become a poet myself and for a time I even added to the prayer I knelt down by my bedside to murmur morning and evening an ardent petition that God would let me write poetry when I grew up. But the Deity had long before refused his consent.

X

SECTARIAN DIFFERENCES

HOWEVER many children might be at home my parents' life continued dedicated day by day to doing God's work in the world. With this purpose in mind my father practiced his profession and my mother managed her family. A hitch in our routine rarely occurred. The children each went his or her own way, making such combinations with the others as naturally arose. From Monday to Saturday we ran along different levels, as it were, attending different schools and cultivating different friends for the most part. Sunday on the other hand was devoted to religion by us all as a family group. The morning began with prayer and reading of the Bible. No excuse other than illness was accepted on Sunday for absence from this rite. After Bible reading followed the decorous walk through the quiet streets to meeting, and the long hours of quietness within the meeting-house walls. Midday dinner, plentiful and luscious, slowly consumed and slowly digested, offered an interval restorative rather than enlivening. Then my father accompanied by a daughter of suitable age took the long streetcar ride down to the Boys' Mission School he conducted in South Baltimore, while my mother rested—her only period for rest during the entire week. My brothers for some reason did not teach in my father's mission school. What they

did on Sunday afternoons I do not know. They were never at home. A meeting for worship again filled the evening hours. No driving, no playing, no reading of stories was allowed: only the hushed rooms at home, the high, evenly lighted hall of the meeting house over which God brooded.

These Sundays followed one another throughout the winter months, their solemn monotony piling up for me, until when spring came around again the restlessness they induced rose by mid-afternoon to an irresistible tide. Then the big house about me was completely silent, as if deserted. Though I listened intently not a sound from my mother's room or the kitchen reached my ears. No longer able to stand staring through the windows, I used sometimes to rush out by myself and wander alone far off through the poorer quarters of the town, past rows of small houses, with three white-painted wooden steps leading up to a closed wooden door. I found some uncomprehended solace in those rows of houses and in those people on the streets who were utterly strange to me. Always I returned home quieted and appeased, and for many years when depressed or lonely I continued to seek equilibrium of spirit by wandering alone through strange streets or along unfrequented country roads.

Any variation in the Sunday routine had for me in my childhood the force of an explosion. Once an English boy scarcely older than I, thirteen or fourteen perhaps, rose up from his seat beside his mother on the women's benches at our formal meeting for worship. With amazement I saw him

149

stand there, erect but small above the high back
of the bench. I could hardly believe my ears when
in his lilting English voice he urged that solemn
congregation to trust in the Lord. Quickly I turned
my cyes to the gallery where the authorized
preachers and elders sat, but the faces ranged above
me were immovably quiet and composed; no smallest change of expression could I detect on even my
father's face or my mother's. Surely they could not
have failed to hear Roger. When meeting was
over and I could find my way through the crowd
of slowly departing Friends to my mother's side,
she checked my excited whispering with a gently
uplifted hand. Not a comment was made until we
had reached home, then at last she said in her
quiet way that Roger was too young to preach in
meeting, and began at once to talk of something
else. What subsequently took place I learned from
chance remarks. The boy's parents were visited by
the head elder of the meeting, old Cousin Edward
Morrison, and were advised to restrain Roger.
This they failed to do. He preached the next Sunday and the one after that. Perhaps they did
earnestly endeavor to control him, or perhaps they
may even have believed their son inspired, as the
Bible said. "Out of the mouths of babes and
sucklings hast thou ordained strength" and again
Christ's words, "Thank thee, O Father, Lord of
heaven and earth, because thou hast hidden these
things from the wise and prudent and hast revealed them unto babes," were texts often quoted
even in our family where the self-expression of
babes and sucklings was shut off with firm dis-

cipline. Whatever the feeling of Roger's parents may have been, they were finally told to keep him away from meeting and this order was obeyed. Roger was clearly an abnormal boy, a case for a nerve specialist. Years later in one of our Western states he ended his own life after shooting a girl who refused to marry him.

More exciting than Roger's preaching even was another strange event that broke the decorous routine of Sunday morning meeting. A visiting woman friend seated in the gallery above my mother began slowly to untie the strings of her Quaker poke bonnet of plum-colored silk. I watched her slowly take it off and lay it on the seat beside her, then rise up to speak. Her face framed only in the thin white ruffle of her undercap shone pale and her eyes gleamed, as she stood for a moment in silence to dominate the congregation. Then speaking in a low intense voice she called to repentance two souls on the benches before her, who writhed there, God had revealed to her, in the torments of unconfessed sin. As she continued to speak her exhortation became more impassioned, until her voice filled the large room with its thrilling vibrations. Though I knew that Hannah Milbrook's words were not meant for a little girl like me, I also writhed on my seat with the sense that I had committed some dreadful sin.

Since she was my parents' guest, Hannah Milbrook returned with them from meeting to our house and while we were all sitting about waiting for dinner she fell asleep in her chair. Immediately the atmosphere grew tense, for we knew of

her power to read people's secret thoughts and of her sometimes divulging them in her sleep. When Grace left the room I crept after her, unable to endure hearing the words that might fall from Hannah Milbrook's lips. The possibility of her going into a trance at any moment and revealing one-could-not-imagine what, made her presence in the house so exciting to my sister Grace that she fell ill: heard voices, bells ringing, lay awake at night trembling with fear. Finally my parents felt it wise to cut short the sojourn of our terrible visitor, prophetess, sibyl, or witch. I remember the relief I felt when her dread presence was removed from the house, though I believe I felt it rather for Grace's sake than my own. My terror of Hannah Milbrook's occult powers had gradually evaporated as I saw her day after day lying with closed eyes on our back-parlor sofa muttering in her sleep and I wondered why Grace continued to be so profoundly disturbed.

At that time I had still a very imperfect idea of my sister's character. I adored her as the fascinating young lady who was such fun to watch; her goodness and kindness I took for granted as well as her religious convictions. I never saw any signs that Grace herself worried about her own gay escapades, or felt remorse for them, though she may of course have done so without my perceiving it. I rather fancy that she felt herself too firmly on the side of religion and morality to bother about little things. Grace had in fact many good deeds to her credit. I knew in a general way that she visited orphan asylums and hospitals and even went to the

prison far downtown to comfort the inmates and soften their hearts, but these activities of hers remained vague for my imagination until one day I happened to hear her tell her most intimate friend about one of her visits to the prison.

The two young girls were talking together in Grace's sitting room, no doubt without noticing that I was present reading in my accustomed corner.

"What's the matter, Grace?" I heard Lettie Tyson ask my sister. "Thee looks terribly pale today."

"I couldn't sleep a wink last night, I had such an awful experience yesterday morning," my sister replied.

"Yesterday was thy day for visiting the prison, wasn't it?" Lettie's voice was excited.

I did not look up from my book, but I listened intently.

"It was all the Warden's fault!" my sister exclaimed in a tense voice. "Mother says I shouldn't have gone to the men's side of the prison, but how could I refuse when the Warden himself asked me? He told me he was worried about a young prisoner who refused to speak, he was in such despair. This young man had just been committed for housebreaking, and though it was his first offense and he had only been a helper, the Judge had given him ten years. The Warden felt that a visit from me would help the poor fellow very much, perhaps keep him from becoming desperate. Of course I agreed to visit him, and went right off with the guard to his cell. I wasn't a bit afraid for I expected to find a very young man, a boy al-

most." Grace paused for a moment, then exclaimed in a voice that vibrated strangely, "Imagine my horror when I saw a grown man with a beard backed into the corner under the grated window and looking at me with burning eyes! Before I could ask the guard not to leave me, I heard the door snap shut behind him; and there I was, locked up alone with that terrible man! He said 'Good morning' to me, but I couldn't answer him, my voice stuck in my throat. I just sat there not saying a word but watching him all the while and straining my ears to hear the footsteps of the guard outside. They sounded fainter and fainter. He was going off down the corridor. Soon I couldn't hear him at all and I thought he'd forgotten me. Then very faintly I heard him again. His footsteps came nearer and nearer. They were right outside the cell. I tried to call but couldn't make a sound. When the door opened and I knew I was rescued I very nearly fainted."

Grace's voice was coming in quick gasps, and for my part I was trembling with excitement. I hardly heard Lettie Tyson's exclamation of horror and sympathy, but I paid attention when my sister spoke once more.

"Mother says she will tell the Warden never to send me again to visit one of the men, but I can't go back to the jail. I couldn't stand being locked up in a cell again. I simply couldn't bear it, not even with a woman!"

Once more I heard the unaccustomed vibration in Grace's voice. It made shivers run up and down my spine. My sister had had a terribly narrow escape. But what an exciting adventure!

My own good deeds, if such they can be called, were in no way exciting. I was never taken or sent to visit orphan asylums or hospitals or shut up in prison cells. It was only Grace, I believe, who helped my mother with her charities.

The duties imposed on me had an annoying way of masquerading as pleasures. Helping with the Meeting Sunday School picnic that took place in the park every spring was considered a disagreeable task by both Frank and me, but our parents spoke of it always as a treat. I remember rushing about in the hot sunlight trying to infuse some spirit into the games that always lagged. Very few children came to the Sunday School picnics, since there were few children in our Meeting, even counting those who lived in the country and the "mission children." To make up, quite a number of older people attended. They liked to see the younger generation enjoy themselves, they said, and they pronounced each and every picnic a great success.

Going to the evening party given during the winter by Great-Aunt Julia Valentine and Aunt Mary Thomas was also an inescapable duty for us. To have a new dress and to go out after supper was exciting, of course, but the parties themselves were awful. Too many older people were present and their benevolent intentions in bringing the country and city young people of the Meeting together were so painfully obvious as quite to defeat their own purpose. I can still see the big parlor lighted by a gas chandelier and Aunt Mary talking vivaciously to a group of embarrassed boys and girls, directing them where they should stand

for the game she was arranging, while Great-Aunt Julia Valentine watched the proceedings with her bright old eyes from her armchair at the end of the room where the other grown-ups clustered. Frank and I, who made up the entire city contingent, felt positive dislike for the boys and girls we saw at these parties, and no doubt our feelings were reciprocated by them.

Throughout their youth our older brothers and sisters had all had friends who were Quakers, either members of our Baltimore Meeting or cousins in Philadelphia. Even after Carey had left home for boarding school and Grace had deserted the Friends Academy, these friendships continued. The boys had gone from a Quaker school to a Quaker college and Margaret's friends were, as I have said, almost exclusively the boys and girls of her class at the Friends Academy. But circumstances brought it about that during our childhood and youth neither Frank nor I ever had an intimate friend who was a Quaker outside our own immediate family. This fact, though it was not perhaps particularly noticed at the time, must have operated to make us different from our older brothers and sisters and like each other in certain ways.

Since I entered Miss Bond's school with my chum, Peggie White, I had no sense of strangeness because I was the only Quaker among the pupils. Indeed, I doubt whether I was ever conscious of that fact. I was well used to Episcopalians and the Episcopal service, since I often went to evensong with Peggie at the parish church in our neigh-

borhood. I enjoyed the singing and the beautiful prayers and collects, some of which I learned by heart through constantly repeating them, but the service never moved me as did the silence and simplicity of our meeting. After I had made friends with other girls at school I sometimes went with them to the churches they attended. I even saw the sister of one baptized by immersion inside a hideous dark church. A tank of artificially heated water struck me as a ridiculous substitute for the River Jordan and I felt that it was far more in accord with the Gospels to omit the outward symbolism of baptism, as Quakers did. To my friend however I made no such comment and the internal sense of superiority I surely had was perhaps somewhat mitigated by being referred to my parents.

Once I did experience a moment of fierce religious antagonism. I was walking peacefully home with a girl whose parents happened to be zealous high-church Episcopalians. Our books under our arms and our hair hanging down our backs in neat braids, we chattered and laughed as we walked, mulling over school gossip. Suddenly changing the subject, Edith broke out:

"My mother says no one can go to heaven without being baptized. Everyone who hasn't been baptized goes straight down to hell when she dies."

Edith's tone was triumphant. It excited in me a violent upsurge of anger. So that was what Edith had been thinking all the time! How about my mother? Had Edith's mother been talking about my mother? Was she to go to hell? These questions went through my mind like a flash of lightning. I

stopped short where I was on the pavement to confront Edith, but instantly the calm, beautiful face of my mother rose up before me. My mother in hell! Impossible! Without deigning to answer Edith by a single word I walked on again, my head in the air. With angry eyes I scrutinized her pretty round face, her dark hair, the tiny pearls in her ears.

"How silly Edith looks," I thought to myself, "with holes burned through her ear lobes to stick pearls in! How terribly silly!"

XI

RESTRICTIONS AND ESCAPES

DASHING in from school one day Frank threw a small package at me. "Here, Nellie, catch," he said. "Hal Howard sent thee this. He hopes thee'll go skating with him again at Black Rock Pond."

Quickly I tore the paper off and lifted the top of the little box. Under a layer of pale blue cotton a gold pencil lay revealed.

"Look, Frank!" I exclaimed, "what a beautiful pencil! Hal can't mean it for me."

"He said I was to give the package to thee. That's all I know."

Together we examined Hal's pencil—the point that twisted out, the fine gold ring to attach to a watch chain, the tiny tube of extra leads.

Frank was obviously greatly taken with it. "I need a pencil very much," he said. "I wish Hal had given it to me, but he's crazy about girls."

Though I was only twelve years old, this comment embarrassed me. Still I did not dream of giving my pencil to my brother.

"If it wasn't a present I'd let thee have it," I placated him. "I can't give away a present," I said as I carried my little box off with me to the safety of my own room.

As I examined it there at my leisure I thought what fun Hal Howard had been the Saturday before. While Frank and I were buckling on our

skates he skimmed up and began doing a figure eight in front of us.

"Wait a minute, Hal, and I'll show you I can do that too," Frank called out as he shuffled to his feet, but without noticing him Hal came to a stop in front of me.

"You'll get cold standing there watching Frank," he said. "Let's skate down the pond."

"But I'm only just learning, Hal, and I fall down every few minutes," I protested. "You'd hate that."

"You won't fall down with me. Come on!" He held out his hands and there I was the next moment skimming by his side over the gleaming ice.

"I knew you would make a fine skater," Hal said, tightening his hold on my hands as we swept about in a great curve at the far end of the pond. "All you need is confidence." He looked at me with his bright eyes.

"How can you say that, Hal, when you just this minute saved me from falling?" I replied. "You needn't pretend you don't know that."

I had regained my balance and was gliding swiftly along again. "Without you I'd have been down like Nancy," I said catching sight of Nancy Holt near the bank shaking from her coat the white ice-dust of a tumble.

It had been glorious fun. Though the day was windless our swift motion made Hal's red scarf stream out behind him and my hair blow about my face. A white mist veiled the horizon, but the sky above our heads was brilliant blue. Bright-

colored figures dotted the pond and the skates flashed in the sunlight.

Happily I recalled all these things before I tucked my pencil back into its box and hid it safely away in my desk. I was terribly pleased with Hal's present.

Not so my father, when I exhibited it to him, as I felt in duty bound to do.

"Did Hal Howard send thee that by Frank?" he asked as he examined the pencil. "Send it back to him in the same way."

"But, Father, why shouldn't I keep it?" I asked. "I like it very much."

My father drew down the corners of his mouth in an ominous manner and slowly shook his head. "Thee cannot keep it, child. That boy ought not to have sent thee such a present. He has never been to the house. Thy mother and I do not know his parents. It is all most unsuitable. No use begging," he added, seeing me about to speak. "I will write a brief note for thee to copy and send with the box. I want Frank to take it back to school with him tomorrow and I shall see that he does not forget." Without waiting for a reply my father walked off with quick short steps.

His firmness overwhelmed me. Usually he was so indulgent, so easy to cajole. I had showed my present to him rather than to my mother for that reason, I suddenly realized. Perhaps she might not have objected after all. Now it was too late; there could be no appeal from my father's decision.

As I copied the stiff little note he soon brought back to me deep discouragement descended upon

me. Hal would guess I could not write such a grown-up letter by myself and he would hate my dragging in my parents. I felt sure he never let his parents know what he did. His gay self-assurance told me that. He would despise me for showing my pencil and be very, very angry. When I thought how angry Hal would be and how he would despise me I could not hold back my tears. Still there was no use in appealing to my father again or to my mother now against my father, I knew that very well. Only after several struggles did I manage to copy my father's letter correctly.

When I handed the box and my neatly addressed envelope to Frank, he jeered at me with all a small boy's malice.

"So Father won't let thee keep thy fine pencil after all! Thee might just as well have given it to me in the first place. Hal will be pretty mad, I bet."

This was on a Monday. Gradually as the days passed a faint hope asserted itself that Hal might possibly understand and forgive me. The cold weather held and on Saturday I went again with Frank to Black Rock Pond.

My first glance showed me that Hal was there. I kept him in view and when he happened to skate by me I smiled at him. I was all ready to wave my hand to him, but his grave stiff bow stopped that gesture short. He must be dreadfully angry to give me such a formal grown-up bow. Then later I saw him across the pond talking and laughing with Bella Sterling and I watched her skate off with him as I myself had skated off the

week before. Bella was a lovely girl and very popular with boys, not stupid and shy like me. The wonder was that Hal had ever noticed me at all. I found comfort in the conviction that he must really have liked me, to send me such a beautiful present. Though I dwelt on this in my mind I could not bring myself to go again to Black Rock Pond. Since Frank liked to skate there and would not change to the Park Pond, skating expeditions were at an end for me.

In the spring I had another disappointment. My parents refused me permission to take part in a play planned by the children next door. Peggie and I had made friends with them, we had visited each other's houses, my father and mother knew their father and mother; the connection was entirely suitable from the social point of view. But, alas! the question of morals came in. Play acting was morally wrong. I was not allowed even to be present as a spectator, and so I found myself excluded from that gay little group of boys and girls. On the afternoons when Peggie was busy at rehearsals I wandered about the garden alone or sat up in my little room feeling very melancholy, but not resentful, I believe, in spite of an occasional impulse to revolt. I was too much under the spell of my mother to resent her decisions. Or perhaps I merely lacked spirit to fight for what I wanted as Grace had fought. But Grace's case was different. She had been led on and no doubt supported by Bond and Harry.

This experience and others like it taught me the uselessness of starting a friendship with anyone not

approved by my parents. Since disappointments upset me profoundly I soon learned to avoid situa-
tions that might lead to them, and I clung to
Peggie White who stood by me "through thick and
thin" with unwavering loyalty.

We had dropped our brothers as playmates or
they had dropped us—it came to the same thing.
No other boys sought out our society. Every now
and then we combined with other girls, but as a
rule we liked to keep to ourselves. And yet our
friendship, exclusive as it continued to be, was
in a way superficial. As small children we had
argued together passionately about religion and
life, each citing her own parents as final authority,
but the differences in our inherited traditions once
explored, we no longer bothered about them.
Whites were Episcopalians and Democrats, the
Thomas family was Quaker and Republican; automatically we discounted all the consequences of
this difference. When I was promoted to the class
above Peggie at Miss Bond's school we could no
longer study our lessons together, and the books
we enjoyed reading and discussing together became
fewer and fewer. In the house we occupied ourselves very happily apart. It was almost entirely
for outside amusement that we joined forces.

In those days no school athletics were provided
for girls. Peggie and I had to have exercise and we
got it by taking long walks. We wandered here
and there over the town, at first in our own district, then by degrees farther and farther afield.
We had no sense of being supervised by our
parents. On the other hand we did feel that they

had put us on our honor to behave in a way they would approve. This fundamental assumption held us in check when the issue was clear. When there was a doubt we usually, I suppose, took the benefit of it.

On bright afternoons in the autumn and spring we often walked as far as Druid Hill Park to watch the team of which Harry was captain play la crosse. Sometimes standing side by side in the wind on the edge of the athletic field we shivered with cold, but we persisted. As the only spectators we were greeted enthusiastically on our arrival. The players waved their la crosse sticks at us; in the pauses of the game Harry ran up to joke with us, but little attention was paid us really by anyone, small school girls that we were in short skirts with pigtails hanging down our backs. The walk to the park was a long walk, but the young men running about the field, leaping high to capture the ball in the narrow nets attached to their sticks were fun to watch, and Harry seemed to feel some special pleasure in seeing us stand there on the side lines. Whatever it was that rewarded us, once a week perhaps during the open season for a year or two we went to look on at the game.

Peggie was ingenious in devising things for us to do, far more ingenious than I. It was she who conceived the idea of disguising ourselves as poor women and seeing how much money we could get from the neighbors by begging. So as darkness began to fall, dressed in old skirts that dragged on the ground, with shawls over our heads shadowing our faces and with fast beating hearts, we rang the

165

bell of a neighbor down the street and asked for the lady of the house. Standing in the shadow of that strange front hall, Peggie made a touching appeal and was rewarded by the gift of a dime. This first triumph encouraged us. Our skill increased with practice; once a kind lady gave us a quarter, so pathetic had Peggie's story become. Not until we had collected nearly two dollars did we boast of our success. Our parents, Whites and Thomases alike, were outraged, as we might have foreseen. They ordered us to return the money we had got under false pretenses. What we had done was no better than stealing; we had disgraced ourselves and we had also disgraced them, they sternly declared. This, of course, we had not meant to do. We were very repentant, but to go back to our victims and make restitution in our own persons seemed to us really too terrible a punishment. After much pleading our sentence was lightened and we were allowed to enclose the sum of each depredation in an apologetic note and leave it with the maid at the door. Though we fussed and complained we really enjoyed humbling ourselves on paper.

Before very long we tried the same trick on Harry, now a student at the Medical School. Our disguises, with which Grace helped us, were cunningly devised. We even had a bit of make-up. When the front door opened to us Peggie asked for Dr. Thomas. She was suffering terrible pain and must see the doctor at once. Our colored maid, coached beforehand in her part, informed us that old Dr. Thomas was out but the young doctor was

JOHN

HARRY

BOND

FRANK

THE THOMAS BROTHERS

at home. She would call the young doctor if we would wait. Harry, talking to Grace in the parlor, was easily found; he must indeed have heard what Peggie said. At first he refused to see us but, Grace urging, he finally came out into the hall.

He was not yet a real doctor, he explained, only a student of medicine. He could do nothing to help.

Peggie took a step forward. "It's me jaw, Doctor. It pains me something terrible," she said in the brogue she had picked up from her mother's maid. "Sure you can give me something for me suffering. Take a look, Doctor, please." She opened her mouth and pointed a finger down her throat.

"Since you are suffering so much," Harry responded in a dignified tone, "perhaps I might give you something to relieve the pain. It is probably your tooth that is causing the trouble." As he bent over to look into Peggie's wide-open mouth a shout of laughter from Grace behind the door betrayed the trick. The sudden change in Harry's self-important expression was terribly funny: I felt a pang of sympathy for him as he glanced about bewildered, but I laughed with the rest. Even the maid down the hall was showing her white teeth in a grin. Quickly pulling himself together, Harry congratulated Peggie on her talent as an actress.

"I had no idea it was you," he said, carrying off his chagrin. "And Helle there too! Come into the light, Helle, and let me see thee."

I thought that Harry minded really very much; the sudden change in his expression haunted me. I was sorry for the trick we had played on him.

From time to time flashes of insight into my brother's feelings came to me and I saw the extreme sensitiveness from which under his gallant gaiety he suffered. On his side he was well aware of my secret emotions, childish feelings of inferiority and shame, personal vanities I tried to conceal, and sometimes he laid them bare with an acute comment in private or even in public before the assembled family, causing me agonies I have never forgotten.

My short fat legs were a dreadful trial to me and gaiters made them look even shorter and fatter. I avoided wearing gaiters whenever I could, so one wet morning when my mother told me to put them on before starting for school I protested.

"I really don't need gaiters, Mother," I said. "The rain is stopping already."

I saw my mother look at the windows down which the raindrops were pouring.

"Go right up to thy room and put thy gaiters on," she said. "It will take only a minute." Her voice was very firm.

As I pushed my chair back from the table to obey Harry remarked to the company in general, "Helle is so proud of her legs, she hates to cover them up." Then speaking directly to me he said, "Thee looks very nice in gaiters. They really set off thy legs."

Though I did not glance about me I was well aware of the smiles his words excited.

This was not the first time Harry had teased me about my legs. He knew very well how I hated them. It hurt me terribly that he should put me

168

to shame in this way. Perhaps he was not really fond of me, after all. Perhaps I only bothered him with my affection. I did not know what to think.

Now that he was a medical student Harry seemed always busy and preoccupied. He spent long hours shut up in his study where there was a ghastly human skull perched on a bookcase, bones lying about on his desk and hanging on the wall the chart of a man without his skin, showing raw red muscles—a hideous object. When Harry emerged from this den he immediately left the house. At meals he was sometimes gay, making little jokes and rallying us good-naturedly in the old manner, but more often there was a rasp of irritation in his banter. What could be the matter with Harry? I knew that he was devoted to Zoe Carey and I felt sure from watching her that she liked him. Being in love made people happy. It could not be anything connected with Zoe. I puzzled my head in vain trying to guess what was upsetting my brother.

Chance enlightened me. One afternoon while I was lying curled up in my favorite place on the back-parlor sofa reading I heard my father come into my mother's sitting room and begin talking to her with unusual vehemence. His voice carried to me distinctly through the curtain that hung in the doorway between the two rooms.

"How can Harry be so foolish as to think of marrying before he has finished his education?" my father said. "A medical student needs his whole time for study, but Harry spends every evening at the Careys'. He won't get far in that way. I have

169

given up all hope of his distinguishing himself in his profession."

"Harry and Zoe both know they are too young to get married now. They expect to wait." Though my mother's voice was low, I could hear what she was saying.

"Why not wait to get engaged then?" My father's indignant question rang out. "It's nonsense for Harry to say he was afraid of losing Zoe. If she really loves him she would have waited. If she does not love him enough to wait without an engagement she had better marry someone else."

The rapid flow of my father's words kept me from remembering that I had no right to listen to my parents' conversation, concealed from them as I was. When his voice stopped, I knew that I ought to creep away.

My mother was speaking again. "Thee cannot expect Harry to look at things as thee does, James. Robert Talcott has proposed to Zoe twice already and he will not give her up until she is engaged to someone else. I do not wonder Harry was afraid to wait."

I had got to my feet and was crossing the room when my father spoke once more. "The truth is I don't like the marriage. I object to the fact that Zoe is an Episcopalian and I object to her being such a near relation on the Carey side." What could my father mean? Curiosity held me lingering by the door while he continued. "The Careys have a streak of supersensitiveness. I suffer from it myself and Harry is dreadfully touchy."

Having heard this much I propelled myself out of earshot at last.

Throughout the conversation I had seemed to see my father's eyes reproaching my mother for Harry's rashness and then for his supersensitiveness, even though that fault was inherited from him. When annoyed by one of his children my father had a peculiar way of looking at my mother with bright darting glances that placed the blame where it belonged, on her.

Poor Harry! I understood his ill-temper now and I forgave him for his stabs at me. I would not betray his secret; whatever the temptation, I would keep my mouth shut. I tried to quiet my shame for eavesdropping by making this resolution very firmly, but it was never put to the test. Harry's engagement to Zoe became public property the very next day.

My father betrayed his disapproval only too clearly. He kept after my brother, asking him frequently how much studying he had managed to do the day before, and once I was present when he complained that Zoe's brother came too frequently to the house.

"I wish thee would not encourage Jasper Carey's visits," my father said to my brother. "He is paying marked attention to Grace. He comes to see her several times a week. One marriage between the two families is quite enough!"

"Jasper is my most intimate friend," Harry replied hotly. "He comes to the house to see me. After all I do live here and surely I may be per-

mitted to receive visits from my friends. Jasper cares nothing for Grace, I assure thee."

Harry was so deeply hurt that he left the room before my father had time to speak again.

Much as I sympathized with Harry in his difficulties I felt that my father was right about Jasper Carey. I felt sure he was in love with Grace.

For some time I had been borrowing and reading the paper-backed novels my sister kept on the bookshelves of her sitting room, *Molly Bawn* by The Duchess, and other such stories. I delighted in the adventures of the lovely heroines and identified them consciously with Grace however much I may unconsciously have slipped into their roles myself. I delighted hardly less in the sufferings of the lovers, so handsome and rich and aristocratic or, as the case might be, so humbly born by comparison with the heroine. I felt not the least sympathy for the agonies endured by these victims of feminine charm. Harry's difficulties were a different matter. I wished he and Zoe could get married at once. Still, since my novels had taught me that the course of true love never runs smooth, I did not worry greatly on my brother's account.

It was probably at about this time that Peggie and I began to attend church weddings. We were never invited of course. Our technique was to arrive at the church very early, slip by the sexton in charge, climb to the gallery and wait hidden there until the guests began to arrive and it was safe to show our heads above the rail. Ostensibly we came to see the flowers and the dresses, the bride's dress above all, to compare the composure

with which the bride and groom spoke their responses, and finally to rate the whole ceremony with others we had attended. These were the things we discussed; secretly I at least was intoxicated by the suspense of waiting for the bride's coming, the thrill of the organ's deep voice announcing her presence, the slow procession up the aisle while the bridegroom awaited his bride at the altar, and the final release of the blessing with the gay march out to the carriages.

The only real adventures that came Peggie's and my way were so carefully arranged for us that they hardly counted as adventures. Several times in June after school was over we made a trip alone together on one of the Whites' steamboats that sailed down the Chesapeake Bay and up the rivers flowing into it. I cannot now date these expeditions. We were surely old enough to be trusted to behave ourselves properly and still young enough not to require a conventional chaperon when they took place. Peggie's father was able to arrange everything for us, since in the intervals of his law practice he managed this line of steamers which his wife had inherited from her parents. He took us on board himself always, introduced us to the captain and handed us over to the stewardess, a capable, middle-aged, colored woman who had been brought up in the White family. He had already instructed us not to bother the captain or be familiar with the underofficers. A taciturn man, severe but just, Peggie's father could rely on our doing exactly what he told us. A word from him controlled the wildest of his sons and neither

Peggie nor I would have dreamed of disobeying him.

The trip up the Rappahannock River lasted three days, and others were shorter; they merge into each other in retrospect. I remember the tiny officers' saloon where, separated from the other passengers, we took our meals, its portholes, the long table crowded up against cushioned benches, the excitement I felt and the cramp in my knees I suffered there. The captain seldom addressed us, we did not dare chatter to each other, our legs were so short they hardly reached the floor but we were thrilled by the strange situation. Nor have the intervening years effaced my memories of flat river banks in hot sunlight passing by monotonously hour after hour, of lush trees, of bells clanging sharply as the boat drew up to one long wooden wharf after the other. Black men ran on and off carrying freight, shouting and singing, black women and children crowded near the gangway, watching. The water was churned into foam, then flowed smoothly by again, flaming with the bright sparkle of sunlight. In the morning when we came on deck the captain always greeted us formally. He took us ashore at Fredericksburg, I remember, and pointed out to us Stonewall Jackson's stone wall with a fervor of emotion that impressed me. It looked much like any other wall to me but I knew that to the captain and to Peggie as Southerners it was an object of veneration. The vision of the square tower of an old church in a tree-shaded street rises up before my eyes. I cannot be sure that it belongs to Fredericksburg.

During the years these sails lasted I looked forward to them with extreme eagerness, but when they ceased I do not remember that I missed them. The passage of time had brought with it other preoccupations.

XII

CAREY'S RETURN HOME

Boxes and trunks stood about the laundry; the bare wooden floor, the ironing table, the tops of the tubs were littered—strewn with piles of books, rolls of photographs, vases, statues, and queer-shaped bundles still unwrapped. From the last of the trunks my eldest sister, Carey, was taking clothes which our laundress, Eliza, received on outstretched brown arms. Carey was at home again after four long years of absence. The tension of her arrival had been great. For five terrible days my parents feared that she had been shipwrecked in a terrific November storm off the banks of Newfoundland, but here she was at home once more, "safe and sound," as they said, and I was helping her unpack. My excitement increased moment by moment as I saw appear one after the other the strange things she had brought with her from abroad. Even the dresses she was taking from the trunk seemed queer and different.

The face of our laundress, usually solemn and cross, was wreathed in smiles as she stood beside Carey supporting the growing pile of dresses on her thin outstretched arms.

"I d'un know, I's sure, Miss Minnie," she said, "where we can put all these duds. There ain't no place left in this here laundry." She looked about at the confusion with obvious enjoyment.

At that moment we heard my mother's voice speaking to the cook and my mother herself appeared at the top of the short flight of steps that led down from the kitchen into the laundry. She still had on her bonnet and cloak; she had come to find Carey the moment she got home from the committee only a stern sense of duty had enabled her to attend. She found it hard, she had declared at breakfast, to leave her returned prodigal for a moment. I saw her smile at my sister as she slowly descended the steep steps.

Carey dropped the frock in her hand and hurried to meet my mother. "I have found the picture I told thee about, Mother," she said. "I want to show it to thee."

From a roll on the ironing table she selected a large photograph and spread it flat for my mother to see. "That is Leonardo da Vinci's picture of the Mona Lisa," she said. "Isn't she beautiful?"

My mother studied the photograph of the strange-looking woman before her for a moment. "I see nothing beautiful in her," she answered at last. "I am thankful that every one of my daughters is better looking than Leonardo's 'Mona Lisa.' " She looked at my sister with a gay little smile.

My mother's remark gave me a shock. I feared its effect on my sister, whose wonderful possessions had impressed me profoundly. What would she think of us at home? The moment of silence seemed long before I heard her laugh; then, when the tension was snapped. I burst out into a shout of glee so unrestrained that it haunted me afterward.

177

Over Raphael's "Sistine Madonna" my mother lingered, declaring it beautiful but objecting that the figures kneeling in adoration on either side savored of Virgin worship. In the end it was the photograph of Mona Lisa that hung framed in brown wood on the walls of our parlor, a strange companion piece to the engraving of Elizabeth Fry that had so long presided there.

In the months which followed I stood very often in front of that large dark photograph studying and studying the face and the figure, puzzling out details of the landscape, the distant hills, the valley, and the brook winding down it. Back and back again I came to stand on the same spot of our carpet and gaze up at the picture. What could it have been that so fascinated the little girl of twelve I then was? Perhaps she felt an unquenched longing to worship the beauty that hung there on the wall above her. Perhaps her persistence may have been due simply to bewilderment: I cannot tell.

Soon after Carey's return Aunt Hannah arrived on one of her flying visits to our house. She had rushed on at the very first opportunity to see her favorite niece. Like my mother, she wholeheartedly shared Carey's enthusiasm for women's education. The two sisters rejoiced together in the final triumph of her winning the degree of Doctor of Philosophy at Zurich University, *summa cum laude,* a great distinction even for a man. My father also was pleased. The atmosphere of rejoicing that pervaded the house—of welcoming home

a conquering heroine—impressed me greatly, elevating my sister further than ever above me.

With Carey's enthusiasm for the arts neither my mother nor my aunt showed any great sympathy, though my mother loved poetry and cultivated a taste for pictures. My mother was sensitive to influences—to Carey's influence and also to the steady pressure of my father's beauty-loving Celtic temperament, his delight in poetry and music and painting. Aunt Hannah, however, was made of sterner stuff. In spite of her children's efforts she had remained firm in her instinctive scorn for art and artists. In her opinion most famous poetry was unintelligible verbiage and most so-called "good pictures" absurd distortions of fact. The paintings of the Madonna and Christ Child she had been taken to see in Italy were her particular abhorrence. They outraged her maternal instincts. She couldn't look at them, she declared, without wanting to snatch up in her arms the poor scrawny, wrinkled baby, hold him comfortably in her arms, and give him a good meal for once. These opinions of Aunt Hannah's were well known in both the Pearsall Smith and the Thomas families. They were deplored by the younger generation, though shouted over too with pleasure because of their vehemence.

Thus it could have been no shock to Carey when one evening during this visit Aunt Hannah attacked her for her excessive love of poetry. Dinner was over, my father had gone off to see a patient, the others also were out, only my mother, Aunt

Hannah, and Carey remained in the lamplighted back parlor, with me in unobtrusive attendance. Passionately on the side of my sister, I listened to the arguments back and forth between my elders.

Finally Aunt Hannah ended the discussion by a direct challenge to my sister. "I don't believe there is a single poem I can understand and enjoy that thee would consider really good," she said. "If there is, now is the time to produce it. I am determined to settle this question in my own mind once for all. If thee with all thy learning and thy reading cannot convince me, nobody can! I shall dismiss the subject of poetry from my mind."

Carey meditated for a moment, her eyes on Aunt Hannah's face, then turning to my mother with a smile that showed her faith in my mother's sympathy she said, "I will read you the most beautiful poem in the English language," and quickly left the room. I heard her climb the stairs to her study.

The book she brought back in her hand was, I instantly saw, a volume of Shelley's poetry. Would my sister choose "The Sensitive Plant," or "I arise from dreams of thee?" Very slowly, it seemed to me, she seated herself at the table where the light from the lamp would fall on her page.

"Shelley's 'Hymn to Intellectual Beauty,'" she announced and began to read in her lovely voice:

The awful shadow of some unseen Power
Floats though unseen among us—visiting
This various world with an inconstant wing
As summer winds that creep from flower to flower,...

The rhythmical stress of my sister's voice lulled me to enchantment as she read on. Though I struggled hard to keep my attention on the meaning only a phrase here and there penetrated to me. When the last words had sounded—

> *Whom, Spirit fair, thy spells did bind*
> *To fear himself, and love all human kind—*

deep silence fell in the room, and I saw that the light of enthusiasm on my sister's face was reflected in the uplifted countenances of my mother and my aunt.

"It's a hymn to God really, Minnie," my mother said, using the old pet name in her emotion. "But what a pity that such a beautiful poem should be so sad! If Shelley had had faith he would not have felt despair but joy instead, and peace that passeth understanding."

Aunt Hannah acknowledged her defeat, gloried in it, she said, but none the less she entered a final protest.

"Why 'Intellectual Beauty'?" she asked my sister. "Isn't the name of 'God' good enough even for Shelley?"

As I examine now one by one my memories of Carey at this time they all glow with her passion for literature and art. In spite of her long years of study at foreign universities and the high honors she had won, I saw her not as a student and scholar but as a lover of books and pictures, of beauty and freedom. In less than four months after her return home she was appointed Dean of the Quaker College for Women soon to be opened

at Bryn Mawr. She was busy planning courses of study, finding a professor for Greek, for history, for the sciences. I must have heard a great deal of talk about these things, have caught glimpses of the important-looking, strange men who came to confer with her, but not one single concrete memory remains of them, while many stories of my sister's travels over Europe are still vivid in my mind. Young women though she and Miss Gwinn were, they made their long journeys always at night, sitting out the slow hours of darkness in day coaches or waiting in stations, to save money since hotels were expensive, my sister explained, and they had fascinating things to do with every penny they could save. Once they arrived in the early morning at a far away Italian town, climbed the hill to the great church that topped it, and saw hanging above its altar a most rare and lovely picture by Giorgione. Again they lifted the curtain of their railway carriage in the early dawning and found themselves gazing out on languid green waves rolling up a long stretch of dark sand—the Adriatic. Beyond, far to the east, lay Greece. They meant to go to Greece if their money held out, and somehow they managed to make it do so.

Thus did my sister kindle in me the fires of imagination. Without surprise, I heard years later my cousin, Logan Pearsall Smith, declare that as a young man he always pictured Carey and Miss Gwinn traveling about dressed like men in coats and trousers with plain felt hats and flowing ties after the manner of George Sand. My sister always

dressed in a perfectly conventional manner, but from the beginning she possessed the power of giving reality to the dreams of young people.

Carey loved to share her pleasures with others on a momentary impulse. I was not long in learning that it paid to be discreetly at hand where her bright eyes could spy me out. One spring afternoon, April by that time it must have been, I saw old black Horace waiting with the dogcart in front of our door and I heard Carey talking with Mamie Gwinn as they came down the stairs. They were already drawing on their gloves when I slipped out through the parlor door into the hall.

My sister's eyes pounced on me. "Run get thy hat," she commanded me. "Thee will not bother us on the back seat. Quickly, child!" I was ready in a flash.

Though I could not see my companions' faces, by turning as much toward them as was safe on that high, unprotected seat I could hear what they said. They were discussing plans for a school in Baltimore to prepare girls for college, for Bryn Mawr in particular. This was thrilling news; I strained my attention to catch every word.

At last Carey addressed me over her shoulder. "Has thee been listening, little Miss Nell?" she asked. "We are going to open a school to teach thee Greek so that thee can read Homer. How will thee like that?"

"Oh, Carey, do. Please do," I said. "But won't it take a long time? Won't I be too old before the school begins?"

Carey laughed. "The school will open a year

from next autumn," she declared. "Thee will have to give up thy bad habit of reading silly novels and work hard to be ready for it."

La Reine began to climb a steep street on the way back to our house, slowly dragging after her the heavy, ill-balanced dogcart. I had to cling tightly to the padded leather bar dividing the front and back seats to keep myself from slipping off onto the cobblestones. A sense of slipping and clutching but triumphantly maintaining my place rises up in my mind as I think of this drive.

Our family routine was naturally affected in many ways by my sister's presence at home. Dinner, which already had taken the place of supper in the evening, now became a ceremonious affair. Nine or ten people often sat down to it. For some reason I felt this fact a great distinction. Table manners began to be subject to stricter censorship: napkins had to be not only unfolded but used, knives and forks properly manipulated, elbows kept off the table. This was highly irksome to Frank, heedless like all small boys and resentful of criticism. My father took his part and from time to time a scene would flare up. I accommodated myself to ceremony more easily than did Frank, but the general effect of the situation on me was to increase my shyness and sharpen my critical faculties. I hardly ever dared say a word myself, fearing the shout of laughter that usually greeted any remark of mine, however seriously meant, but I watched and listened to my elders, noting and comparing, pronouncing judgment on one or the other in the silence of my own mind.

None of my brothers or sisters cared to hear the opinions of the smallest girl in the family; still less would they tolerate criticism from me. The affection that they showed me I could return in kind, love for love, only not criticism for criticism, though I was myself often the subject of remarks that pierced to my heart like daggers.

Many lively discussions took place about the dinner table. Most I have forgotten, a few made a deep impression on me.

"Thee must acknowledge one thing, Carey," my father said. "Women have as yet done nothing to prove themselves the equals of men in originality or in power of mind. Men have always governed the world, they have made the scientific discoveries, thought out the systems of philosophy, composed the music, built the buildings, painted the pictures and also they have written the great books."

"Don't forget Jane Austen, Father," Harry filled up my father's pause, looking at Carey with a gleam of malice in his brown eyes. Though he was devoted to her, he sometimes took my father's side against her. "There is always Jane Austen; we must make our bow to Jane Austen."

Carey's frown showed that she was annoyed. "There is also George Eliot and Sappho, probably the greatest poet the Greeks ever had," she admonished Harry a little sharply, "also Queen Elizabeth and—"

My father did not wait for Carey to complete her list. Having got his breath he continued with the momentum of the practiced preacher. "Spirit-

ually and morally women are the equals of men, their superiors in fact. A good woman is more unselfish, more loving, far purer than the best of men, but there is no man so abandoned, so lost to all sense of decency as a bad woman.''

My mother spoke from her end of the table. "We have heard too much about that, James. Bad women are not the fallen angels become fiends men like to think them. They are poor weak creatures, the victims of the men who have corrupted them for their own purposes."

"That is not the whole story, Mary," my father replied. "And even supposing it were, women have allowed themselves to be corrupted. Thee cannot deny that," my father, looking up and down the table, collected the approving glances of his sons, Harry, Bond, and Frank.

"I do deny absolutely that women fall to lower depths of evil than men," my mother, herself a practiced speaker, knew how to stick to her point. "Men overlook in other men what makes women outcasts forever in their eyes."

Carey broke in, "How can women show what they are capable of intellectually, when they are denied education, denied all opportunity? They have to use their energy in fighting for what men get as a matter of course. Take my own case"— she turned on my father with a certain fierceness.

Harry spoke up quickly. "That is true, Carey, we all acknowledge that. Father means only that we must wait to see what they can do, when they have a fair chance."

"Nobody denies that women can learn anything

they set themselves to learn," my father began again in a more conciliatory tone. "But can they work things out for themselves?—that is the question."

"What about mathematics?" Carey asked. "Did not Dr. Sylvester maintain the other day here at this very table that no woman can understand a mathematical problem? Their minds are incapable, it appears, of grasping an abstract proposition. He forgot Sonia Kovalevsky, as I pointed out to him."

Grace's voice was now heard. "May it not be that women's minds are different from men's minds as their bodies are different?" she asked. "They may always have to depend on men mentally as well as physically." She turned to Bond for approval as she spoke.

Carey had only time to dart a scornful look at Grace before my mother's calm voice intervened. "All that women are asking," she said, "is the opportunity to show what they can do. Prejudgment is one of the greatest obstacles they have to meet. But they will overcome even that," she added, smiling as if she knew she were herself prejudging. Harry's answering smile seemed to show that he understood. I loved him always for his sympathy with my mother.

Busy as she was, Carey did not neglect my education. Among the books she put into my hands was George Sand's *Consuelo,* a little pile of volumes, three or four perhaps, bound in pale green paper. She urged me to begin reading them at once though they were in French. "Do not stop to look up many words in the dictionary," she ad-

187

vised me. "Just get the sense. When thee has read *Consuelo* thee will find thee knows French, and then I will give thee a volume by Balzac, the greatest novelist that ever lived. I learned French myself by reading him."

This was terribly thrilling. *Consuelo*, George Sand, Balzac, all new and fascinating names. I set to work with enthusiasm. At first the going was hard but soon, enthralled by Consuelo's adventures, I sped along. For hours at a time I lay curled up on the back-parlor sofa that was flooded by light from the garden window. Not even the clanging bells of fire engines clattering by our house could distract me for more than a moment. I heard the engines, of course, but felt no impulse to dash to the front window to see them, much less to snatch my hat and follow down the street. Carey was pleased when I told her of this amazing proof that I really enjoyed reading French. It was important to impress her with my good deeds since I was conscious of certain lapses from the standard she set me.

I had not in fact wholly given up my habit, my bad habit she called it, of reading silly English novels. I enjoyed them too much for that. Molly Bawn, one of the heroines whose name I remember, was very different from Consuelo but her unreal love affairs thrilled me as much, almost, as Consuelo's adventures. I wanted to please my sister and I wanted also to please myself. So whenever I indulged myself with a book of the wrong kind, I kept another of the right kind close at

hand. Should Carey chance to enter the room I could snatch it up and answer "Bacon's *Essays,* Carey," in reply to her inevitable question, "What is thee reading, Miss Nell?" Not that I felt easy practicing deceit on my sister, far though I had come since the days of my early literal-minded conscientiousness; but by this device I avoided verbal lying, from which I still shrank, and I escaped a scolding. Harry, always alert, soon became suspicious. Creeping up behind me one day he read over my shoulder the name of the book in which I was absorbed and spied out the volume that stuck up between the cushion and the arm of the chair, convenient to my hand. He laughed at me unmercifully of course; he even went so far as to congratulate me in front of Carey on my passion for Bacon's *Essays,* but he did not actually betray me. It amused him, I suspect, to see Carey delighted by her success in training my literary taste, all the while both he and I knew she was flattering herself. Even Harry did not dare make fun of Carey. As soon would he have put his head in the mouth of a lioness! After this incident I was so deeply ashamed of myself that I made a real effort to read the volume of Bacon's *Essays* through, a dreadfully heavy task that left me with a lifelong dislike of Bacon.

From time to time the white Arabian horses that had so delighted Frank and me as little children stood waiting in front of our house. When I caught sight of them I knew that Miss Garrett must be upstairs attending a committee meeting of

the Bryn Mawr School. A small group of their intimate friends had joined Carey and Miss Gwinn in founding the school and since it concerned me nearly I noted their presence upstairs with satisfaction, but my attention was solicited by too many people and things as I moved about day after day, looking, listening, questioning, to allow of my dreaming over faraway deserts.

Grace still intrigued me. She was a heroine to me still, different from Carey, but fascinating. Free to wander in and out of the small upstairs parlor where she entertained her friends, I saw clearly enough that the young men who gathered there vied with each other for her favor. One afternoon I went into the room with my pencil in hand to borrow a knife. Tom Worthington produced his from his waistcoat pocket, opened the blade and holding it by the point gave it carefully to me. I was preparing to sharpen my pencil where I stood, letting the bits of wood and powderings of lead fall on Grace's carpet instead of into the wastepaper basket by the window as she asked me, when, before I realized what he was doing, Tom took knife and pencil from me, carried them across the room and did the sharpening himself so that the basket caught every scrap. I ran after him and looked up into his face to protest. His large gray eyes looked through me, took no notice of me, intent on something else. Amazed and abashed by his strange, intent seriousness I glanced across at Grace, standing by the piano with Jasper Carey. She was smiling quietly, her eyes on the sheet of music she held. But I knew that she was conscious

of every movement Tom Worthington made. I took my pencil from his hand in silence and in silence left the room. And somehow after this I felt less inclination to run in and out of Grace's room when she had company.

XIII

REFORMING THE WORLD

During the first winter after Carey's return home in November, 1883, or it may have been the second winter, a national convention of the Women's Christian Temperance Union was held in Baltimore. My mother, who was president of the Maryland Branch, entertained as many of the delegates as our house would hold. There were certain domestic details to which my mother herself always attended when guests were expected and as little children we had greatly enjoyed these preparations. A flock of us, boys as well as girls, used to follow her about the house and into the kitchen, running errands and doing, with delight, little tasks she assigned to us, for she had a way of making us feel that we were really helping her. She set our mistakes right quickly and without finding fault, laughed at our jokes and capped them with jokes of her own. Moreover many little treats fell to our share. When my mother prepared the special salad dressing for which she used the yolks of hard-boiled eggs she let us peel off the egg shells, and as a reward for doing it neatly she gave us the whites to eat, though they should have been kept to garnish her platter, and she looked the other way when we purloined for ourselves some of the almonds required for the company almond blanc-mange. Year by year my mother's accompanying

train of children had diminished until now it consisted usually only of Margaret and me. Indeed the rite of preparation itself had been largely discontinued. Ice cream and charlotte russe bought at the confectioner's had long ago taken the place of my mother's almond blancmange and the cook now mixed the salad dressing without supervision, but my mother still inspected the rooms of her guests and got out the solid silver from the depths of her locked closet where it was safely hidden away from burglars, as we used to assure each other, with childish thrills of excitement and fear.

On the day before her ladies arrived for their Temperance Convention I was on hand to help my mother with whatever she had to do. Surrounded as she usually was by throngs of people, my only chance of being alone with her was to do things with her when occasion arose. Margaret happened to be otherwise occupied on this particular afternoon. I rejoiced that I was to have my mother entirely to myself. She moved about the house with all her old swiftness and activity in spite of her increased weight. In a flash she had inspected the dressing-table drawers and the closets I held open for her and had whisked the furniture into just the right places without waiting for my assistance, but she no longer kneeled down herself on the floor in front of her silver chest. It was my part now to take from its depths the pieces she indicated, hers to receive them, and she left me to unwrap them and carry them down to the pantry, while she started off exactly on time for the Women's Bible Class she conducted.

Every morning my mother took her guests to
their convention and brought them home again
in the late afternoon together with other ladies
for dinner. They talked with each other in the
liveliest manner, laughing a great deal in spite of
the serious nature of the subjects they discussed.
I was struck by my mother's gaiety. One evening I
came upon her already dressed in her bonnet and
cloak, waiting alone in the front hall, and I heard
her call up the stairs, "Come, girls, hurry! It is
time to start! Frances, do not forget you are to
take the chair. We must not be late." I was amazed
by her calling her guests "girls," when they were
really old ladies. And how gaily her summons rang
out! Often since that night my mother's happy
voice has sounded in my ears calling, "Come, girls,
hurry, hurry! We must not be late."

This was the first, and I think the only time I
saw Frances Willard, the leader adored by so many
earnest women of my mother's generation and in
particular by my Aunt Hannah. She was a slim
woman with a narrow pale face and eyeglasses
astride a small nose. The lusterless blond hair that
bounded her ivory-white forehead on either side
was artificially waved, I noticed at once. This arti-
ficial waving of Miss Willard's dust-colored hair
struck me as out of keeping with the intense gaze
she fixed on me through her eyeglasses. The impression of extreme concentration she produced
on me put me off.

My mother, however, promoted the cause of
Temperance with no less zeal than did Miss Willard herself. Since God had created Man in His

own image, my mother believed that men and women were really capable of virtue. Christ's admonition to his disciples—"Be ye therefore perfect even as your father in heaven is perfect"—she cited not only as a command but also as a promise. Believing thus in the possibility of perfection for human beings, she hated drunkenness as the most powerful cause of depravity. With terrible quickness drink could extinguish the divine spark in man, she asserted, reducing him to the level of the beasts. His very body was destroyed by it. To show the dreadful physical effects of alcohol, my mother possessed a set of charts which she displayed at meetings and also at home to her children. I found it hard to believe that the discolored, shapeless mass of putrescence labeled "Drunkard's Stomach" on the chart could be the same organ as the smooth, pink pouch assigned to the "Total Abstainer." Comparing the two, I felt that only an idiot would knowingly give himself a stomach like the drunkard's stomach.

For my mother total abstinence was not a question merely of protecting others weaker than herself—"Cause not thy brother to offend." She had experienced the temptation of drink in her own person, she explained to us. Once long ago in the early years of her marriage the doctor had ordered for her a daily glass of champagne to recruit her strength after a difficult confinement, and she had found herself looking forward to her dinner with greater and greater impatience until one day, lifting her glass to her lips, she perceived as in a flash of revelation the true cause of her eagerness. It

was not food for which she longed, it was the champagne that went with it. Back down on the tray she put the glass she had so eagerly seized and, trembling with a sense of the awful danger that confronted her, she determined then and there never so long as she lived to drink another drop of intoxicating liquor. Had it not been for this sudden revelation my mother would have been a drunkard. Gazing at her face I could not believe in any such possibility, but my mother's earnest voice left no doubt of her own conviction. She felt it a sacred duty, she said, to save others, especially young people, from the temptation she herself had experienced. The Women's Temperance Campaign in Maryland, of which my mother was the leading spirit, proved highly effective. They even succeeded in having antialcohol propaganda, as we should now call it, inserted in the physiology textbooks used throughout the state in our public schools. This victory was a cause of great satisfaction to my mother.

Her horror and detestation of alcohol communicated themselves to me. If the scene in Geneva when Frank broke his pledge with my father's permission even occurred to me at this time, I surely thought of it only as a failure of consistency on my father's part, not relevant in any way to the general question of total abstinence. I had of course no suspicion that grave dangers might lurk in the repressions imposed by my parents' strict code. The tide of puritan morality was everywhere rising and very few people, certainly not my parents, foresaw that after reaching its high-water mark it would

suffer retrogression into an ebb tide and leave the next generation stranded far down on the shore. With many other earnest reformers my father and mother rode on the crest of the wave, sure that the changes they advocated and promoted would result in permanent progress for the human race. Fortunately for them, they closed their eyes on this world before the tide had begun to turn.

My father's efforts were directed largely to helping and reforming men and boys. His particular concern was with the Young Men's Christian Association, the State Manual Labor School, the Society for the Prevention of Vice, and the Sunday Afternoon Mission School for the boys of South Baltimore he himself had organized. He also from time to time preached or lectured to various men's associations or clubs and more regularly to the patients in the Baltimore hospitals. In addition to the work my parents each did separately, they worked together for the Society of Friends. They watched over and occasionally visited the isolated groups of Friends that were under the jurisdiction of Baltimore Yearly Meeting. Sometimes they stayed away for several days conducting series of meetings in one of these communities. The Friends Meeting at Richmond, Virginia, must have been a special concern of theirs, for I remember their being absent in Richmond several times during my childhood. My mother's participation in such "pastoral visits" depended of course on the good health of her children. Often at the last moment she had to let my father go off without

her while she remained at home to nurse a sore throat or a violent stomach-ache. My mother's enjoyment of these trips was so obvious that even at the time I hated to see her deprived of them.

With Carey's return from Europe another enthusiastic reformer was added to our already well-stocked circle. Her zeal was as great as the zeal of my parents, but its aim was different. Carey, who shared so much with my mother, did not share her religious enthusiasms, though at the time I was hardly conscious, I believe, of this lack of agreement between them. My sister never in my presence discussed religious doctrines with either of my parents; indeed she never talked about religion at all that I remember. Her enthusiasm, not her lack of enthusiasm, caught my attention. I found her praise of poetry and painting, her stories of travel highly exciting, and I had a personal interest in her schemes for reforming the education of women since I expected to attend both the school and the college she was so busily organizing at this time.

The attention of everyone in the house became more and more keenly concentrated on education. As the months followed each other in rapid succession individual ambitions flared up like flames. The first actual crisis arose in Harry's affairs. It happened that his work at the Medical School was almost finished and he planned as a matter of course to settle down to practice medicine as a family physician immediately after he got his degree. But this prospect seemed to offer little hope of distinction for Harry. My mother and Carey

urged on him the advantages of a year's further study in Germany where new methods as yet little known in America had been developed. From this plan for Harry my father disassociated himself. I heard him discuss the matter with my mother on several occasions.

"There was a time when thee might profitably have used thy influence with Harry," he reproached her. "Having encouraged him to engage himself to marry Zoe, thee should not now urge him to run off to Germany and leave her. He has taken on himself the responsibility for Zoe's future and should devote himself at once to providing for her by practicing his profession in the best way he can. That is my idea of his duty."

It was also Harry's idea of his duty as well as of his pleasure. He showed no desire to separate himself from his adored ladylove. By what arguments he was persuaded I do not know, but I fancy that Zoe herself did the job in the end. Before very long "Mother's plan for Harry" as we called it, had been accepted by him, and Zoe herself was hard at work studying for the entrance examinations to Bryn Mawr College, where it had been decided that she could most pleasantly spend the time of Harry's absence, together with Grace and Margaret and the Whitall cousins.

Carey was enchanted with her new recruit and set herself to make preparation for the entrance examination easy and pleasant for Zoe. She planned out courses of study not only for her and Grace, but also for other young women who had been getting themselves ready to enter the new

Quaker college and were upset by the unexpectedly difficult entrance requirements. Some of them, not satisfied with Carey's written instructions, came to our house to consult her in person, spending a night or two with us.

Groups of young girls, lively and gay in spite of their worries, were often to be found gathered about Carey in my mother's writing room off the parlor. Into their midst I insinuated myself, keen to listen and keen to watch. However vehement their complaints, Carey never for a moment admitted the possibility of lowering the standard she had set up for Bryn Mawr College. It was to be the equal of any man's college in scholarly requirements and was to serve as a demonstration of woman's intellectual equality with men. Even a small concession might imply feminine inferiority, she pointed out, and that she would not tolerate. But this major premise once accepted, Carey approached each individual problem with the intention of solving it. Before her ingenuity and the enthusiasm she inspired difficulties faded away; the prospect of hard work became exciting, became delightful. She made going to college seem a great adventure. My mother, busy at her writing table, followed the argument and at crucial moments looked up from her work to interject a remark. Even when she was silent her mere presence was a help. We all knew that she took delight in our having opportunities she herself had never had.

One morning my father's Aunt Julia happened in on one of these conferences.

"I cannot understand why young girls of the

present day want to leave home and go to college," she said in a sharp voice. "*I* never had any desire to leave my parents. I stayed at home and did my duty. All this talk about higher education is wicked nonsense. Living at home is the best and highest education for a woman."

Aunt Julia's words impressed no one, least of all her great-nieces. Long ago we had learned to discount her opinions though we dreaded her sharp tongue. She disapproved always of our being allowed any privilege she had been denied, approving only of our having what she herself had had. She obviously felt that we could not do better than follow her example in every detail.

"Give the child a cup of coffee if she wants it, Mary." She had intervened in my behalf not long before at breakfast. "It would put a little color into her pale cheeks. Coffee is good for young people. Every morning since I was five years old I have had a cup with my breakfast. Thee cannot maintain that it hurt me, whatever thy newfangled notions may be."

Aunt Julia's glance challenged my mother. Delighted for once to accept my great-aunt as a model, I fixed expectant eyes on my mother. She, however, continued to sit quietly behind the breakfast tray, making no motion to fill a cup with coffee for me, and from his end of the table my father pronounced sentence.

"Coffee clearly has done thee no harm, Aunt Julia," he said, "but none the less I think milk is better for Nellie."

Aunt Julia uttered not another word. My father

was always able to silence her if he really wished to do so.

Study was now the order of the day for all the young people in the house except for Frank, who was too young perhaps to feel Carey's dominating influence, or perhaps just old enough to react against it. When I wandered down the hall now from my room to Grace's little parlor I often found my charming sister seated all alone at her desk turning over the pages of a Latin dictionary. The sight of her so occupied never failed to give me a little shock. Though I was not exactly surprised that Grace had made up her mind to go to college, since everyone else was going and it was such a wonderful privilege, still as a student she did not seem to me natural. She had always been for me the young lady triumphant, skilled in all the arts of elegance, and I was not alone in taking this view of her. Everyone was impressed by Grace's accomplishments. Her umbrella was famous for being faultlessly rolled, slender and smooth as a walking stick. Her frocks, fashionable without being extreme, were even considered by some critical spirits so very becoming as to show undue attention for her appearance. Grace never carried a bundle, however many things she might buy. During this particular season when bustles were worn, young girls affected the "Grecian bend," leaning forward at a fascinating angle as they walked. Grace's rendering of this gait was acclaimed as the height of perfection. I sometimes heard her called worldly, a snob even, because she believed in correct behavior and was proud of the

Southern traditions of my father's family. It was in fact principally from Grace that I learned about my Thomas ancestors. They had been Southern landed proprietors at a time when my mother's people were farmers or small merchants in New Jersey and Pennsylvania. If a Thomas was forced to make money himself, he entered a profession, while the Whitall men invariably went into business. We were poor compared to our Whitall cousins, but Grace intimated that perhaps we had other advantages.

I doubt whether at this time I really understood the importance of "family," though I perceived that my sister valued it highly. The Baltimoreans with whom Grace associated put great stress on their ancestors as all Southerners do, and my sister naturally developed keen pride in hers. No doubt she needed every bit of personal prestige she could find to help her bear the exclusions our Quaker code imposed on her. But five years her junior, and without the least social experience, I for my part was not interested in my pedigree. I was familiar, of course, as we were all familiar, with the roll of parchment paper on which the Fox family was depicted through many generations as a tall tree with widespreading branches. As a small child I had enjoyed searching for and finding the remote twig that bore the leaf on which my father's name was inscribed, but I attached no importance to this game. And I regarded as a huge joke the Thomas crest, a raven with one claw lifted, done in stained glass and set in a window where we saw it many times every day after our house was al-

tered. The motto or legend on the scroll under-neath this family bird, *Deus pascit corvos,* seemed deliciously appropriate. God feeds the crows—we were as numerous as crows and as hungry! That other members of the family took the crest more seriously than I did, in spite of their joking, seems to me probable. Its presence there in the window and the Fox genealogical tree show all too clearly the pride my father felt in his descent. He could perhaps hardly have escaped this prepossession, growing up as he did under the influence of Great-Aunt Julia, who carried about with her under her plain bonnet a mine of family lore. She loved to tell family stories, most of which concerned the high-born ladies brought into the Thomas family by successive heads of the house, or so I under-stood. I had heard of these events only in general since by the time I came along my great-aunt must have been weary of telling stories to children, for she never told any to me. When Grace took me in hand at last my mind was too full of other things to bother with family history or even to dwell much on contradictions. Still, though I covered it up by joking, I had a keen sense that heraldic dis-plays were out of place in our Quaker household.

XIV

COUNTRY HOUSE

ONE afternoon in the autumn of 1884 nearly a hundred ladies sat crowded together on rows of chairs in our front parlor. Facing them with her back to the fireplace stood my cousin, Mary Pearsall Smith. She had come all the way down from Radcliffe, where she was a student, to expound her philosophy of life to us in Baltimore. Tall, golden-haired and lovely, she seemed not in the least disturbed either by the size or the age of her audience as she announced her subject: "The Duty of Self-Development."

From the corner I had found for myself I gazed at my cousin with all my eyes. I had heard many tales of Mary's fascination, but I was totally unprepared for the reality. Her radiant beauty and a kind of vital force I felt emanating from her bowled me over. Even the costume of green velvet she wore seemed alive. Where the light from the window struck the folds of the skirt they took on the shimmery color of leaves and the yellow rose in her girdle shone like her hair. A slight lisp broke her speech with momentary pauses that reminded me of the pauses in a bird's song. I stood staring at her, hypnotized by her charm.

I was still only thirteen, but in the year that Carey had been at home my mind had developed rapidly. Thus when I began to pay attention to

my cousin's speech I was keenly interested in the points she made. She stressed them strongly, repeating them in various forms.

Our highest duty is to develop our own gifts. Only by doing this can we be of use to others and attain happiness for ourselves, Mary insisted. The pleasure we take in a course of action may be considered as the measure of our power to succeed in it. If after giving it a fair trial any particular task continues to be disagreeable, we can be sure it is not the right task for us. Our duty to society and to ourselves lies in finding something we can do with pleasure and then in pursuing it wholeheartedly. Congenial activity is successful activity.

Mary's audience was remarkably attentive. Even the older ladies sat transfixed in their chairs, and when the lecture was over they thronged about her. I heard them flattering her, saying that she had a decided gift for speaking, that they had been deeply interested, but I noticed that they went away very quietly. Only a few of the younger women remained to ask questions and discuss points, as invited. Even my mother quickly disappeared, but before she left she paused to address the group clustered about Mary.

"I agree with our speaker," she said, "that we do things better when they give us pleasure, and that it is our duty to cultivate the talents with which God has endowed each one of us. But in any particular case our pleasure in following a course of action cannot be considered a proof that it is right. Not all our impulses are good and some duties must be done however hard and unpleasant

they may seem to us." Having borne her testimony to this effect, my mother left the room, nodding to me to follow her.

Mary's lecture enlightened me about certain things. She was the leading spirit in the group of Whitall cousins to which Bond and Grace belonged. They were both influenced by her opinions, Bond even more than Grace, since he was in love with Mary's intimate friend, Edith Carpenter, engaged to her secretly in fact, as I knew. Unfamiliar phrases used recently by my brother and sister now took on definite meaning for me. When Grace spoke of "the higher selfishness" I knew what she meant and I made out that doing things "for the sake of one's character" was another way of saying doing what gives one pleasure. That my mother disapproved of Mary's ideas I had of course inferred from her remarks after the lecture and later I heard her ask Aunt Hannah not to let Mary write about her "advanced notions" to any of the Baltimore girls. Still I found Mary's advanced notions by no means unattractive.

During this eventful winter Aunt Hannah's visits to us were unusually frequent. She and my mother together had decided to build a country house as a joint refuge for their two families. Land had been bought in the Blue Ridge Mountains almost equally distant from Philadelphia and Baltimore and a house was in process of construction. Details of every sort had to be discussed and settled between Aunt Hannah and my parents, and on every point Carey, keenly interested in planning and building Coombe Edge, was called in

for consultation. How any one of them found time for all this I cannot imagine, since neither Aunt Hannah nor my parents ever neglected their multifarious religious duties and my sister had on her hands the organization of a new school as well as of Bryn Mawr College. The girls too were occupied from morning till night preparing for their entrance examinations; but in spite of their heroic efforts they were obliged to take great boxes of books along with them when we journeyed up to the mountains late in June.

We moved into Coombe Edge on the day set long before, but we moved in without Aunt Hannah's family. A sudden catastrophe had sent all the Pearsall Smiths sailing away to England. Sometime during the winter Mary had fallen in love with a strange Irishman lecturing for a few weeks at Harvard and had announced to her parents her intention of marrying him and settling in London. At her mother's entreaty she had consented not to engage herself formally until she had seen her lover again and met his people. However, everyone now knew that Mary's mind was made up. The rapid fire of letters she and her lover exchanged across the Atlantic had settled the matter. Briliant, entrancing letters they were reported to be. In my imagination they figured as probably the most wonderful love letters ever written. Thus it came about that the refuge planned by my mother and her sister to take the place of "The Cedars" as a center for the Whitall relatives was occupied only by us. From the first it seemed, to me at least, ex-

clusively ours and in the end it did become my mother's sole property.

The house stood on an abrupt little hilltop that fell steeply away to level fields. It commanded a wide view and was open to all the winds of heaven. To the northeast we looked over a narrow valley between wooded hills toward Gettysburg in Pennsylvania and on the other side sun and moon set behind the mountains of Maryland, three miles distant perhaps. A row of locust trees grew on the edge of the knoll where the house stood and farther from it were some ancient cherry trees and a magnificent tall pine with widespreading branches, deep blue in the waving shadows. Though large, the house was very simple, built of wood with wide piazzas on two sides and in the center a big brick chimney. The long French windows with doors opening on the piazza were Carey's contribution to the builder's plans, while the chimney had been contrived by my father. He took immense pleasure in the place, declaring it had the most beautiful view and the coolest breezes for miles about. Returning home after an absence he always sighed with satisfaction when he felt his brow fanned by his own wind. He was delighted too with his share in the plans, and always explained to visitors how he had anchored the house to the chimney, showing them the fireplaces that opened from it into room after room upstairs as well as down. Invariably on these occasions he employed the very same phrases without being aware of the repetition, I fancy, until by ill luck he overheard me

use his words when I was showing one of my friends about. Exasperated by my impertinent mimicry, he gave me as severe a scolding as I ever received from him.

My mother's great delight was in the untamed wildness of the countryside. She often declared her preference for "Nature with her hair uncombed," still she had yielded to my father's desire to prune and to plant within the boundaries of the place, and herself cherished the desire for a "pleached walk" of lindens like one she had seen in England. Already on the day of our moving in we drove from the gate to the house between rows of little spiky linden trees. The road led to a side porch and then, turning about a heart-shaped plot of ground, went off to the stable which stood on the edge of the highway, much to the scandal of the country people, as we soon learned. The plot of ground by the house had been ploughed up and sown with grass seed, a flower bed had been planted in its center and in one curving corner already stood a tiny silver birch tree with small, pointed, shivering leaves. Because of its shape we called this plot in the turn of our driveway "the family heart." It soon became the custom for my mother to lead a squad of us out in the coolness of late afternoon to clear away the weeds that settled down on its loosened soil like flocks of birds. With a small watering pot she herself refreshed the honeysuckle vines that were beginning to creep up the pillars of the piazza. In addition to his flower beds my father had laid out a large vegetable garden in the field below the knoll. Already

it showed signs of flourishing, for my father had what is called the green hand. Even the neighboring farmer who worked for him acknowledged this gift of my father's, although he had been utterly scornful at first of a city doctor's directions. This country man and his family were from the very first day an important part of our life at Coombe Edge, and succeeding generations on both sides were to cherish the connection.

We found the house not only entirely free from workmen, but also comfortably furnished, a miracle performed by my mother. She had picked up what was absolutely necessary during the winter at auction sales. Her bargains proved a source of constant amusement to us all. Among the lots she had bought she recognized certain pieces as having belonged to various friends and we liked to imagine the feelings of these former owners, should any of them come to call at Coombe Edge. Taking the leading role in my mind, where alone I possessed it, I sometimes pictured myself welcoming Miss Johnson, for instance. "Won't you sit down on the divan?" I would imagine myself saying to her with distinguished politeness, as I steered her to the large piece of furniture that had once stood in her own father's hall. "You'll find it comfortable, I think." The china was of a cheerful blue and white pattern with storks poised on one leg, but it was constructed of stone and very heavy. When we passed a plate at table we groaned as if lifting it were a tremendous effort. This was a favorite joke. But about our beds we did not joke.

"My mattress is stuffed with corncobs, really it

is, Mother," one or the other of us would complain. "They stick into my back so terribly I can't get a wink of sleep."

"Nonsense, child!" my mother would reply, "thy difficulty is not in sleeping but in waking up. Thee was late for breakfast again this morning." Thus my mother would send us off laughing.

Once settled in the country we found ourselves taking a keen interest in the whole region about us. By the high road not many miles away from our house stood a weatherworn milestone, set up before the Civil War to mark Mason and Dixon's line. The country was the border country between North and South, a region of wooded hills rising here and there to mountains and interspersed with fertile valleys. The upland fields immediately about us, however, were not fertile. A scanty population managed somehow to subsist on their dry soil, and the only really prosperous farmer within a radius of some miles was a Pennsylvania Dutchman with a flock of hard-worked children and a poor thin drudge of a wife.

One afternoon my father was summoned to give first aid at this farm. When he had stopped the flow of blood from an ax wound one of the smaller boys had inflicted on himself, he used his authority as a physician to remonstrate sternly with Farmer Nagel.

"You can see for yourself," he said while he adjusted the bandage, "that the boy has almost cut off his foot. He is much too young to use an ax. You should not give an ax to such a small child. I might not be able to help another time."

212

Farmer Nagel's thin lips tightened. "He's old enough, Doctor. Jim's plenty old enough," he insisted. "The boy can play all right, can't he? Any boy or girl that's old enough to play is old enough to work. That's my rule. I won't have no idle children hanging 'round my farm. Them saplings had to be cleared. They ain't so big Jim couldn't 'a' handled 'em. He's careless and he's terrible lazy. His mother spoils him. That's what it is!"

Mrs. Nagel, who stood by the boy helping my father in silence, fixed anxious eyes on his face as if to implore him to disregard her husband's tirade. With difficulty my father controlled his indignation. Ignoring Farmer Nagel, he collected his instruments, gave Mrs. Nagel a few simple directions for the care of the boy, and as he got into his carriage he spoke quietly but firmly to the angry old man.

"I shall come tomorrow to see your son, Mr. Nagel. He will have to stay in bed, of course, until the wound heals and he can do no work of any kind for the rest of the summer. I am his doctor and I expect my orders to be obeyed." Without waiting for an answer my father drove off.

Described to us in dramatic detail, this scene filled us with horror. We liked Mrs. Nagel, who sometimes stole away to get sympathy and advice from my mother, but we hated Farmer Nagel and refused to speak to him when we went to his place for chickens or eggs. Still somehow his words became family sayings with us. "You're old enough to play, ain't you?" we would ask each other. "Then get to work on the tennis court with that

roller"—or it might be the long taproot of our enemy, the Canada thistle, that had to be dug out with a tool we particularly hated, called a spud.

The natives lived for the most part in log cabins, picturesque but dreadfully primitive. How they managed to exist was difficult for us to imagine. The men did some logging in the winter or hunted rattlesnakes for their oil, and in the summer a few of them worked by the day for the two small hotels, or for the city people who owned houses. When they could get it their wives took in washing, kept scrawny chickens or a pig perhaps, a cow also occasionally. The rough land about the log cabins and their blank windows produced an impression of sordid poverty, yet out of one of them we sometimes saw come a young man, obviously a gentleman, dressed in loose tweeds and with a Tam o' Shanter on his head. He had a handsome pale face and his way of walking was quite unlike the shuffle of the natives. He was ill with consumption, I was told, obliged to remain both summer and winter in the mountains and being poor, though a Raleigh of Baltimore, he had left the hotel to live at smaller cost with a native family. This explanation satisfied my curiosity at the time but from chance remarks I soon learned there was more to it than that. Though he was delicate, Charlie Raleigh's real trouble was not tuberculosis but drink, and he had moved to Widow Haskins' cabin because of her daughter, a common country girl.

Very pretty she seemed to me when at last I caught sight of her carrying a pail of water across the road to her house on the hillside above. As we

drove past I turned my head to watch her climb quickly up the rough ground. She had dark curling hair, shining eyes, and a lovely wild rose color in her young face. Though shocked by her behavior, the implications of which I understood, I was attracted by her beauty. It was Charlie Raleigh from whom I shrank. His behavior was in fact the scandal of the neighborhood. All the city people cut him and they shunned the members of the Haskins family, as if they had had the plague. My mother, however, soon visited their cabin to offer work to Mrs. Haskins and also to the girl in the hope of rescuing her. Though they expressed gratitude for her kindness, mother and daughter alike refused her offer of work.

On the other side of the railroad from us in a long white house, vine covered and cool, lived a family from Virginia, four beautiful girls with their mother. Their servants were negroes, former slaves who shared with them what remained of their lost fortune. Though the Civil War had ended so many years before that only the mother and the old servants could have remembered it, the thoughts of all these women still centered around its horror and injustice. They were bitter against my father's cousin, Francis King, whose house was not far from ours, because he hung out the Stars and Stripes on the Fourth of July when they displayed the Confederate flag. They called all Republicans "Yankees" and regarded them as personal enemies, just as my father in moments of passion spoke of Democrats as rebels and distrusted them always. Aware of the Middletons' feelings,

we were particularly discreet and cordial when they paid us their first ceremonious visit of welcome and as it happened we never hung out a flag since my mother disapproved displays of patriotism. The Middletons found themselves able to accept us and we on our side were charmed by their pretty looks and the soft Southern voices in which they chattered so volubly. Visiting each other and going on an occasional picnic together, the two families maintained friendly relations, but never saw much of each other. Had Grace and Margaret been less absorbed in study or had there been a Middleton boy or girl of suitable age for Frank and me, we might possibly have become intimate in spite of our different traditions.

XV

POETRY AND GOOD WORKS

ALL summer long there was a constant coming and going at Coombe Edge. Guests arrived and departed and every morning from Monday to Friday my father took the early train for town, breakfasting before the family by himself unless some child was up sufficiently early to join him. He never delayed his departure for a moment; anyone who wanted to go to the station with him had to be in the carriage before he appeared on the porch with his hat on his head and his coat over his arm. I loved these drives with my father in the early mornings when the dew still glistened on the grass and the birds sang gaily. Meeting the train when he returned in the afternoons was a family ceremony. My mother usually waited in the carriage, but some of the children were always on the platform to watch the engine puff up the incline, throwing clouds of black smoke high into the air as it drew to a stop. The moment my father stepped from the train we took his packages from him, eager to see what he might have brought us.

Once back on our hilltop my father liked to visit his garden, watching day by day the growth of his plants; vines, flowers, vegetables, and grass, he cherished them all and he liked companionship on his rounds of inspection. Whoever else was busy, I followed him down the hill into the vegetable garden, which stretched in rows from side to

217

side of the open field below the house. Stepping carefully, my father would bend down to examine one after the other his lettuce plants, his cabbages, his carrots, his peas and bean vines twisted about their supporting sticks, the stalks of his sweet corn that grew day by day with miraculous speed until, flowering at the top, they bore the tasseled corn-cobs. Usually I kept close behind him but some-times I lingered to gaze out at the distant hills and at the great white clouds floating high above them. On windy days flying shadows swept over us, dark-ening the field momentarily, the wind rustled in the trees, a partridge whistled "Bob-o-link." I stood motionless forgetting the garden and my father until I heard his voice calling me from the end of the row. He too loved the blue of the hills, the sun and the wind; we shared our pleasure without need of words. On Saturday afternoon, which was a holiday for everyone, even the students, my father sometimes led a climb up Blue Mountain or he took us on a long walk to inspect one of the geological marvels left in our neighborhood by the glacial period, I believe. Though I stood in the group he gathered about him, I paid little atten-tion to my father's explanation. I was not at all interested in what had caused the "Devil's Race Course," a river of stones that completely filled up a long narrow valley and was the haunt of rattle-snakes, nor had I any curiosity about the particu-lar upheaval that had dropped two great boulders of similar shape miles away from each other on either side of Rouserville. They were called "Devil's Shoes" and the Devil had lost them in his

monstrous striding across country. My father's costume in itself was enough to give these expeditions a peculiar charm. In a gray flannel shirt and gray trousers, with a black leather belt about his wide waist, a stout ash staff in his hand, and on his head a countryman's hat, he looked very different from usual, and his agility amazed us. We all watched over him a little, admonished by my mother who felt unable to take part herself in such strenuous exertion. My father was a big man, weighing nearly two hundred pounds; though he protested that he felt as young and vigorous as ever, he really was grateful, we found, for help up the steep places.

My mother took her exercise on the piazza that bordered two sides of the house. Careful measurements had been made to determine how many times back and forth went to make up a mile, and after breakfast a line of us with her at its head often told off the required number. My mother's soft white morning frock swept the floor behind her energetic figure, causing a gap between her and the child who was her immediate follower. As often as I could manage it I was that immediate follower. Then I measured my stride so that automatically I avoided stepping on her train and gave my whole attention to my mother, who seemed always to look her loveliest in the morning. Occasionally one or the other of us would drop out of line to sit on the edge of the piazza in the narrow strip of sunlight that slanted under its roof at that hour. Grace and Margaret and Zoe usually made a quick dash down the road between the spiky linden trees and back, racing each other before going

upstairs for their morning's work in the big room set aside for the students. In the back building, this room was reached by a bridge from the second story and occupied the whole space above the kitchen and storerooms. Very hot it must have been in spite of its size and its windows opening in every direction, but the girls did not complain. They were too much interested in working together there, too anxious about their examinations, I suppose, to notice the heat. Immediately after breakfast Carey went to work at the desk in her study where Miss Gwinn, settled in the neighborhood, soon joined her. Being proficient in languages, Miss Gwinn helped the students also by reading French with them. My mother, her daily exercise over, went off to consult the cook in the kitchen and then to write her letters or her reports in her own particular corner of the parlor behind the closed double doors. Frank and I were left to amuse ourselves alone, free as birds—too free perhaps.

There was in fact little for us to do, especially for an energetic small boy like Frank. Used to playing with other boys, he found me a wholly unsatisfactory companion while I found him uninteresting. When he ran off to follow old Fitz at his work, or it might be to hunt up some boy at the hotel, he left me and I saw him go without regret. I enjoyed pottering about in the sunshine by myself and I enjoyed sitting for hours perched high up in an old apple tree reading a book, often what Carey called a bad book. *The Leavenworth Case* was, I remember, one of the bad books that, fla-

vored with the smell and taste of ripe apples, seemed superlatively good to me. However, with Miss Gwinn's permission I joined her French class and also read some French by myself. Thus I was never bored, but Frank quite frequently complained to my father that Coombe Edge was a dreadfully dull place.

After dinner the family often sat about together in the fading light on the piazza or on the grass to talk a little. Once a week at least to please my mother we would repeat poetry. If Carey joined the group at all she did not stay for long; she would recite a few lines from Shelley or Swinburne or Wordsworth or perhaps a short passage from Victor Hugo, then off she would go again upstairs to work late into the night. Grace knew Elizabeth Barrett Browning's "Bertha in the Lane" by heart from beginning to end and recited parts of it in a low emotional voice, while Margaret's rendering of Tennyson's lyrics, taught her at school, was dramatic in the extreme. Her "Blow, bugles, blow!" rang out like a trumpet call. Even Frank said his piece. Very unwillingly and with much coaching he had learned a poem about a wolf that lost its wildness in a storm to become mild as a sheep. "Little one come to my knee, Hark how the rain is pouring," were the first lines. Once he had committed it to memory, Frank enjoyed reciting this poem, especially as he had no fear of getting stuck. If he hesitated for the fraction of a second over a word, it was supplied him in a whisper by the one of us who happened to be near him. We all knew the poem by heart and

were all interested in Frank's giving the perfect performance that so greatly delighted my father.

Choosing what I should recite was my difficulty. I found memorizing poetry a great amusement, but, alas! no one seemed to want to listen to me for long at a time. The chorus of "Atalanta in Calydon" or "To a Skylark" was spoiled by being cut; I fell back upon shorter poems like Longfellow's "I stood on the bridge at midnight," or "St. Agnes's Eve" by Tennyson. They were well received, but Shelley's "I arise from dreams of thee, In the first sweet sleep of night" proved an unfortunate choice. After the first verse which, carried away by the beat of the rhythm, I repeated with fervor, my mother interrupted. It was late, she said, and getting up from her chair she led the way into the house. Puzzled by her interruption and even more by the tone of her voice, I went slowly up to my room and without lighting the lamp, undressed slowly, thinking things over. For some reason my mother did not like love poetry, I decided, and determined to avoid annoying her in future by the poems I recited.

One night when the harvest moon shone on our hilltop from a cloudless sky, even Carey lingered late with the rest of us under its beauty. The faraway mountains, no longer massive as in the daytime, seemed pale barriers on either side of a gulf of light that was the valley. There was not the faintest stir of wind. Our great pine tree stood a dark pillar motionless in the bright field; nearer at hand the leaves of the locust trees shone in silver radiance while under their branches black

shadows lay deep. In the flower beds the flowers
were strangely distinct and strangely pale, and the
grass at our feet was a golden gleaming. Hardly
aware of each other, we sat in silence until my
father's voice broke into our enchantment, repeating a description of moonlight from Byron. Passage
followed passage in praise of the moon, more
Byron, then Tennyson, Shakespeare, Milton:

> *Now glowed the firmament*
> *With living sapphires: Hesperus, that led*
> *The starry host, rode brightest, till the moon*
> *Rising in clouded majesty, at length,*
> *Apparent queen, unveiled her peerless light*
> *And o'er the dark her silver mantle threw.*

When my father's voice ceased no one spoke for
a long time. The rhythm of Milton's verse beat in
my mind: the stately pauses, the irresistible on-
ward flow, the majestic words—I had never heard
anything like them before.

At last my mother rose from her chair. "Thee
knows more poetry than any of thy children,
James," she said; "not even Carey can equal
thee."

Another of these evening symposiums was
broken in on harshly by my brother John, who
was spending his holiday at Coombe Edge, together with his wife and child. Some reference
had been made to his early youth and he seized the
opportunity to reproach my mother with her
cruelty to him as a small boy. She had never understood him, he insisted, and had punished him
with unjust severity. He had always been over-
looked and disregarded and finally he had been

refused the opportunity to study medicine and forced into business. He had wanted to be a doctor quite as much as Harry.

All this came out in a rush before anyone could intervene. As I watched my mother's face grow sad under John's reproaches, fierce anger against him rose up in me. How could John reproach my mother when she had done her best for him and for all her children? She was tiring herself out now entertaining his family. Only that morning she had spent an hour in the kitchen helping Mamie make a ridiculous jelly roll. I sat on the edge of the piazza at my mother's feet, trembling with rage.

This was the worst of John's offenses, at least the worst that I witnessed, but quite frequently I heard him speak to my mother in a way that I thought unkind. Only once in my presence did she make any real response.

They were sitting together not far from the hammock in which I was reading. My mother had the baby in her arms and she and John were chatting cheerfully about him. I paid no attention to them until a sudden note of gravity in my mother's voice struck me. Instantly I was on the alert.

"Thee must try to remember, John," my mother was saying, "how young I was when thee was a child. Then perhaps thee will be able to forgive the mistakes I made. Thee was my eldest son, and I have always loved thee as thee loves thy little Jimmie. Try to remember that I loved thee dearly even when I punished thee with unwise severity. 'Spare the rod and spoil the child' was the rule everyone went by in those days. Mamie and thee

are fortunate in being free from any such idea." My mother's voice had lost its gravity as she spoke and taken on the gay note that was so endearing.

Cautiously turning my head, I saw John get up from his chair and kiss my mother and I heard him say he was sorry he had distressed her, but my heart was not softened toward him. I did not trust him in the least. Grace and Margaret were too busy to entertain visitors. I felt it was up to me to protect my mother from John and to take his wife and baby off her hands as much as possible. I exerted myself with such zeal that my mother, who greatly enjoyed having the baby with her, was forced more than once to drive me away. No doubt she thought I was mad about little Jimmie. I did like him, but baby infatuation was not my chief motive in hanging around him. For John at this time and for years afterwards I felt not the least sympathy. Only much later did I come to understand that he said such bitter things to my mother because he adored her and was dreadfully jealous of his younger brothers.

On Sunday mornings it was Margaret's and my duty to draw together the shutters of the hall windows, to arrange the chairs in a wide circle and to drive out the flies before the meeting for worship that was held in our house at eleven o'clock. By the time Cousin Francis King and his daughters drove up the room was cool and free from flies, due to our energetic attacks on them with folded newspapers. We were ready dressed in our Sunday clothes always a few minutes before the hour to allow of a final inspection and a few last swishes

and slaps, should necessity be. The Kings invariably arrived before the other members of the little congregation. Very solemn and decorous Cousin Francis King looked in his "plain coat," a testimony to Quaker principle I was glad my father did not feel the need of making; Cousin Mary and Cousin Annie were simply but elegantly dressed, even Cousin Bessie, the youngest sister, showed on Sundays only the faintest signs of unconventionality in the color of her frock and the flop of her large hat. I observed Cousin Bessie always with particular interest; she was an intimate friend of Carey's, one of the inner group, and she was a painter. Nobody else who attended our meeting interested me so much, not even gentle blind Mrs. Giddings and her lovely daughter, Mrs. Reid, who sometimes came, though they were members of the Episcopal Church.

Getting the room ready and watching people arrive was exciting, but the hour of the meeting itself passed for me in a dream that was hardly broken into even by my mother's voice. If a stray fly buzzed or bothered I was worried for a moment, leaned forward in my chair perhaps, but unable to do anything, resumed the motionless hypnotic quietness to which I was trained by long years of attending meeting.

Quite different were the religious services held by my parents for the community at large. Deeply shocked by the lack of religious instruction provided for the country people, they had set about remedying this condition immediately after their arrival. A large hall used as a bowling alley and

ballroom by one of the hotels was requisitioned for Sunday nights and a general invitation sent out. The service began with the singing of hymns, my father leading while Grace or some other young lady accompanied on the piano. Then my father preached a simple mission sermon and before the people dispersed he and my mother went about speaking to them individually. Soon the farmers and their wives from miles about began coming to these evening services. The hall was crowded and my father spoke with eloquence and power. Sometimes as I listened to him, his words, or the tone of his voice, thrilled through my nerves and exalted my spirit. On the way home in the open carriage I looked up at the stars with a feeling of worship, undefined but intense, and as we passed dim figures of men and women walking along the road back to their homes I felt in harmony with them and with the night. I was profoundly happy and at peace.

Margaret and I took part in my mother's Bible class for the country women and children, teaching each her own little group of girls. We found it no easy task. Our pupils were not only completely ignorant of the Bible but also, it seemed to us, of everything else. This was my first missionary effort and I remember my horror that such ignorance could exist in an American countryside. I invited my girls to come to the house twice a month, fed them cake, talked to them, and sometimes read them little stories. Since we were all of about the same age, I felt no impulse to preach to them. I wanted to give them a little fun along with a little

227

general information. In some obscure way I was ashamed of my greater good fortune.

Harry's departure for Germany took place in the early autumn. He had spent the summer helping my father look after his patients in Baltimore, coming up to Coombe Edge off and on for brief visits. But before sailing away he stayed a week or two with us. He devoted himself almost wholly to Zoe. When she was working, as she often had to be, Harry wandered about restlessly, hunting in the fields and along the brooks for rare flowers to give her. Seeing him waiting alone in the wavering shade of the locust trees, I sometimes joined him and once he explained to me what the different flowers of his bouquet were meant to express to Zoe. He never asked me to go along with him on his solitary walks, although formerly he had always been glad of my companionship. Now it seemed he cared only for Zoe.

The young men who spent week ends with us from time to time during the summer were ostensibly family friends, but really they came to see Grace, for my charming sister had not entirely merged the young lady in the student. During spare moments she had found time to decorate the sitting room with Japanese umbrellas fastened over mirrors and Japanese fans spread out on the white walls to display their fantastic oriental scenes. Finally in the autumn above the baseboard on a side wall she tacked up a row of cattails alternating with their sword-shaped leaves to make a frieze, after the fashion of Oscar Wilde, she informed me when I exclaimed over the strange

ZOE AND HARRY AT COOMBE EDGE

effect. For special occasions, notably when she expected a visit from some young man, Grace used to put a single sunflower in a glass vase near a window. I enjoyed dashing down the road with a pair of scissors to get a perfect one for her from the great hedge of sunflowers my father had planted by the stable. I asked no questions and made no comments but did Grace's errands with an inner excitement that I kept to myself. My mother discouraged all teasing of Grace about her admirers, objecting even to our speaking of them as "Grace's beaux," according to the usual Southern custom. It was one of these beaux, I have forgotten which, who helped her hunt out the marshy places where the reeds she so much admired were to be found, and who gathered them for her. I saw his soaked, muddy boots drying in front of the kitchen stove, but when I put Grace's shoes away they were quite clean, even the soles were dry.

The examination date drew nearer and nearer. Carey took her final departure and the pressure of work increased day by day for the students. Finally at the last possible moment Grace and Margaret and Zoe went off to face their ordeal at Bryn Mawr, leaving my mother to pack up and close the house at Coombe Edge with no assistance but mine. I was far from efficient but I worked with zeal and managed after many struggles to fit the oil lamps so snugly into their barrel that for the future they became my special charge. The moves from town to country and back again were always exceedingly burdensome. They overtaxed even my mother's energy.

XVI

BRYN MAWR COLLEGE AND SCHOOL

BACK in Baltimore I found my little room there a sad change, with its window opening onto a city garden tucked down between high walls. Gone was my wide view over fields to the distant mountains. I could not see the sun nor moon nor a single star shining in the bit of oblique sky, without leaning far out over the window sill. Yet I spent much time in the solitude of its four walls and closed door, reading and studying, tormented with anxiety over my new school, the strange, new school Carey and her friends had founded. As the days passed slowly by I became more and more worried. I had never as yet had serious difficulty with my lessons but then they had always been easy: the standards of the Bryn Mawr School would be another matter. And even at Miss Bond's school I had not been a particularly shining success. Occasional praise from my teachers for some special stunt, a few intimate friends, easily counted on one hand were all I had to my credit. Grace and Margaret were different. The dazzling superiority of Grace did not bother me for Grace was a being apart, but I was really discouraged when I reflected how much better Margaret seemed to get on than I did.

Perhaps my untidy appearance was to blame, perhaps the first sight of me put people off. I fixed

on this point with relief. I had turned over the pages of my old schoolbooks at random but not knowing where to begin had put them back on their shelf. I could, however, do something about my appearance. I determined to make at once certain reforms that had long been urged on me. I would not fail to keep my hands clean or to cut my fingernails as soon as they needed cutting, though I particularly hated that operation. I would be careful to fasten my collar on straight and never to forget my handkerchief. I would even wear gloves though that would be a trial, as I liked having my hands free. Years before I had asked my mother to buy me a pair of kid gloves for Sundays, but she had refused. "Little girls should not have their minds fixed on such things," she had said. "Elsie plays with her gloves all during Sunday school, taking them off, smoothing them out and putting them on again, paying no attention to the lesson. I should be sorry to see thee do that." So I had gone barehanded with a sense of superior virtue, lately replaced by a furtive sense of shame, since gloves had now been supplied me. Fortunately my new school dress was very pretty, a brown and blue plaid. I would pay particular attention to adjusting the belt in the way Grace had shown me. Grace had a charming smile. I would brush my teeth until they gleamed white as pearls like Grace's teeth. I stood in front of my mirror for a long time dreaming, until at last I failed to notice the image reflected there, saw rather a vision of myself dressed in my new frock and smiling so enchantingly that people would fall at my feet.

But, alas! dreaming would not help me. I must set about doing something. My hair was my most troublesome problem. Terribly thick and wiry, it twisted itself into nasty snarls and never failed to attract attention because of its bright color. My father often scolded me about it. Just a little while before, meeting me on the stairs, he had said to me, "Every lady spends twenty minutes a day brushing out her hair," and had pointed his remark with a sharp glance at the top of my unfortunate head. I would begin with my hair.

Fixing clear eyes now on the looking glass, I undid my braid—my pigtail, Frank called it—combed out even the least little tangle, underneath as well as on top, straightened the part and then began on the brushing with long, slow strokes. Very, very slowly five minutes marked themselves out on the face of my clock. Abandoning my dressing table I walked over to the window and stood where I could see the garden while I brushed and brushed. A long time passed. I glanced over my shoulder at the clock face. Five more minutes, that made ten minutes in all. It was enough! Twenty minutes a day for hair brushing was ridiculous. My father had exaggerated. I wanted to look like a lady but really there was a limit to the time I could waste.

My anxiety was kept alive by the constant talk about my new school that I heard at home. Its standards were to be in their way as high as the standards of Bryn Mawr College, which was destined to revolutionize women's education. Establishing such a school for girls in our Southern

town was a bold experiment but Carey and her friends were determined to keep it open however small the attendance. Now to the amazement of everyone the "best families of Baltimore" were rushing to enroll their daughters. For some reason the school had suddenly become popular, almost fashionable. Perhaps its novelty worked the miracle—no finishing courses and Latin required— perhaps and more probably it was interest in the young women who were running it, all of whom belonged to well-known families, an interest founded on curiosity. Day by day the enrollment was checked up by my parents. I felt the excitement of taking part in such an experiment, but I also felt my responsibility. My sister had warned me half in joke not to disgrace her. If I ever did, that would be truly dreadful.

Discussion of education was no new development in our family. From as far back as I could remember my parents had been active in education, my father as trustee of the Johns Hopkins University and Haverford College and my mother as one of the managers of the Friends Academy in Baltimore, and more recently my father had been a member of the Board of Trustees of Bryn Mawr College. All these institutions were Quaker institutions in the sense of having been founded by Quakers. My parents were proud of the great interest Friends took in promoting education, and they praised Johns Hopkins' liberality in making the university he founded effectively undenominational by not restricting his Board of Trustees to Quakers. However, the Johns Hopkins University

was closed to women, even its graduate department. After leaving Cornell, my sister Carey had knocked at its doors in vain. As a personal favor to her and partly perhaps to my father, certain professors had given her advanced instruction, but she had been definitely excluded from the University. The founder of Bryn Mawr College, Dr. Taylor, had been more liberal than Johns Hopkins in providing for the higher education of women. On the other hand he had decreed that only members of the Society of Friends should serve on his Board of Trustees. Dr. Taylor was a Philadelphian and the majority of the trustees he appointed were conservative Quakers in the strict Philadelphia tradition. Still even among the Philadelphians there were several liberal-minded men, notably the President of the College, Dr. James E. Rhoads, while Cousin Francis King and my father, who were the Baltimore trustees, had both been won over to the higher education of women by their daughters. The liberal members of the board, Philadelphians and Baltimoreans together, forming a powerful minority, had induced the conservative majority to join with them in appointing Carey Dean of the Faculty.

That my sister should be considered for some position at Bryn Mawr College was inevitable. She was a birthright member of the Society of Friends, nearly related to several of the trustees, my mother's brother, Uncle James Whitall among them, and was well known to every member of the board, if only by reputation. Moreover she was clearly competent since she had graduated bril-

liantly from Cornell University and had won high honors at the University of Zurich.

On the other hand Carey had shown an alarming independence of spirit in going abroad to study at foreign universities for men. The more conservative trustees could not have failed to suspect that her ideals for her sex were far from being the ideals they themselves thought desirable. Then Carey was only twenty-eight years old, too young for so responsible a position as Dean of the Faculty. Had not Dr. Rhoads strongly favored her appointment she would almost certainly have been rejected. All the members of the board without exception respected Dr. Rhoads and trusted his wisdom. Those who distrusted my sister no doubt believed that Dr. Rhoads as President would have the deciding voice in all important matters. The Dean would be merely his assistant and to deny the President the assistant he asked for would have been difficult, so, no doubt reluctantly, they accepted Carey.

Used as I was to the difference in strictness between Philadelphia and Baltimore Friends, I failed to understand how anyone, even the old gentlemen on the Board of Trustees, could object to my sister. Though I sometimes found it impossible to live up to the standards she imposed on me, I never doubted that they were the right standards. Carey was anxious only that I should do what was best for me myself. I had fallen completely under my sister's spell.

She was in fact a fascinating person. Her very appearance arrested attention. If I had to rely on

memory alone I could not visualize her as she was at this time, so many later memories have blurred the impression. Fortunately photographs of Carey taken just before her return from abroad are still in existence. One of her seated in a chair shows a small compact figure surmounted by a remarkable head. The smooth hair, parted and drawn closely back, reveals a finely arched skull, the nose is straight, the eyelids lowered, the mouth determined and composed. This photograph produces an impression of nunlike self-discipline and self-dedication. Another taken in London by Hollyer reveals more of my sister's charm. The fine shape of the head and profile are the same, but the hair drawn back more loosely seems softer, the eyes are lowered and the expression, though composed, is somehow gentler. In looking at this picture one is impressed by the charm and intelligence of the sitter rather than by her force of will. Later when Carey was older her personality in no way suggested renunciation, rather it spoke of readiness to act instantly and with power on whatever was before her. You felt that if you could enlist her sympathy she would help you with all the energy she had, but if she disagreed and a battle was in order you knew that she would fight on until victory fell to her side. The tension with which her small hands rested on the arm of her chair or grasped a book showed force of will. Such certainly was the impression that in later years she made on me, obliterating other more youthful impressions. What remains most vividly in my memory from the period immediately following my sister's return home is her beautiful voice repeat-

ing Shelley, singing the praises of Greek, and calling me little Miss Nell.

Together with the others I traveled on to Bryn Mawr for the opening exercises of the College. Even Frank was taken along, quite uninterested as he must have been. For me, destined in my turn to become a student at Bryn Mawr, the experience was terribly thrilling, but too multitudinous and confused for sharp impressions. I do, however, remember seeing James Russell Lowell, a small, bewhiskered old gentleman, seated on the platform next to President Rhoads, and I remember thinking him very disappointing as a poet. Since he was so famous and Carey had been so anxious for his presence I tried to listen to his speech, but failed through excitement. Later I learned that the humorous lightness with which he had referred to "Quakers" had displeased the authorities. Dr. Rhoads had felt obliged to apologize for it to a distinguished English Friend, Bevan Braithwaite, who had honored the ceremony by his presence.

During the rush from one thing to another there was an interval of waiting alone with my mother in the bare square room in Merion Hall that was to serve Margaret and her chum for a study. After we had examined their writing tables and chairs in the study, the beds in the narrow adjoining bedrooms, and I had peered into the queer yellow wooden wardrobes in one of which some day my own clothes might hang, we sat down to rest on the sunny window seat of the study and then my mother turned her attention on me.

"Child, look at thy fingernails!" she exclaimed.

"Run get Margaret's scissors off her dressing table so that I can cut them for thee. They need it." Then, the process over, she bade me pick up the bits that lay about, strewn over the rug.

"It would hardly do to leave such a visiting card for Margaret," my mother said with a gay laugh.

She did not take the matter seriously but I was terribly ashamed. Though almost a young lady and in spite of all my good resolutions, I had once again let my nails grow until they disgraced me. I despaired of myself and dreaded my new school more than ever.

But the first days of school proved so thrilling that I had no time to worry about myself. Four other girls and I were assigned to the Fifth Grade, the highest class in the school that first year. Unchallenged by newcomers, we were to remain at the top of the school as the Sixth and finally the Seventh Grade, from which we graduated. I found no difficulty in making friends with four girls, even though they were all older than I. We began Greek together and together struggled with algebra under a severe young woman, a Vassar graduate, quite unlike any teacher any of us had ever had. History and English, taught by modern methods, proved easier than at Miss Bond's school because more interesting. The Fourth Grade joined us for French, making up a fairly large class which our teacher, a middle-aged French lady of good birth and impeccable accent, proved unable to control. Poor Madame Thibaut! Large and impressive-looking as she was, she quite failed to win our respect. I can still hear her deep voice as, exas-

perated beyond endurance by our whispering and giggling, she shouted at us:

"I am not a bulldog. If you will not behave like well-elevated young ladies I can teach you nossing, nossing. I am not a bulldog. Remember that, young ladies, if you please."

The joke of it was that she looked just like a bulldog to us. We misbehaved for the fun of hearing her growl.

From the first the young English woman who was principal of the school as well as teacher of English singled me out for notice. Her frequent references to "Your sister, Miss Thomas" prevented my being personally flattered, but she was very pretty and I was fascinated by her. Alone in a strange country, Miss Andrews was in need of a confidant; before long she was pouring into my excited ears the story of her broken heart. She trusted me, she said, to repeat what she told me to no one, not even to my sister, and I never did. It seems to me now that she took a great risk but she probably knew that children flattered by being trusted are faithful as dogs.

Mme. Thibaut made difficulty for me by stressing my name in her complaints to the managing board. Carey remonstrated and I found myself forced to desert my comrades of the French class, nor did I dare take an active part in a general strike that soon resulted from a new rule imposed on the school. After recess one day all the pupils filed into the assembly room a few minutes early, took their places behind the desks and slammed down the lids in unison for a full five minutes by

the watch of Elise Harding, our ringleader. The noise was terrific. Miss Andrews ran as fast as she could from her office to the platform but did not succeed in quelling the tumult before the appointed signal. When the situation was brought to the attention of Carey, she blamed me for not giving Miss Andrews a hint of what was brewing. On my side, while I acknowledged that I had been aware of the plans, I pleaded that I had not myself taken part in the lid-slamming, even though I considered the new rule unfair. I had held back because of her. This plea only increased my sister's annoyance. She accused me of disloyalty in not accepting as just the decisions of the committee. "I am very much disappointed in thy lack of loyalty," she repeated over and over. "I thought I could trust thee at least to be loyal." In the end, I stood speechless and with burning cheeks before her, convicted of disloyalty.

And yet in my heart I was puzzled as to what I should have done. Surely Carey could not expect me to tell tales on the other girls. She herself would never have done that, I was sure. I tried to puzzle out what she would have done, but in vain; I merely felt that she would not have betrayed her comrades.

My real crime was, of course, sympathizing with my fellow pupils and not with the authorities. We had all been ordering our lunch sent in at recess time from a confectioner's shop near by and a few girls had been also receiving presents of cakes from gallant boyish admirers. They were delivered along with the other packages, and one day so large a pack-

age came for Elise Harding, who was pretty as well as high spirited, that it attracted attention. Enormous really, it must have been, since Elise had treated the whole school to currant buns. An investigation at the confectioner's followed and the privilege of receiving any packages at all was withdrawn. The lid-slamming had been planned to show how unjust we thought this prohibition. Of course, the girls had been insubordinate; I had not quite approved the violence of their protest, though I had secretly enjoyed the rumpus. Carey declared that the receipt of packages from boys, even boys whom one knew well, constituted a serious offense, and that the slamming of desk lids was unladylike. Such practises if continued would ruin the school. I was a foolish, ignorant child, quite unfit, she told me, to have an opinion of my own about such things.

My mother mitigated this judgment for me a little. She thought it natural that I should be carried away by my companions, she said, but she pointed out to me that we were all of us really very young and inexperienced, and we were thinking only of our own pleasure, whereas Carey and the committee had the good of the school at heart. If I would reflect a little I would see, she was sure, that it must be very embarrassing for Carey in the committee meetings to have her own sister reported for insubordination.

So henceforth I devoted myself wholly to my studies in which there was no catch that I could see. They were difficult enough to tax my energies and they were interesting. I particularly enjoyed

the English and history classes in connection with which geography was taught. As yet Latin was largely a matter of grammar and syntax for me, though I had begun it two years before in a special class at Miss Bond's, while beginning Greek was wholly memory work, but with exciting vistas ahead. We pushed rapidly along to become at last involved in the subtleties of the aorist. Both Greek and Latin were constantly compared with English to avoid the teaching of English grammar as a separate study. All languages were instruments for expression; Greek was best from every point of view, Latin came next in precision and exactness, we were told. In this way the learning of languages was made interesting, but even so I found grappling with three different grammars and three vocabularies at a time a heavy job. Only by dint of hard work did I manage to stand well in my classes and instead of blame to win occasional praise from Carey.

XVII

TOLSTOI'S MY RELIGION

I WAS now the eldest child and the only daughter at home, but it took me some time to realize the advantages of my new supremacy. Indeed, so far as my father was concerned, it was of little consequence since he already had the habit of taking me about with him and Frank, of course, still remained first in his affections. The absence of my three older sisters did, however, make a great difference in my relations with my mother. Now when she had a free afternoon it was I who went with her for the drive in the park which was almost her only recreation, and rare at that. I remember the joy of sitting beside her in the open carriage, but nothing of what she said. At home in the late afternoons she was more likely to talk seriously with me, I found, and I made a point of wandering into her room after I got back from my walk, or had finished my lessons perhaps. I would pause beside her table in the hope that she might ask me to stay, but if I saw that she was busy, off I would go again without a word. Gradually from my mother's stories of the people she helped, I learned something of the life that lay beyond and underneath my own sheltered existence. Most terrible to my imagination was the fate of a half-witted girl no older than I, who had been attacked by a brutal man when she was returning across an empty lot

243

to her own home. This poor creature was too stupid to defend herself, my mother said.

"In any case, stupid or clever, girls should not walk in lonely places. It is not safe," my mother admonished me, and fell into silence.

"Is the girl going to have a baby, Mother?" I asked her quietly.

My mother looked at me for a moment in silence. "That is just what has happened, though I did not mean to tell thee," she answered in her gentle voice, and after another pause she continued. "It is hard to believe that any man alive can be so wicked as to take advantage of a half-witted child, but that is what happened in this case. I have questioned the girl carefully several times and I am convinced she is telling the truth. Now we must take care of her and of her baby. It is impossible to punish the man, since she cannot describe him. She was terribly frightened and it was growing dark."

I struggled to control the horror that rose up in me like a wave of nausea as my imagination filled out these details. I knew that my mother would hesitate to confide in me if I let her see how deeply I was moved. I wanted her to feel that there was nothing she could not tell me, so I managed somehow to choke down my emotion.

Very often she talked to me of Tolstoi, whose book, *My Religion,* just translated into English, lay on her desk. She herself believed that the Sermon on the Mount should be put literally into practice. Tolstoi's account of his experience was a great comfort and inspiration to her. "We should

244

all reëxamine our conduct in the light of what Tolstoi has been able to do," I heard my mother say to my father, and she became more scrupulous than ever in doing what she thought was right. Finally my father remonstrated with her.

"It is very foolish, Mary, to give to every beggar who comes along," he said one day at luncheon. "The man I saw waiting in the hall this morning was obviously a drunkard. Any child would know that he wanted money to get a drink."

"I warned him against doing that," my mother replied. "I told him that Christ had died to save just such sinners as he is from their temptations. He kneeled down and prayed with me before he left."

My father said nothing more on that occasion. But the stream of derelicts that flocked to our house in constantly increasing numbers was more than he could bear with patience. No doubt he argued with my mother about the matter in private, and one day he broke out again at table.

"Do show a little common sense," he urged her in an irritated tone. "Those rascals of thine tell each other where they can always get money for a drink. Thee does not sufficiently consider the consequences of what thee is doing. I admire Tolstoi in many ways, but he has no common sense, and he lives in the country."

My mother looked genuinely hurt and grieved by this remonstrance and her voice when she answered had a note of reproach in it. "The Society of Friends has always held that Christians should obey the teachings of Christ literally. Tolstoi is

doing in Russia only what we are trying to do here. Christ commanded us to give to him that asketh. He did not tell us to take thought for the consequences in this world. Had Jesus what thee calls common sense, James?"

My father made no reply to this question but I thought he looked annoyed rather than convinced.

Finally my mother herself must have decided that it was a mistake to give money at the door. Instead of dimes she began to hand out tickets for food and lodging at a charitable lodginghouse, but she still accompanied every gift with a serious exhortation. "At least they are forced to listen to me," she once said with her gay smile, but seeing Frank and me about to laugh she added quickly, "it really is no joking matter. Sometime in some crisis one of them may remember my words and be helped by them. Words are like seeds, they take root."

Under the new treatment my mother's beggars soon began to decrease in number until finally no more at all came. This seemed to prove that my father was right, but somehow I felt it did not prove that my mother was wrong. I recognized in her a spiritual sincerity that I respected. She made a determined effort to obey Christ's commands and she had complete faith in his promises. My father's way was somehow different. He said much the same things that my mother said, cited the same texts from the Bible, but he seemed able to make an easier adjustment between beliefs and actions. He was not bothered by inconsistency as my mother was bothered. The beggars were frauds,

of course, and a horrid nuisance crowding the hall, but for me they symbolized my mother's goodness.

I did not attempt to piece all these impressions together; I had not yet got to the point of considering the effect, whether for good or evil, of unattainable ideals on human character; my mother's constant effort to live by a counsel of perfection fostered in me a dislike of living as though one's ideals and one's actions belonged to two different worlds. Even as a child I saw people valuing themselves for their beliefs, however much they failed to live by them. This I called hypocrisy and judged with all the harshness of inexperience. For my father, it is true, I made instinctive allowances. I knew him to be really good and kind in spite of certain obvious contradictions, but I drew no general conclusions from this fact. I was entirely capable of taking advantage of his tolerance toward my shortcomings while I condemned the concessions that made his leniency possible. I relied on his sympathy and enjoyed sharing my pleasure with him.

The four burners of the chandelier were turned up to their highest point and the double reading lamp on the parlor table was also shining brightly. My father leaned back in the big easy chair which he filled so completely while I stood before him with my back to the blazing logs of the fire.

"How does thee like my new coat and hat, Father?" I asked, turning about to display them.

"The coat and hat look very well to me," he said and examined me attentively, his gray head

drooped toward one shoulder, as was habitual with him in serious moods. "What about that blue bow under thy left ear?" he asked after a moment. "Is that the style?"

I stopped short in my gyration. "Thee always asks 'is it the style,' before thee will admire anything, Daddie," I said laughing. "This time it really is the style, the very latest style. The best-dressed girls at school are wearing ribbons under their coat collars with a bow at the side. I did not have to tell Mother that. And the curl of cock feathers on my hat is all the style, too. I hated the plain velvet band so Mother bought the cock feathers and put them on for me. How did she know just the right feathers and just the right place for them? I watched her sew them on and she did not hesitate for a single second, though she never seems to think about fashions."

"Thy mother is a remarkable woman," my father commented with a smile, then gave a full minute more to contemplation of my costume before pronouncing judgment. "The brown hat and coat go well with thy hair, and the blue bow adds just the right contrast of color. Thee looks very nice. Now give me a kiss and turn out the gas before thee goes. It makes the room too hot with the fire."

There was a trace of teasing in my father's voice, but I did not mind. I knew he was really interested. I turned off the gas, kissed him on the top of his head, gave him a little pat for good measure, and left him in the subdued glow of the lamplight to continue his interrupted reading.

I was myself extremely pleased with my cock feathers and my blue bow and above all with my new coat. Somehow I had never expected to possess so fine and expensive a garment. I knew my mother was bothered about bills and I had been amazed when she ordered the coat that had taken my fancy instead of a cheaper one that would have served the purpose. Perhaps she felt the time had come to pay more attention to my clothes. I was growing up at last.

This winter my father took me with him on Sunday afternoons to teach my first class of boys in his Mission School in South Baltimore. For many years he had maintained this school; hundreds of boys passed through it and went on to live out their lives, some in other cities and states. When my father traveled, strange young men occasionally greeted him by name on the streets and in railway cars. Well used to this at home, he was always surprised by it in faraway places. Once on the back platform of a St. Louis streetcar the conductor suddenly spoke to him.

"I am glad to see you in St. Louis, Dr. Thomas. You don't recognize me, but I would know you anywhere. I am one of your boys and I'll never forget your talks to us on Sunday afternoons. St. Louis is a fine big town, Doctor. I hope you'll enjoy it."

My father liked to tell this story. "That boy wanted to impress on me that St. Louis is just as fine a town as Baltimore, and finer too, though he spared my feelings by not putting it in so many words," he would comment with a smile. "That's

the proper American spirit. I am proud to have
been a help to such a boy."

At first I found teaching in my father's school
difficult. My boys were older than I, most of them,
and after my slow-witted country girls their city
sharpness amazed me; to cope with it I was forced
to gather together all my energy. During the three
years my classes continued they made Sunday afternoon exciting for me. Set down now after such an
interval of time in the big room of the Mission
Meeting House, I could still find my way to the
place where in the noisy, jostling crowd of boys
my particular group used to gather about me,
under a high window on the left-hand side as you
entered. The light of early winter afternoons,
though usually sufficient for seeing, had a dim,
dreamlike quality. When the yellow-varnished
doors at the far end of the long room were once
shut they enclosed us there inescapably between
the walls. Time seemed hardly to move, lengthen-
ing out immeasurably the half hour of the lesson
before we turned our chairs toward the upper end
of the hall from which my father addressed the
whole school. His broad figure occupied the raised
platform powerfully, his arms moved in swift
emphatic gestures, his sonorous voice rolling out
his sentences came to a pause always on the right
word. Practical and direct as my father's preaching
to the boys was, his voice and his gestures produced
a kind of exaltation in his audience.

One face of the many faces that gathered about
me I can still see. Strong-featured it is, with eager,
intelligent eyes and a firm chin. A smooth white

throat rises above the unbuttoned shirt collar. The ears are small and high set. This particular boy showed his ambition by reading in rapid succession through the lending library I carried down with me on the streetcar journey from our part of town. He preferred *Lincoln's Boyhood, Arctic Explorations,* books about strange countries, to which the other boys were indifferent, but he also devoured their adventure stories. All during one winter I spent much time finding books that might interest him, and for years his face would rise up suddenly before me and I would wonder for a moment where he was and what he was doing.

Frank never taught in my father's school or did missionary work of any kind. He was well-endowed mentally as well as physically but like most high-spirited boys he was bent on amusing himself. That my father would make allowances for almost anything he might do he was well aware, and he seemed hardly to feel my mother's influence. At the time I accepted this state of things without surprise, since it had always been part of my life. Musing on it now, I wonder whether the intimate relation between my father and Frank may not perhaps have been for them both a kind of masculine refuge from overpowering feminine influence. They were alike in possessing to a high degree the strong egotism of the male. Then also my father had for Frank a kind of sympathetic tenderness that left no need of his boyish nature unsatisfied. There was no place really in his heart for my mother.

A gay story my brother was fond of telling shows

clearly his failure to take my mother seriously. She had remonstrated with him earnestly about some misdeed or other, and then had sat him down on a chair near her writing table to meditate for an hour upon what she had said. Shortly after establishing him for his penance, she was called away but promised to come back at the end of the hour to release him. Her table stood in a bay window just above the street. For a while Frank gazed out through the glass, watching his friends play ball on the sidewalk outside, then he threw up the window sash, crawled out, clung by his hands, dropped down, an easy feat for him, and joined in the ball game. When my mother appeared once more Frank was back again in his chair solemnly waiting for her.

Only once that I can remember did I ever see my father thoroughly exasperated with Frank. His school reports had been unsatisfactory, especially his Latin report, and my father, who helped us all crack the hard nut of Latin grammar, was devoting an afternoon interval to drilling him. My mother and I came into the room together just in time to hear my father say, "Really, Frank, thee must be either deaf or an idiot! Thee cannot parse the simplest sentence however often I have explained it to thee. Do stop yawning and pay attention. Thy lack of attention surpasses anything I have ever experienced."

My father's eyes were fixed with irritation on the boy who sat opposite him poking holes with his pencil point in a scrawled-over sheet of paper. Frank's head was lowered and his cheeks flushed; he looked dreadfully hurt by my father's vehe-

mence. My mother stopped on the threshold of the door, and following her example I stopped too, stifling with difficulty the exclamation of sympathy for Frank that rose to my lips. I knew that once thoroughly irritated my father kept on at his victim, and I also knew from my own experience that helping Frank with his lessons was a highly exasperating job. I was tempted to create a diversion in my brother's favor by offering him protection against my father in the very words I had heard my father himself use when condemning the outrageous severity to Frank of Mr. Capper, his Latin teacher. But I managed to refrain out of deference to my mother. My impertinence to my father made her blush with shame, she had more than once told me.

Very gravely she surveyed the group before her, but even when my father turned his head to look at her, she offered no comment. In silence she left the room, I after her.

My mother's silent departure seemed to me the strongest possible protest against my father's management of Frank. I was so used to my parents commenting freely on each other's behavior and openly discussing their differences of opinion that this wordless scene between them struck me as strange. Still I laid no particular stress on it. If my mother had anything to say to my father about Frank, she would say it to him in private.

My parents had the habit of sitting together before the fire in the back parlor late into the night, each in a favorite chair. The evening hours after their children had gone upstairs were the only

253

time they had together free from interruption, they explained. Once when I had come down late to ask my mother some question, she had put me off.

"That can wait until tomorrow," she told me. "Thee seems to forget that thy father and I like to have a little time alone."

I must have looked crestfallen, for my mother smiled at me sympathetically, though she did not relent and ask me to stay.

My mother and father might differ about what was wise for Frank, but I felt sure there were no reservations between them.

XVIII

PAST AND PRESENT

AT Christmas time every room from top to bottom of the half-empty house was occupied once more. Where silence had reigned during most of the day, footsteps now echoed on the stairs, the doorbell rang, lively voices and music and laughter sounded from morning till night and sometimes the cry of a baby rang out, for John and his wife had brought little Jim and his baby brother to visit their grandparents. Only Harry, far off in Germany, failed to return home for the festival. Automatically I fell back into my old place in the family, revolving once more in an outer orbit. But busy as I was all day long, I hardly noticed the change. My mother had assigned to Margaret and me the duty of decorating the rooms with ropes of evergreens and with holly wreaths. We also checked over the presents and dashed downtown to supply what had been forgotten. We wrapped packages in the traditional manner, less elaborate than later became the fashion, but still a dreadfully time-consuming job. We took charge of trimming the Christmas tree and even superintended setting the table for dinner, though Katie, our mulatto waitress and chambermaid, needed no help. These tasks fell naturally to Margaret and me since Grace had many callers and would be at home for a few days only before she went off to visit the Phila-

delphia cousins, while important matters always pressed upon Carey to the exclusion of family concerns. Our elder sisters confined themselves to suggestions and comments while Margaret and I did the work.

When it came to hanging the mistletoe, an innovation this Christmas if memory serves me, the whole family took part. My father directed operations. He had himself provided the mistletoe, picking out from a great heap in the market branches so studded with white waxen berries that we all exclaimed over their beauty. Every possible place to display his treasure had to be tried. Old black Horace brought the tall ladder in from the carriage house and moved it here and there. Frank mounted it to hold the bunch in the place my father indicated, while the rest of us, including Carey for once, stood about craning our necks to judge of the effect from every point of view, gaily disputing the advantages and disadvantages. Only my mother sat quietly at her desk, undisturbed by the commotion. At last the center of the wide doorway between the front and back parlors was agreed on as absolutely the best place. Anyone could have foreseen this result from the first, but we enjoyed reaching it with due ceremony and deliberation.

On feast days it was my father who played the leading role. He loved presents—books, trifles for the house or for his own use, flowers, especially at Easter time. Any gift, however small, delighted him, and my mother, who refused presents herself, declaring that she had more possessions already than she wanted, greatly enjoyed my father's pleas-

ure. It was almost as though she regarded him as one of the children at such times.

Christmas day began by my father's reading aloud to us from the gospels the beautiful story of the Nativity. Then later in the morning he presided over the distribution of gifts, though no longer disguised as Santa Claus. He not only carved the huge turkey, he enjoyed it himself as much as anyone, together with the chestnut stuffing and the scalloped oysters. He also led our singing, keeping us on the key as nearly as was at all possible. My mother never attempted to sing, the Whitalls not being musically gifted, but she encouraged all her children to join in the family chorus, especially the younger children. She had herself provided for our musical education by supplying a singing teacher with an infallible method, a middle-aged Scotchwoman, Miss Campbell by name, expounder of the "sol fa system." Whether this lean, precise Scottish spinster was employed by my mother because of her need for pupils or because of her method, is an open question. Her success with us was not striking. Even my father occasionally winced when we lifted up our voices in song as a family, while Zoe Carey at the piano could hardly continue with the accompaniment. On such occasions we were a bit shamefaced before Zoe, but at other times her musical gift was a joy to us, especially to my father.

John's children, too young to take part in the festivities, stayed in the sunny room where they slept except for ceremonious visits downstairs to the parlor. Since Mamie had left her nurse behind

in Philadelphia, I found myself obliged to spend a good deal of time keeping her company in the nursery. Always very tender to their grandchildren, my father and my mother regretted the cutting short of John's and Mamie's visit before New Year's Day, but for my part I rejoiced. When I saw them packed into the carriage, babies, bags, and presents, actually starting off for the train, I heaved a deep sigh of relief. They must have been gratified by the energy with which I waved to them from the doorstep.

My own presents this Christmas appear to have delighted me, since among my papers I still find a list of them graded according to my preference. The *Poems of Algernon Charles Swinburne,* complete in one volume, my parents' gift, stands at its head marked with a double star. It was procured for me, I feel sure, by Carey's influence. This book I had long coveted and half expected to receive, now that I was fifteen years old, but Mamie Gwinn's gift, a reproduction of Verrocchio's head of a girl, a line drawing, was a complete surprise. I loved it from the very first glance and hung it in my little room over my bed where I could see it constantly and delight in the down-bent profile, the lowered eyelids, the winged ornament in the hair so subtly drawn as almost to escape notice. Mamie Gwinn's sending me this picture without comment, as if sure it would please me, explains in a way the fascination she exerted over me and over many other young people.

Grace constantly entertained visitors in her own upstairs parlor. Tom Worthington, Zoe's brother,

George Carey, and other young men came and went, but I did not join myself to the company as once I would have done. I was not greatly excited even by a scrap of conversation I chanced to overhear after lunch one day.

My mother's gay voice came to me through the curtain that separated her writing room from the back parlor where I was reading.

"I think I ought to tell thee, Grace, of a little talk I had with John Collins yesterday, since it concerns thee." There was a pause and then my mother's voice went on. "He sought me out especially to ask whether I objected to his frequent visits to thee in view of the fact that he was not sure of his own feelings. He had great difficulty in expressing himself, poor boy, but that is the gist of what he said."

"And what did thee say to him, Mother?" I heard Grace ask in a cool voice.

"I told him I had not the least objection to his coming as often as he liked. If he felt that he could take care of himself, I was sure thee could."

My mother laughed lightly and after a moment Grace laughed too, but her voice did not sound amused when she said, "I am much obliged to John for his thoughtfulness."

I chuckled to myself over my mother's reply. "Poor John," I thought as I turned the page of my book, "he is too conscientious by half!" but that was all I thought. I quite failed to perceive that a crisis in my sister's life was at hand. I no longer followed her about, absorbed as I now was in my own affairs.

During this holiday I was preparing a paper for my history teacher on the rise of democracy in Rome, an *original* paper to be put together from big standard histories. With much trepidation I had made my first visit to the Peabody Library to hunt out my authorities. Mounting the wide stone steps all alone, consulting the catalogue, handing in my slip to the young men behind the desk, taking my seat at a corner table and waiting for my books to be brought—every incident of the adventure had terrified me, in spite of Miss Harrison's careful instructions; and when the books came I had been too much excited to understand what I read. But on my second visit I settled down quickly to work with the agreeable ease of an initiate and was soon absorbed in the struggle between the common people of Rome and the senators. On the side of the Tribunes of the People from the first, I adored the Gracchi who remained for years my favorite heroes.

Up to this time I had taken little interest in the past. A year of English history at Miss Bond's school had, it is true, left in my mind certain picturesque figures like King Alfred, the Black Prince, Henry VIII, and Mary, Queen of Scots. In American history I had not had, and as it turned out was never to have, a particle of instruction. I knew of course the most famous stories about our national heroes and had picked up a few general facts, but my ignorance and my lack of curiosity about my own country were appalling and had already brought disgrace down on my head.

During Yearly Meeting the autumn before, I

had been assigned to guide a visiting English Friend down our street to Cousin Francis King's house. As I walked along beside him in silence I felt very proud of companioning such a tall, handsome man, a distinguished stranger. But, alas, the street sign on a lamppost we were passing caught his eye!

"Why do Americans honor Madison so greatly?" he asked me, gazing at the sign. "In every town I have visited there is an avenue or a public square named after Madison. What did he do to become such a hero?"

He smiled down at me, waiting for my answer.

With burning cheeks I gazed up at my Englishman. The pause seemed hours long before I managed to stammer out the information that Madison was a very great man in American history.

Though my companion did not insist, though he dropped the subject at once, I remembered the walk with horror. How could I have lived all my life on a street named after Madison and know absolutely nothing about him? The surprised face of that Englishman had a trick of flashing up in my mind to make my cheeks burn.

Not for worlds would I have mentioned my disgrace to anyone, least of all to my father, but by questioning him discreetly I learned that Madison had been the fourth President of the United States. This discovery did little to comfort me.

What general knowledge I possessed I had picked up from my father. He liked to read out to us Burke's speeches in defense of the American colonists, so that our Revolution was first pre-

sented to me as a quarrel between liberals and conservatives in England as well as in the Colonies. Lincoln my father revered as the emancipator of the slaves and the preserver of the Union, but he revered almost as much the English Quaker, John Bright, who had supported the side of the Northern States in our Civil War. Inevitably I thought of Americans and English as essentially one people though I knew of course that we in the United States were American, not English, citizens. It never occurred to me that English literature was not part of my birthright, that Shelley, Swinburne, and Tennyson were not as much mine as Longfellow, Whittier, and Poe. Thus when I first met it in England, the repudiation of Americans as legitimate sharers in the glories of English literature gave me a severe shock. I resented especially the scornful denial of our right even in Chaucer and Shakespeare, who lived long before the Declaration of Independence.

Only my information about the history of the Society of Friends was at all detailed. I knew a great deal about George Fox, its founder, and loved him in part because of an old engraving we possessed of him with eyes up-rolled and hands uplifted in an ecstasy. I liked to laugh over Charles II's witty rebuke to him for wearing his hat in the royal presence. William Penn, surrounded by his feathered savages and himself so primly and carefully dressed, was a far less sympathetic figure; still I was proud of William Penn's justice to the Indians, unconsciously reckoning it up for righteousness in the sum of our own family inheritance. On

the other hand, I boiled with indignation against the early Pilgrims for their persecution of peaceable Quakers, their whipping at cart tails of decent Quaker women, and their shameful expelling of them from towns. The burning of witches also flamed on the Northern horizon in my imagination. The Puritans, it seemed, had fled from bigotry and intolerance in England only to establish their own kind of bigotry and intolerance in New England. Our Catholic founders of Maryland, Englishmen too, had done better than that, Catholics though they were. I felt very critical of the Yankees and very superior to them, and no doubt I enjoyed sharing in this way the local hatred of the North without disloyalty to the Union.

Thus my ideas of the world had been formed at haphazard by family and local prepossessions. In that old quarrel between the Roman senators and the Tribunes of the People I could not have failed to be on the side of the common people against the aristocrats, of the poor against the rich. And yet investigating for myself a question so remote from my daily life gave me the sense of arriving at my own judgments. This study of the past, superficial and biased as it was, initiated a slight change in my mental attitude, hard to define and yet very real. It was not exactly a sense of historical sequence that I acquired, though I was amazed to find democratic ideals and Christian virtues in pagans born long before Christ; rather it was the dawning in my mind of a suspicion that many surprising and important things had happened in the past, of which I was ignorant. They were written

down and recorded in books, waiting for me to discover them. At the moment, busy as I was, I could not follow the trail.

When the holidays were over and school began again, my Greek and my Latin and my French lessons pressed upon me day by day. Nor could my algebra and English composition be neglected. Science, too, claimed its toll of time. At no point in all this studying could I linger for a moment, since I had to get over so much ground in so short a time. To wander from the direct path was to risk falling behind, and this risk I was unwilling to take.

The days and weeks flew by, spring was quickly upon us, bringing my sisters home again for Easter. Of this holiday I remember only the unusual beauty of my father's flowers. He kept his bulbs stored away in the cellar during the winter months, and when they were potted and brought upstairs he tended them himself. Standing in a sunny window, they were a kind of private flower show. This year his great success was his rubrum lilies. The curled-back petals of the flowers, spotted and streaked with pink, the bold outjutting clusters of pistils and stamen were admired by us all and were praised by visitors, to my father's great pleasure.

He and my mother, forced to go off to some important meeting, missed the last days of my sisters' holiday at home, and after the girls too had left, the house reverberated with emptiness. Thus when I heard the carriage drive up to the door, bringing my parents from the station at last, I dashed

out into the hall to welcome them and I followed my mother upstairs, eager to be with her while I could.

As I entered the room behind her a square white envelope propped against the pincushion on her dressing table caught my eye. Quickly my mother took it up, tore it open and read the letter it contained, then stood with the open page in her hand, her face very grave.

During the long interval of silence my anxiety mounted. "What is the matter, Mother?" I asked. "Has anything terrible happened?"

"Grace has engaged herself to marry Tom Worthington," my mother replied and then added as if speaking to herself, "Before I left home she promised me to wait. She is too young to make such an irrevocable decision and I am not at all sure that Tom is the right husband for Grace."

Grace engaged and to Tom Worthington! I had not expected Grace to marry so soon. I was greatly excited.

My sister came home, the very next week end I believe it was, summoned so that my parents might talk the matter over with her and Tom together. The conference took place behind closed doors after dinner. I started downstairs from my room to ask Katie for something I had mislaid without the least expectation of meeting anyone, but as I reached the head of the stairs I caught sight of the lovers in the front hall under the lighted chandelier. Grace stood close to Tom, her left hand at arm's length clasped in his right hand, her side strained against his side, her face lifted up to his

face bending down to meet it. I dashed back into my own room, my errand completely forgotten. The passionate emotion of my sister's attitude appalled me. She was terribly in love. It was not a question of the heroine's merely yielding, as in my novels. Grace met her lover's emotion with a surge of feeling as powerful as his own. I sat at my table for a long time contemplating what I had seen.

At my parents' insistence, Grace and Tom agreed to wait until he got his doctor's degree at the University before they married. A year's engagement would not be too long. After the wedding the young couple could go abroad for further study, if Tom wished it. Meanwhile Grace, who was not yet twenty years old, was to continue on as a student at Bryn Mawr College. Everything seemed happily settled.

Presents from Tom immediately began to shower down on my sister. He fitted rings on her fingers—diamond, sapphire, ruby rings—he gave her brooches, he hunted out rare books for her. He even presented her with an Irish setter of unimpeachable pedigree. There was no end to his gifts. Twice every day he wrote Grace when they were separated, taking the letters himself to the box in the railway station, the quickest method of reaching her, as he explained. Everything Tom did had the emphasis of intensity. The week ends he and Grace spent together at Bryn Mawr or at home.

It fell to my lot every now and then to companion my new "brother" in an interval of his waiting for my sister. He talked to me mostly

about political and philosophical ideas. Though I was greatly flattered by his taking me so seriously, I could not follow his expositions and finally honesty compelled me to tell him so.

"I'm terribly stupid, Tom," I interrupted the flow of his talk, "but really though I nod my head I don't understand a word thee is saying."

Nonplussed for a moment, Tom recovered himself quickly.

"Thee has not got a clear idea of the universe, that's the trouble," he assured me. "If thee will make a plan of the universe everything will fit together, but thee must have a general plan."

"Does thee think I really could make a plan of the universe?" I asked. "That would be marvelous!"

"It will take time and much thought, of course, but I'll help thee," Tom smiled at me encouragingly.

I was delighted by his suggestion and in an unguarded moment boasted of it to my father, hoping to impress him, but my father shook his head, drawing down the corners of his mouth even farther than usual in repudiation.

"I never heard of such nonsense! Tom might as well tell thee to sit down at thy table and make a map of Pekin out of thy mind. Does thee think thee, or Tom Worthington himself, could do that?"

"Thee's dreadfully hard on Tom, Father," I protested, but my father only smiled without replying, and when I thought it over I could not help seeing that he was right.

Still, though I was no longer impressed by Tom's "map of Pekin," I continued to enjoy my conversations with him then and later. He was full of interesting ideas. His large gray eyes fixed in a distant gaze, he often pondered silently, but he took pleasure also in pouring out his thoughts to a sympathetic listener, which was where I came in. He was a very handsome young man, tall and slender and pale, with finely chiseled features. I admired him exceedingly and was greatly flattered by the attention he paid to me.

The presence of two pairs of lovers made our second summer at Coombe Edge very different from the first summer of strenuous study. Harry, back again from Germany, spent as much time as he could with Zoe Carey, who was again our guest, and Tom Worthington came frequently to visit Grace. Carey was absent traveling in Europe. The whole atmosphere of the house was surcharged with passionate young emotion, though the lovers kept much to themselves. Once I had learned not to dash into rooms without warning and to avoid the piazza when the moon shone, I put them out of my mind as much as possible. My newly awakened interest in serious reading was the refuge to which I retreated, though I remained alert always to help my mother when I could with her multifarious household duties, and I still followed my father about on his inspections of the garden, which bored Frank.

Often, armed with a stout stick, I carried my book down the mountainside to a stream that flowed through the gorge and sat for hours in the

flickering light under a great chestnut tree on its bank. Before I settled myself I searched about carefully to make sure that no snake was curled up in the neighborhood, for the woods were infested with copperheads. They never attacked unless disturbed, and if by chance my foot should stir one up, he would be, I knew, easy to maim by a single sharp blow with my stick anywhere on his long thin back. No one of us ever ventured into the woods without a stick. I had seen several copperheads killed and knew just how it was done. I was not really afraid, and the sense of danger gave a thrill to reading in the woods.

Elizabeth Barrett Browning's *Aurora Leigh* proved the great excitement of my summer. Page after page I devoured it, and I meditated earnestly on the questions it raised concerning the destiny of women. Passages that impressed me strongly are underscored by a heavy black line in my copy of the book that still stands on my shelves. Though few people now remember the existence of this poem and still fewer attempt to read it, in 1887 it fell inevitably into my hands. Mrs. Browning was an often-cited contemporary example of feminine accomplishment, and in *Aurora Leigh* she wrote of women in a way that thrilled my generation. Long as it was, the poem was not too long for our enjoyment. During the course of the summer I also read Frederick Denison Maurice's *The Natural Law of the Spiritual World,* but that was rather in the nature of a stunt. My parents valued the book as a modern scientific vindication of their faith and often quoted from it. What I remember

about reading it is my pride in having finished so serious and important a book. No sense of excited interest in its contents remains as in the case of *Aurora Leigh*. It may have helped me on my way; at least it kept me busily occupied and ministered to my self-respect.

I still wanted to be a writer though my first hope of becoming a poet had long ago evaporated. I recognized my complete lack of a gift for poetry, still I sometimes thought that I might perhaps be able to write novels. I had brought up to the mountains several volumes of Dickens and Scott with the vague intention of studying them. However, lured on by the story, I dashed through them at such a rapid pace that I could not pretend even to myself that I got anything out of them except amusement.

Meanwhile from June to September visitors surged through the house, relatives and friends of one or the other of us. John and his family stayed for the usual two weeks. A big vigorous Englishwoman, Miss Chamberlain by name, came for a long visit to read French with us, at Carey's suggestion lest the summer be completely wasted. The high point of our entertaining was a week-end visit in June from the President of Johns Hopkins University, Mr. Gilman, and the Professor of Pathology at the Hospital, the great Dr. William H. Welch. The importance of these gentlemen was impressed on us strongly by my father's repeated instructions beforehand concerning our behavior during this visit. Unfortunately while they were at Coombe Edge our hilltop was poured on by one

of the violent rain storms which last for days in that mountain region and my parents were put to it to entertain their guests. I can still see Mr. Gilman's stately, erect march by my mother's side up and down, up and down the protected piazza, and Dr. Welch's short heavy figure following behind with my father, who was of much the same build, though heavier. Mr. Gilman inspired awe, while Dr. Welch proved to be genial and entertaining. During meals in the big, damp, rain-darkened dining room he told stories at which the young people gathered about the table could laugh. I liked him, though of course I did not dare say a word in his presence. No sooner had our guests driven off to the station than the sun broke through the clouds. It shone on brightly for many days, during which my poor father, looking out over his view, deplored the miscarriage of all his plans for his visitors. It was dreadfully hard luck of course, but with the impatience of youth I felt my father made too much of his disappointment.

XIX

BALTIMORE GHOSTS

IT'S a comfort to be in town again, isn't it, Mother, where things can be ordered by telephone?" I said to my mother one morning after breakfast. "I don't see how thee manages to get food for all those people in the mountains."

I spoke with feeling, remembering how bitterly cold Margaret and I had been on our last drive down into the Cumberland Valley for creamery butter. It fell to Margaret and me usually to help my mother out in an emergency, and on this occasion we had failed to take wraps enough. The sun had already set when we began the slow climb back up the mountain to Monterey and by the time we reached home our hands were so stiff with cold we could hardly hold the reins, though we took turns in driving. There is something about cold hands one doesn't forget.

"The expense is the worst of it," my mother said glancing anxiously at the papers piled up on her writing table. "I haven't money left in the bank to pay all these bills. Fortunately the country people don't mind waiting. I'll settle with them all when my next check comes from Philadelphia." My mother's voice had grown cheerful as she talked.

"They know thee is as safe as the Bank of England," I assured her gaily, but my heart sank.

New bills would be piling up and next month my mother would have to make the tour of the butcher and baker, the shoemaker too perhaps, asking them in their turn to wait.

I had gone on such a tour with her the winter before and I had hated to hear my mother beg the shopkeepers so solicitously for time, though they had been charming to her. When I had asked her if she really needed to go about like that, she had answered, "The shopkeepers must know when their money is coming in. They have bills of their own. It is not right really for me to make them wait, but I don't seem able to help it, hard as I try."

"Thee and Father do too much for your children. We're to blame." I had tried to comfort her and had determined then and there to husband my own weekly allowance so that I need never again appeal to my mother when anything extra came up. I was distressed now to find that this winter would be no easier financially for my mother than last winter had been.

My mother plunged into her many activities immediately after her return to town, and I thought that she enjoyed them greatly. She seemed more energetic and gayer than she had been at Coombe Edge. She talked more at mealtimes, discussing with my father the various causes in which they were interested. Only three of their children were left at home to sit about the family board, and Harry was often preoccupied, though he sometimes told amusing stories of his work at the State Insane Asylum, while Frank and I were too busy

273

eating to chatter or interrupt very much. My parents had an opportunity for quiet conversation together at dinner when the day's work was done, such as they could not have enjoyed since the early years of their marriage.

I listened to what they said, learning many things from their discussions, and when a subject happened to interest me, forming my own impressions. My father and mother felt it part of their duty as Quakers to bring people of diverse opinions together, which explained in a way the wide diffusion of their energies. My mother seemed to me better fitted for the role of mediator than my father, who made concessions up to a certain point but stood firm when that point was reached. Not even my mother could persuade him to yield another inch.

Both my parents believed in faith cure, though not to the same degree. In his practice of medicine my father had found faith in prayer of great value in certain cases. Being a minister of the Gospel, a pastor really as well as a physician, he did not neglect the spiritual side of his art, but his training and his experience alike taught him that there were certain organic disturbances of the body that required physical treatment. He prescribed quinine for malaria and called in a surgeon to set broken bones and to operate when an operation seemed necessary. With the mind-curists' contention that there is no such thing as physical disease he had not a particle of patience. My mother on the other hand, while not a mind-curist, was convinced by her study of the New Testament that

faith in God could work miracles. Christ had given his disciples power to heal the sick and she believed that this power was still possessed by followers of Christ who had sufficient faith. This belief was a part of my mother's basic conviction that Christ meant what he said to be taken literally. She was unwilling to pick and choose between either his commands or his promises, to regard some as seriously meant and others as symbolical. This easy accommodation seemed to her destructive of true faith.

The illness of my mother's sister, Aunt Sarah Nicholson, had made strikingly clear to me the difference in my parents' opinions in regard to faith cure. Aunt Sarah herself felt that her long invalidism was due to "a false conception of God," as I heard my mother tell my father. His face was very grave as he replied:

"I greatly fear that Sarah is suffering from some deep-seated physical malady. What she needs is not a faith-curist but the most skilful doctor in Philadelphia."

"Sally has consulted the best doctors and they can do nothing for her. She must put her trust in God, who alone can help her," my mother answered and my father did not insist further.

When Aunt Sarah died my mother was deeply saddened but her faith was not shaken. Unable on account of her poor health to be active herself, Aunt Sarah had sustained her two active sisters by her unfailing sympathy and her interest in all they did. Her weekly letters had been "a mainstay" to my mother, as she herself said. For a long time

after Aunt Sarah's death her face became sad when she examined her morning post, but she never spoke of her grief.

Interest in occult forces and powers was widespread at this time. The attention of the public had become fixed not only on faith cure and mind cure but also on such subjects as hypnotism, thought transference, communication between the living and the dead, the return of spirits to the scene of their earthly existence. Eastern mysticism had swept like a wave over the West. Madame Blavatsky, after spending years in India and Tibet, had founded the Theosophical Society in London where she had many followers, and in the United States also she exerted a dominating influence. Other enthusiasts searched the buildings of antiquity for prophecies. The great pyramid in Egypt had been measured, its dimensions, its orientation, and its passage ways interpreted to explain the course of history in a widely read book, a copy of which we possessed. Cryptograms were found in famous works of literature. Bacon was proved to be Shakespeare to the satisfaction of many people.

The doctrine of Divine Guidance and the Inner Light, soberly held by the Society of Friends, had little in common with the current forms of spiritualism, and yet certain Quakers seemed predisposed to accept them. My impression is that I first heard of mediums and spirit manifestations, of occultism and astral bodies, while listening to my Aunt Hannah talk to my mother. She had met Mme. Blavatsky in England and many of her friends, both English and American, belonged to

276

strange religious sects. She described these extraordinary people with such a combination of common sense and zest that her listeners never forgot her stories about them. However, even without Aunt Hannah we at home could not have escaped the current excitements. Baltimore, though a small provincial city, had its table rappers, its clairvoyants, and its haunted houses.

A well-known schoolmaster of Baltimore boys was reputed to be followed about by a ghostly attendant in the shape of a wizened little old man. Several people testified to having seen this apparition, and the victim of his attentions, questioned about the matter, had merely smiled, refusing either to confirm or deny. Then a professor at the Johns Hopkins University, an Englishman with an English wife, had found the house he rented not far from us on Lanvale Street already occupied by a ghost. It was a quite ordinary house, small and one of a row, but it proved to be haunted just as much as if it had been an ancient castle with the thick walls and long-echoing galleries of the ghost stories I had read.

This professor and his wife, both Quakers, were friends of my parents and I happened to be present when Mrs. Hunter described to my mother how intensely she had felt the presence of an unhappy spirit in the dining room that very morning while she and her husband were at breakfast.

"I spoke words of comfort to him," she said, "and I exhorted him to tell us his secret. When he did not answer I kneeled down by the table and prayed for him. Richard felt as certain as I did

that he was there close to us, though neither of us saw him."

Once, looking over her shoulder as she went up-stairs, she had, however, caught a glimpse of a small bent figure following her, Mrs. Hunter assured my mother, and she had often heard his deep sighing.

I listened enthralled to this story, but even at the time it seemed to me funny rather than terrifying. Mrs. Hunter was a tall, angular woman with prominent teeth and the picture evoked of her kneeling down to plead with someone who was not there struck me as comic. Moreover, my mother did not seem to me greatly impressed.

It was, I believe, my father's skepticism that held us all in check. He mistrusted prepossessions, illuminations, and visions, and he frequently warned us that there were charlatans about ready to victimize credulous people. Though shows of all sorts were forbidden to Quakers, he took us himself to see Herman Keller, the great contemporary "magician," that we might learn how easily impossible things could be done by trickery. Also he exacted from his children a promise never to allow themselves to be mesmerized, stressing the danger of abandoning our wills to the control of others, and he would not permit table rapping in his house. Once indeed at a family gathering, unable to resist our urging or perhaps disliking our hints that he was illiberal, he allowed us to make a single experiment. We asked the table how many apples and oranges were in the fruit dish always left after dinner on the sideboard by Katie; then trooping

all together into the dining room behind my father we counted the fruit and found that the answer rapped out by the table was correct. My father was greatly upset. Though he maintained that this success was a coincidence, he seemed also to fear that there were evil spirits about. This was so unlike my father that it worried us all. We never bothered him again with table rapping, and my impression is that no one of us ever took the least interest in it. The general feeling seemed to be that skepticism was the proper approach to such subjects, and no doubt we prided ourselves on not being dupes. I believe that I at least cherished some such sense of superiority.

Harry studied hypnotism as part of a modern physician's technique and my father himself engaged in an informal survey of thought transference in a little group composed of Stanley Hall, then still a professor at the Johns Hopkins University, and another professor whose name I have forgotten. These gentlemen came sometimes to our house for their deliberations, impressing me greatly and exciting my curiosity. One day after they had left I waylaid my father in the hall to find out what conclusions they had reached.

"It's much too soon to reach any conclusions," my father said, putting me off as I thought.

"But, Father, you must surely have found out something after so many meetings. Please tell me what you think."

Smiling at my eagerness, my father interrupted his rapid progress to the front door.

"Thee is too impatient, child," he admonished

279

me. "First of all we have to make sure that thought transference occurs in any real sense. But this much I can tell thee, if it does actually occur we are convinced there is some natural explanation of it."

"What could the explanation be? Do tell me what you think." I rewarded my father's patience by insisting, holding him fast by the front of his coat.

"It is conceivable that we make certain slight muscular movements of which we are unconscious but which convey meaning to other people also without their being aware of the process."

My father seemed really interested as he made this explanation, so quickly I attacked him again. "What kind of movements could they be, Father? It's terribly interesting."

"Well, thee knows that some people can move their ears. Perhaps they express their feelings by ear-wiggling."

Having made me laugh, my father hurried off to his appointment.

Though I realized of course that the ear-wiggling explanation was just a device to get rid of me, I was left with a conviction that somehow or other the most mysterious things could be explained.

During the course of this winter, 1886–87, John Hazelton, a disciple of my father's, came from Cincinnati to consult him. This young man was an earnest Y.M.C.A. worker, "socially minded" as we would now say, and when his manufacturing business had begun to prosper he had inaugurated a

system for sharing his profits with the employees.
My father had encouraged John to undertake this
experiment in which he had great faith, hoping it
might provide a solution for labor difficulties. All
had gone well until a slump in the business, cutting the profits, had also cut the workingmen's
share. They had refused to accept any decrease in
their dividends, which they regarded as permanent
additions to their wages, and were threatening a
strike against the unfair treatment of their em-
ployer. I remember John Hazelton's stocky figure,
his dark, rather ugly, earnest face, and his devotion to my father. After much discussion they decided that the employees should be called together
once more, the facts explained to them again and
the decision left in their hands. My father shook
his head over the unreasonableness of workingmen
when he heard that John's employees had voted
almost unanimously for a return to the old fixed-
wage system.

Politics was almost the only subject of common
interest not discussed in our family; the feelings
aroused by it were too passionate for safety. The
trouble had begun several years before during
Cleveland's Mugwump campaign when Harry and
Bond each cast his first vote for president. Three
separate candidates were favored in the family that
year, the Republican supported by my father, the
Prohibition candidate earnestly advocated by my
mother, who of course had no vote, and Cleveland,
in whom Bond believed with all the fervor of
youthful revolt. Harry, though strongly Republican by conviction, voted the Prohibition ticket

281

because of a chivalrous belief that a man's first vote belonged to his mother. My father was outraged by a situation that made ineffective his opposition to the Democratic party, the rebel party of the Civil War. He firmly believed that Cleveland, if elected, would bring ruin on the United States, and he denounced Bond as a traitor to his country. The Prohibition party had not the least chance of winning. Harry's vote was a mere gesture. It was intolerable, my father said, that his own vote should be cancelled by Bond's vote. My father's vehement denunciations of Bond were very painful to us all, especially to my mother. She urged Harry to vote according to his own convictions, thus pairing off with Bond and releasing my father's vote, so to speak, but Harry refused. He was determined to pay my mother the tribute he had planned in his boyhood.

I remember feeling bitter against both Bond and my father, especially against my father. I had often heard him say that women did not need the suffrage to influence public affairs. Their influence could be exerted most effectively in the home, he maintained, and he even expressed the fear that their husbands and sons would pay less attention to their advice if women themselves had the power to vote. Now in spite of all this my father was making my mother unhappy because she influenced one single vote once in her life! I well knew she would never influence another, nor did I feel it right that she should. Her due was a vote of her own.

During the course of the winter our new sister-

in-law, Bond's wife, Edith, came to pay us her first visit as a member of the family, arriving before Bond, who could not get away from business until Saturday afternoon. She was an exciting addition to our circle, a New Englander, not a Quaker, beautiful and talented both as a painter and a writer. Bond was mad about her. He had from the first pointed out to us that she possessed the profile of a Renaissance picture and he often hinted that she was a genius. He let it be known that they planned to live on a high intellectual plane in the seclusion of their small manufacturing New Jersey village and that they had not the least intention of bringing up a family. Bond would be forced to give most of his time to the glass factory, but by economy they would soon save enough even from his small salary to permit of his retiring and their devoting themselves to writing books in London or Paris or New York. All this was very exciting. I had admired Edith's appearance when I had first seen her the year before, her slender erect figure, her deep-set gray eyes, her fine, thin nose like the blade of a sword, and her soft dark hair, even though it seemed a bit scanty to a well-endowed Thomas. I was quite willing to believe that she was the marvel Bond thought her.

Anxious as my mother was to spare Edith all fuss, she felt obliged to introduce her to certain of our relatives. Tea had been served in the front parlor and after the guests had gone Grace and Edith settled themselves in a corner to talk things over. Eager to hear what they were saying, I joined them just as Edith remarked to Grace, "How could

you admire that awful hat so enthusiastically! I don't think much of your taste!"

"It's hideous, of course," Grace replied, "but when Cousin Eliza asked me how I liked her new hat I couldn't hurt her feelings by telling her so."

"I suspected as much," Edith laughed. "Lying for the sake of being agreeable seems to be a part of your Southern good manners I've heard so much about."

Grace flushed. "Really, Edith," she protested, "you can't call it lying not to criticize a hat you do not happen to admire. Tastes do sometimes differ."

"Call it 'fibbing,' if you like that word better. Polite lies are a particularly cowardly kind of insincerity, and ruin the character. You owe it to yourself to be sincere, Grace."

I looked at Edith in amazement. If she was teasing Grace she was overdoing it badly, but I instantly saw from her earnest expression that she was entirely serious.

Edith seemed to take everything she said and did seriously. There was a kind of effort even in her erect posture and she explained that she walked lightly on the balls of her feet because that is the way Indians walk. We soon learned that "Cousin Mary Foote" was Edith's final authority on all questions of manners. She gave us the benefit of that lady's expert opinion whenever she felt we needed correction. Nothing in Baltimore seemed to impress Edith much. Harry, exerting himself to entertain her, procured for her an invitation to the Sketch Club, where original sketches were dis-

played. The sketch Edith took with her was not up to her usual standard, she said, but added that it had compared favorably with the others. Harry himself took her to one of our Baltimore assemblies that went by the name of "Germans" and were celebrated for their brilliancy throughout the South. She had enjoyed it, she told Harry the next day, because it was so much like dances she had been to in New Hampshire.

"I felt as if I were back in Concord," she said.

This was too much for Harry, I saw by his expression. "Concord is a large town, I believe. I'm sorry I have never had the privilege of visiting it," he said in his most courteous tone of voice.

"It's the capital of the state and the assemblies are very formal affairs. People come to them from miles about."

Harry let the subject drop. It was clear to me that he did not like Edith.

What Grace felt about her I could not quite decide. She knew Edith well, having seen her many times at the Pearsall Smiths', and since she was Bond's favorite sister and no doubt his confidante, she was naturally anxious to please his wife. Grace had cut her Friday classes to be at home for Edith's visit, but when Bond arrived late on Saturday I thought she seemed relieved. For my part I kept in the background, observing and drawing conclusions. I refrained for once from interjecting the sharp comments by which I sometimes drew attention to myself. Edith interested me and I believe I would have accepted her wholeheartedly, if she had not insisted on calling my mother "Matouska."

The name "Mother" belonged to her own mother, Edith explained to us, and seemed very much pleased with herself for having found in the Russian novels she was reading a suitable appellation for Bond's mother. It meant "little mother" and was a term of endearment. This information quite failed to appease us. We all shuddered when we heard Edith call my mother "Matouska" though she herself declared that she liked her new name. Intent on winning the affection of Bond's wife, she was incapable of letting such a trifling matter as a name interfere with her purpose. My father also was charming to his new daughter-in-law but I saw him look at her keenly on several occasions and once I heard him say that he feared Edith had a nervous, high-strung temperament.

Later in the winter a scene occurred that must have confirmed my father's judgment. Aunt Hannah was paying us a farewell visit before she left America finally to settle near Mary in England. Our whole family gathered to do her honor on the last day of her visit. My three older sisters came on from Bryn Mawr, bringing Aunt Hannah's daughter Alys with them; John and Mamie even were present, and of course Bond and Edith. Bond was almost like a son of the Pearsall Smith family and Edith, being Mary's friend, was well known to Mary's mother.

At dinner Aunt Hannah sat on my father's right hand, Edith across the table from her on his left. My place was at my mother's end of the table facing Aunt Hannah. She looked exceedingly handsome, I thought, in her stately black velvet

frock. Already she wore a lace cap on her pale gold hair, but she showed no signs of age. As she looked at the young people seated up and down the long table her face beamed with an affection that was full of energy. My part was to keep Tom Worthington amused and I devoted myself to it until toward the middle of dinner a sharpness of tone in the conversation drew my attention to the group about my father.

Edith was leaning across him over the table toward Aunt Hannah.

"I do not mean that Mary is intentionally cruel," I heard her say, "but she does lead men on to fall in love with her. An atmosphere of adoration seems necessary for her happiness."

Absorbed in analyzing her friend, Edith quite failed to notice that Aunt Hannah had grown pale with anger, for after a moment's pause she went on, "Mary finds a new love affair stimulating. She is very much like Goethe in temperament."

"How dare you say such a thing to me, Edith!" Aunt Hannah's voice rang out, silencing all conversation down the table. "You call yourself Mary's friend and you compare her to Goethe, the most notoriously immoral man who ever lived."

"Mother," Alys leaned forward from her place to intervene, "thee did not understand what Edith—"

But Aunt Hannah paid no attention to Alys. She went right on addressing Edith, dreadfully pale now under Aunt Hannah's fierce eyes. "Mary is an angel of goodness. She cannot help it if men fall in love with her, but she uses her power over

287

them only for their own good, to lead them to higher things, and you dare to tell me she is like Goethe. Take that back, Edith, and apologize or I will never speak to you again."

The tears were streaming down Edith's face. She could hardly control her voice. "Mary is my dearest friend," she stammered. "I never meant to say anything against her. I apologize if I have."

She pushed back her chair and rushed from the room, Alys and Grace after her.

We were all greatly distressed by the scene. Though Edith had come to us as it were from Aunt Hannah's house, still it was in our house that the incident happened. For my part I began to perceive that Edith was totally unconscious of the effect her words produced on people. She was far from wishing to annoy Aunt Hannah, I knew, and I pitied her for her incredible stupidity. Then a little later when I met Mrs. Carpenter and observed Edith's devotion to her I began to have an uneasy sense that we on our side were both stupid and unkind in objecting to Edith's reserving the name she had always called her mother inviolate for her own mother. I knew how I myself would feel in her situation.

XX

SOCIAL FAILURE

WITH the preliminary college entrance examinations impending, my school work was very heavy this year. I enjoyed doing it, and when I had time I enjoyed reading the books Carey had left behind her in her sitting room on the top floor of the house. Some of them were fascinating looking yellow-backed French novels but I did not disturb these since at the moment I read for recreation only. When I was alone safe from oversight in Carey's room the little girl attitude developed in me by my position in the family dropped away. I was a free individual eagerly forming my own opinions of people and the world with the help of Thackeray and George Eliot.

I had made friends with the four other girls in my class at school the year before, though I was not really intimate with any one of them. We took walks together and visited each other's houses without exchanging personal confidences that I remember. Our talk was of school events, the usual gossip and jokes. Sometimes we did our lessons together, but I found that I got on more quickly by myself. I worked with greater concentration than they, perhaps I was more mature intellectually, though they far excelled me in social competence, as I well knew.

At fifteen, the age I had reached, many Balti-

more girls were already finished young ladies. Harry's fiancée, Zoe Carey, and her sister had both been belles before they were sixteen and the same was true, though to a less degree, of Grace in spite of the restrictions imposed on her. Margaret was behind Grace in worldly experience, but if she was ever shy and embarrassed in company I did not perceive it. She was accustomed to dealing with the boys in her class at school, while all my friends were girls. The young men who came to the house to visit my older brothers and sisters paid no attention to me. I suppose I accepted this as a matter of course since I cannot remember being distressed by their neglect. I was silent and shy in the presence of strangers, especially of young men, and made my escape from their company as soon as I could. Success in my studies was the achievement on which my heart was set and that I attained to a sufficient degree. My belief is that I was happy and gay at this particular time.

I even enjoyed a dance given by Carey's friend, Miss Garrett, to a visiting cousin of hers, a girl not much older than I. This was, I consider, something of a feat, since I was, and knew beforehand that I was destined to be, a wallflower. Never having been sent to dancing school, I had managed to pick up only the waltz step, and in executing it I had had almost no practice, except by myself with a chair for partner. At Miss Garrett's party I made no attempt to join in the dancing; still I had a new dress for the occasion and felt that I did look very "nice" in it, as they had told me at home. The spectacle of Miss Garrett's long picture gallery

decorated with flowers and crowded with gay young people amused me; there was always someone to whom I could talk, a chaperon or one of my school friends unengaged for the moment. The reigning belle of the dance proved to be a girl in the class below me at school, of whom I was fond. I rejoiced in her success and broke off my conversation with a young man supplied me by Miss Garrett to introduce him to Alix Pennington, taking much the same pleasure in doing so, I fancy, that an unathletic college boy takes when he displays his intimacy with a football star. That I envied Alix a little I do not deny, for I remember with telltale vividness the eager pleasure on this young man's face as he danced off with her, leaving me standing alone to stare after them.

Later during the winter my equanimity was shattered by my brother Harry's unkindness, as it then seemed to me, though I did not hold it against him since I knew that he was genuinely fond of me. Like many clear-sighted, sensitive people, Harry had a way of exposing with devastating clarity the weaknesses of others, even the people he loved, when they annoyed him or when, as in my case no doubt, he felt it would do them good. He could not yet have had sufficient experience to know that the mistakes of young people, however annoying to their elders, should sometimes be passed over without comment.

One afternoon this brother of mine took me with him to visit the laboratory where he worked three times a week on some problem or other. As we entered the room the two young men seated at

a long table under high bare windows jumped up quickly and greeted me with gallantry as if I were a young lady. One in particular showed me the slide under his microscope and when I looked down the brass tube, shutting my left eye as directed, he adjusted the focus for me and pointed out to me the tiny object "in the center of the field." I really did see it, though I had never looked into a microscope before, and I managed to ask a shy question or two about it. We did not stay long, but I was greatly pleased with the visit and the two handsome young men who had been so charming to me.

After dinner Harry and I settled ourselves in the back parlor to talk over the day's adventure. Harry expressed gratification that I had been so much interested in the laboratory and then he proceeded to comment on my behavior.

"I cannot imagine what made thee speak in such an affected tone of voice and stand with thy shoulders raised up almost to the level of thy ears. Thee doesn't look particularly fascinating in that attitude."

The glance Harry fixed on me expressed not so much wonder as annoyance. I felt my cheeks burn hotly under his eyes as I realized that in my shyness and desire to make a good impression I had made a fool of myself. I had been really interested and it had not entered my head, consciously, that I could "fascinate" the young men, as Harry said. My humiliation was intense. From that moment I avoided young men, telling myself that they were no concern of mine and never would be. Thus I

SOCIAL FAILURE

constructed a suspension bridge of indifference to
walk on above the turmoils of humiliation.

Grace's wedding took place in the spring. The
date originally insisted on by my parents had been
advanced without much discussion. She was clearly
not profiting by college and moreover her health
was suffering from the strain of the situation.
Grace was married at home, since the wedding ac-
cessories on which her heart was set—a maid of
honor and a bevy of bridesmaids and ushers—
would have been impossible in the meeting house.
Even at home there would be no music, no wedding march to float on, but Grace was a good
Quaker at heart and made no complaint. In so far
as was possible, everything was arranged to please
her. My mother helped her to choose lovely clothes
and to list the wedding presents that came in bewildering numbers. I remember my mother's amazing efficiency at this time. Like a strong wind her
cheerful energy carried the family straight through
the pre-wedding confusion.

In the kindness of her heart Grace invited me
to be one of her bridesmaids. I was really too young
for the part, but I would have been dreadfully
hurt had she passed me over and I am still grateful
to my sister for having spared me this particular
disappointment.

The wedding day passed in a nightmarish maze.
My attention was no doubt concentrated on playing my part properly and helping my mother.
Only when the bride in her traveling costume
paused on the stairs to toss her bouquet down into
the group of bridesmaids below did I feel emotion.

Then a sob rose in my throat as I realized that the demure figure standing there above me was the sister who had been a romantic heroine for me all during my childhood and that she was leaving home forever. I turned to look at my mother. In that moment of general concentration on the bride she had relaxed her reserve. Her expression was so profoundly sad that it shocked me, banishing from my mind all thought of my own feelings.

The expense of Grace's wedding had been great. When she left she had, as I expressed it, "given the family a parting kick that set us back two years." The amusement with which this remark of mine was repeated in the family showed how gaily we took our chronic financial difficulties, but none the less I knew they weighed on my parents.

My mother returned to her public activities immediately after Grace's marriage. They seemed constantly to increase. At this time she was busy with a new crusade, the White Cross Movement, endorsed by the Baltimore Women's Christian Temperance Union at the last annual convention, over which my mother presided. This movement had been initiated in England by a band of "White Cross Knights" to promote the equal standard of morality for men and women.

A copy of her presidential address which chance has recently put in my hands enables me to quote the exposition of the subject she herself gave to the ladies of the W.C.T.U. "These Knights wearing the white flower of a blameless life have pledged themselves to purity, chivalry, and self-restraint. They hold the divine truth that a man

ought to be as pure as a woman and they believe that what a man *ought* to be, that he *can* be and that they *mean* to be. Nothing could be more fitting than that this association which represents the motherhood and the sisterhood of our country should take hold of this work and adopt the White Cross as a pendant to the white ribbon." With this peroration my mother ended her speech.

I was not greatly interested in the White Cross Movement at the time—it was just one more cause to me. I remember hearing the phrase "equal standard," the meaning of which I perfectly understood, but there was nothing in it to surprise me. I took for granted that what was right for women was also right for men, and I also believed that people could do what they ought to do. These two propositions were axioms in my upbringing.

Though I could not possibly follow my mother's activities in detail, day by day, however busy I was with my school work, I kept track of where she was and anxiety for her flared up in me as easily as it had done in my early childhood. Thus I was dreadfully bothered one day on my return from school when I learned from Katie that she had been shut up in her bedroom all morning long. Through her closed door she told me that she wanted no lunch and asked me not to knock again. She wished to be left quite undisturbed. My father had gone out of town to see a patient, I knew; my mother had seized the chance of his absence to shut herself up alone, a thing she had never done before. What could be the reason? At intervals all afternoon I went out of my room to stand on the

landing at the turn of the stairs from which I could see my mother's door. Behind it I pictured my mother on her knees praying, praying to God, but I could form no idea what might be the subject of her intercession. At last a little before dinnertime I heard her go down the stairs to her writing room. I did not follow her for I knew she would not want to be questioned. At dinner she seemed just as usual, talking over with my father his journey to the country, and if she perceived my anxiety she gave no sign. For a long time after this I was haunted by a sense of impending disaster, of some secret threat to my mother's peace of mind. I imagined that my mother seemed a little graver than usual, that her cheerfulness was perhaps a little forced, but since nothing happened, gradually my anxiety faded away.

The preliminary examinations, when at last the day for them came, seemed to me very severe, but I passed them better than I had dared hope, so that I went up to Coombe Edge feeling happy and free from care. Our household was small for the summer. Early in June Grace and Tom had sailed away for Tom's year of study abroad. Carey too was in Europe again traveling about with Miss Gwinn, while Harry remained most of the time in town doing his own work and much of my father's as well. Margaret, however, passed the whole summer at Coombe Edge except for a visit or two. In our quiet routine letters from the travelers were exciting events and the visit of John and his family seemed to give my mother unusual pleasure. She spent a great deal of time with the two little

boys and even revived a hobby of her youth to make pencil drawings of them crawling about in their rompers or playing under a tree. Edith's and Bond's visit however was spoiled by Edith's horror of snakes. This was due, she explained, to an over-mastering prenatal impression and, alas! it was I who brought about the crisis by telling her that our mountains swarmed with rattlesnakes and copperheads. Everyone reproached me for my idle chattering, but how was I to guess Edith's phobia? She seemed so gallant and brave with her horse-back riding and her great Dane dog of whom she showed us pictures that I never dreamed she might be afraid of snakes. When I made this defense to my mother she smiled quietly and asked me whether I had not been trying to impress Edith with my fearlessness by enlarging on the snake-infested woods through which I wandered all alone. My mother's question gave me a shock, but thinking it over for a moment I saw that she was right.

"I really was boasting, Mother. I see that now! How awful of me. I've driven Edith away, I'm afraid."

"They are leaving tomorrow. But don't be too repentant. Edith was sure to hear of the snakes from someone."

"Thee's an angel, Mother," I said, restraining with difficulty the impulse to throw my arms about her neck.

After our strenuous winter we were all, I fancy, glad of a respite. I studied and read and wandered about the countryside and was happy. Sometimes

the two horses were harnessed to the light carriage
and we all took a long drive together. I think of
my mother and father rather than of Margaret and
Frank as my companions. I cannot say how my
sister and brother amused themselves. If there was
any special excitement in their lives it escaped my
attention. The only day out of the long procession
of summer days I especially remember is my six-
teenth birthday which fell in mid-August. By my
breakfast plate in the morning I found a full-
blown red rose with a poem to me left by my
father as a greeting before he drove off to the
station. Then before dinner in the evening a little ceremony was made of presenting me with a
gold watch as a token that I had now reached maturity. Though all my sisters had been given gold
watches at sixteen (twenty-one was the age for the
boys) this gift surprised me greatly. I knew that
my parents were worried about money. Indeed,
they had warned us all that strict economy must
be practiced for some time to come. I had taken it
for granted that I would have to wait for my
watch, but when I opened the box my father
handed me, there it was shining and beautiful
with a little gold chain ending in a ball attached
to its ring. I was overcome by astonishment as
much as by joy.

My mother smiled at me, understanding my
feelings. "Don't worry, child. My last check was
larger than I expected," she said as she kissed me.

I valued my watch enormously, the more perhaps because of the circumstances in which I received it, but for a long time I worried as to how

THE AUTHOR AT SEVENTEEN

the bill was to be paid. No doubt I exaggerated my parents' anxieties, since they talked about economy rather than practiced it.

By now my skirts had reached the ground and my pigtail was a thing of the past. I practiced doing my hair in becoming ways and often I wore a rose in it or a pale yellow rosette-like blossom plucked from one of my father's hollyhock stalks. He liked us to wear the flowers he cultivated and always praised the effect. I had this excuse for adorning myself with flowers, trying different color effects before my mirror. My mother rarely praised her daughters' appearance. "Thee will pass in a crowd," she used to say to us when we displayed ourselves to her. But I never had to blush for the clothes my mother chose for me. Only the best materials pleased her, as being the cheapest in the end, she said, and she had an unerring eye for the fashion. Thus I grew up into a young lady not wholly unmindful of her appearance, though a confirmed bluestocking.

XXI

CATASTROPHE

M Y last year at school began under halcyon
skies. Day followed October day clear and beautiful; the great trees in the Park glowed with color.
On our afternoon drives my father and I rejoiced
in the golden tulip-poplar trees, the most beautiful and tallest of native American trees, he liked
to remind me. Maples and chestnuts flamed scarlet
or yellow, widespreading oaks day by day became
a deeper red and the beech grove we loved became
pale gold. Scarlet patches nearer the ground were
dogwood trees, as beautiful in the fall of the year,
we said to each other, as when they were decked
out in their spring blossoms. If time remained after
my father had visited the last patient on his list
we drove swiftly through the Park out into the
country, choosing roads where high autumn grasses
stood unharvested. Though my father told me
their botanical names I paid attention only to
the way the light shone on their feathery tops, pale
brown or a strange red color at once faded and
deep, or I watched their swaying back and forth
in the wind. A certain road we both loved descended a steep grade, crossed a rattling plank
bridge, and then curved to the left about the foot
of a hill covered with wild grasses that ran up in
long undulations under the wind to the bright sky
of evening. We drove between stubble fields where

the cornstalks were bound together into stacks with the dried spiked flowers on top. They reminded me of wigwams, calling up images of the feathered chieftains who had once roved the countryside. Often it was cold when the wind blew but again still days came, the hushed days of Indian summer. Leaves hung motionless then from their branches and the fields were still. Except when he designated by name an unusual tree or a rare variety of grass my father kept silent. Seated side by side in his open carriage, warmly wrapped up in our rugs, we communicated with each other only by a smile or by a glance that was the meeting of eyes almost alike, the eyes of father and daughter.

In spite of the lovely weather my mother had not taken a drive since our return to town. Always she put off the suggestion that she should go in my stead by declaring that she was far too busy. And then suddenly the weather changed. During the week that Yearly Meeting lasted it was very cold and on some days a chill rain fell. Absorbed in preparing my lessons, I was less conscious than ever before of our Yearly Meeting guests. The house was full as usual, but Frank and I were left in undisturbed possession of our little rooms. I brought my schoolbooks and papers from Grace's deserted sitting room into which I had expanded, shut the door of my cubbyhole and worked as usual. In my free afternoon hours, I helped Katie decorate the elongated table for dinner, and I stood by while my mother changed her dress in the late afternoon, ready to run an errand or con-

vey any order that might be required. Very lovely and very stately I thought my mother looked in her ceremonious black silk frock that swept the ground behind and showed in front a panel of soft black velvet where the princess overdress flared open from waist to hem. Her hair was as bright as ever it had been and waved as softly. Immediately after dinner every night I went up to my room to puzzle out the lines of Herodotus or read the pages of *Heroes and Hero Worship* assigned for the next day's lesson. Thus I lived through the week of Yearly Meeting quite unconscious that my mother was not well. Later I was to suffer bitter self-reproach because I had been blind to the effort she was making.

On the day after our guests left I learned when I got back from school that my mother had moved from her own room and established herself in the front room. I found her lying stretched out in bed.

"Mother, what is the matter?" I asked. "Katie told me thee was here in the guest room, but not that thee was ill."

"I have taken cold," my mother informed me. "I take cold easily, as thee knows, and the weather has been very bad."

"But, Mother, thee never goes to bed with a cold. It must be something more than that. Please tell me what is the matter."

"I really have got a cold, but in my back this time. I cannot stand up, so I have to lie in bed," my mother explained cheerfully, but seeing me, no doubt, still look unsatisfied, she continued, "Father

says it is lumbago, got from waiting for the street-car yesterday in an icy wind."

"Dearest Mother, why will thee expose thyself in that way!" I said, but instantly sorry for reproaching her, hurried on, "let me do something for thee. Is there nothing thee wants? Fortunately I had extra time in school to study tomorrow's lessons, so I'm quite free. I have not a thing to do this afternoon except to nurse thee."

"That is splendid," my mother said. "I have been waiting for thee to bring me some papers from downstairs. On my table thee will find a rough copy of my report on the Orphan Asylum, and thee might bring up also the printed report for last year. It should be on the shelf at the right. The Annual Meeting comes the end of next week."

"I'll find them for thee," I assured her. "But wouldn't thee like to have thy lunch right away before Father comes in? I'll tell Katie to bring it."

My mother shook her head. "I will wait for thy father, but I should like to have the report at once. I have only just time enough to get it ready."

I ran quickly downstairs and brought her the papers. Then I went off again to see that the cook and the waitress knew about her lunch. My father had already given the necessary orders, there was nothing further I could do, so I went back to my mother's room and was pretending to read but really watching her when my father came in at last. From the door he glanced anxiously at her face and he spoke rather sharply to me when she winced with pain while I was arranging her pil-

low so that she could sit up a little behind her tray.

The moment she was settled my mother sent us off to get our own luncheon, telling us with a cheerful smile that she was quite comfortable.

"Is Mother very ill?" I asked, as my father and I went down the stairs together.

"She has got a severe attack of lumbago, but I hope she will soon be better. Thee must take good care to see that she keeps warm and doesn't over-tire herself. She needs a rest."

Fearing to distress my father, I asked no more questions. That he was oppressed by anxiety I perceived, but then he always took illness in his family hard, as is the way with doctors. My father himself often pointed out that doctors lose their heads completely where their wives and children are concerned, and ought not to look after their own families. Still my mother had never since I could remember been so ill that she stayed in bed for a whole day. I had an uneasy sense that this time my father's anxiety was justified.

My mother soon began to get better, however. Before many days had passed she was able to sit up and to rest on the couch. I delighted to do little things for her and I rejoiced at every improvement. She was getting well more slowly than I had hoped, but still surely.

Every day immediately on my return from school I went up to her room, which had now become the front room, to ask how she had passed the morning. Usually she gave me a cheerful report. But the day came when instead of replying

to my question she told me to bring up a chair and sit down while she talked to me. She was lying on a low couch with her back to the window, a pink and gray knitted afghan over her. I thought she looked very pale in the bright light that fell on her face.

"I have something to tell thee," she said, and before there was time to do more than feel the presence of doom hanging over me, she opened the front of her gown, uncovering her left breast, and pointed with her hand to an angry redness spread out there. Then she took my hand and laid it on her breast.

Very hard and rough the lump was under my fingers. I withdrew my hand from it and turned my eyes away to look into my mother's eyes. They were clear and dry and her face, though grave, was composed.

"What can it be, Mother?" I asked her. "It feels dreadfully hard."

"It is a cancer." My mother made this awful announcement in a calm voice. "But God can cure even a cancer. Thee must help me by having faith."

Breathless from the shock for a moment and hardly yet understanding, "What does Father say?" I asked her. "Has thee consulted a doctor?"

"Dr. Tiffany was here yesterday morning while thee was at school. Thy father thought that Dr. Tiffany might be able to cut out the lump, but he says there is nothing to be hoped for from an operation."

As I looked at my mother I remembered suddenly the afternoon she had shut herself up in her

room to pray. Months and months ago in the early spring she must have known that she had cancer.

"Dearest," I cried, "why did thee wait for so long before consulting a doctor?"

My mother caressed my cheek with her soft hand. "Do not be so distressed, little daughter," she said. "It is never too late for God. In His own good time He can cure me, if it is His will. If it is His will to take me to Himself now, then that is best for me and for us all. Thee must not upset thy father by weeping. It is hardest for him. Sometimes when the pain is severe I cannot conceal it from him."

Instantly I stopped my sobbing. "Thee can always tell me, Mother," I said. "I can bear anything except thy not telling me. Is thee suffering at this moment? Tell me the truth."

My mother smiled at me. "No," she assured me. "I have no pain now, but sometimes there are sharp stabs like a knife thrust that make me wince before I know it, and there is itching and often my arm aches."

I struggled to keep my self-control. "Dearest, why can't I have the pain instead of thee?" I managed to say before sobs burst from my throat. Half-blinded with tears, I tucked the afghan closer about my mother and left the room and flung myself on my bed in a passion of weeping.

When I heard my father's slow step mounting the stairs I controlled my sobs, bathed my face hurriedly in cold water, smoothed my hair, and went down to lunch. The dining room, warm and bright with sunlight, was empty: Harry never

lunched at home and Frank had not yet got back from school. As my father entered he gave one glance at my face and then turned his eyes away.

"Frank doesn't seem able to be on time for lunch. We had better begin," he said, and took his seat at his end of the table.

I rang the bell for Katie, and sat down in Frank's chair. I could not occupy my mother's place, as I had been doing while she was upstairs.

After lunch was over my father led the way across my mother's sitting room through the back parlor into his office, closed the door behind me, drew up a chair for me beside his desk chair and took his seat.

"Thy mother has told thee the true nature of her illness," he said without looking at me. "Thee must be brave as thee can. Carey and Margaret are coming home from Bryn Mawr this afternoon for the week end. Thy mother has already written them. Thee can help everyone by keeping control of thyself."

I was not looking at my father; I gazed instead out of the window following with my eyes the pattern made by the bare magnolia branches against the bright blue sky, noticing every detail of them with sharp unconscious attention, but when his voice ceased I turned quickly to him.

"Father, is there really nothing that can be done?" I had to ask him. "Surely some doctor somewhere can do something to cure Mother."

"It is too late," my father said in a toneless voice. "If only she had consented to consult a surgeon earlier there might possibly have been some hope,

but she absolutely refused. I could not persuade her."

My father laid his arms on the desk, hiding his face away from me. "Darling Father," I leaned over to touch his shoulder, "it is more awful for thee than for any of us. I do not see how thee can bear it. I will do everything I can to help. Thee can trust me, Father." At last my father raised his head. "I must not break down," he murmured, and sat erect. "Thy mother ought to take a rest after her lunch," he reminded me.

"I will go upstairs to her immediately," I assured him, and left his office.

The sight of his despair had strengthened my self-command. I felt able to do whatever there might be for me to do. Only I must not think. Never, never must I allow myself a moment for thinking.

When she reached home Carey absolutely refused to accept the verdict of the local doctor or to leave my mother's case in the hands of faith-curists as my mother herself desired. Grieved beyond measure by the unimaginable threat to the person she loved best in the world, Carey did not for a moment lose hope or initiative. She insisted that my mother must without further loss of time consult the best specialist in the country. Dr. Tiffany himself had wanted a second opinion, recommending Dr. Delafield in New York as consultant, but my father and Harry, convinced that my mother's cancer was inoperable, felt that she should be spared the fatigue and distress of such a journey. Secretly they feared, as I now believe, that Carey

would insist on an operation however great the danger and however faint the hope of success. But on the surface a consultation seemed so highly desirable that Carey was able to bear down all objections to it, even my mother's. It was agreed that as soon as her lumbago permitted, my mother was to go to New York to be examined by Dr. Delafield. The three days' holiday at Thanksgiving was tentatively fixed upon for the journey.

Until Dr. Delafield had given his opinion we were justified in hoping that my mother's life could be saved, Carey assured Margaret and me. Though she did not criticize my father in words, it was clear that she blamed him for not taking action earlier. "I am convinced that Father has known about Mother's cancer for a long time, but was unable to face the fact. We must say nothing about it. It's too terrible to speak about."

Though I had no share in the deliberations of my elders and could influence their decision in no way, I was passionately on Carey's side. Something could and must be done to save my mother. It was utterly impossible that she should be doomed to die at fifty-three. Such a terrible thing could not happen to my mother.

She continued to gain strength day by day and was soon able to come downstairs again for her meals. On the Wednesday before Thanksgiving she started off to New York accompanied by my father and Harry and by Carey, who joined the party at Philadelphia. Margaret and Frank and I remained at home. We succeeded in keeping externally cheerful during the first two days though

they stretched themselves out immeasurably, but by Friday night our courage had worn thin. We separated early and shut up alone in my little room I faced my anxiety by myself. The very best we could hope for was an operation, and an operation which had at first seemed salvation now loomed up in my mind menacing terrible risks. "No one can tell in what an operation would end, Carey," I had heard Harry say in a low voice to my sister, without really understanding what he meant. I had not thought of Harry's words again but now when my mind presented them to me I perceived their significance. My mother might die in New York.

Somehow Friday night passed and on Saturday morning I settled myself down in the room where my mother always worked. There by her table I felt nearer to her than anywhere else in the big empty house. With my books spread around me I could give myself up to thinking of her.

As I looked about the room it seemed full of my mother's presence and yet it was hardly more than a common passage way. Katie had just gone by me from the dining room into my father's office to answer the telephone. Doors opened into my mother's room from three directions and through them the household traffic continually flowed. At her table in the window recess on the street side where I was now seated my mother was somewhat withdrawn from this coming and going, but she faced it none the less. It seemed not to disturb her. Indeed all of us, my father, the children, and the servants, were free to appeal to her

if occasion arose, for she had the power of returning to her work instantly and without irritation
after interruptions. She never complained of being
disturbed; on the contrary she often expressed satisfaction in having her own special table for working with shelves for her books and drawers in a
desk for keeping her papers.

Until the house had been enlarged just a few
years ago she had had no settled working place of
her own, I reflected. Now this alcove was really
hers and such was the power and charm of her personality that the long narrow room across which
everyone tramped seemed also absolutely hers. My
mind swerved away from the thought of what it
would be like without my mother in it. I fixed my
eyes upon the huge white plaster head of Hermes
after Praxiteles that stood on the high desk against
the left-hand wall. Carey had brought it back from
her last trip abroad as a present for my mother. I
remembered the unpacking of the immense box
and the discussion of where the head would show
to the best advantage. It was very big for my mother's room but looked well from the dining room
when the double doors were open. Now for the
first time I felt it unbearably oppressive even
though the serenity and beauty of the countenance
suggested my mother. Perhaps Carey had chosen
it for that reason. I gazed up at the great face with
a sense of utter desolation.

At last just before lunch time a telegram from
my father arrived. Margaret came running downstairs to tear open the envelope. They would reach
Baltimore at 5.45 that afternoon. Horace was to

meet them at the station. That was all. No word about the doctor's decision. Margaret and I tried to encourage each other. Perhaps my mother had been sent home to grow stronger before undergoing an operation, we said, but we knew in our hearts that her doom had been pronounced. Her case was hopeless. Instinctive though my impulse was under stress of emotion to ask God's help, I did not pray for my mother. If her own prayers had not sufficed, what use could there be in my praying?

Margaret and Frank and I were waiting in the hall when the carriage drove up. We could judge nothing from my mother's smile or my father's composed face. He and Harry went upstairs with her immediately, but Carey lingered for a moment. We had read the truth in her face before she spoke. Dr. Delafield had been immovable in advising against an operation. The effort to save my mother had come too late.

CHAPTER XXII

FEBRUARY TWENTY-SECOND

DESPAIR now seized on us all. We could not imagine life without my mother. On the surface we succeeded in maintaining the composure to which we were trained by our Quaker tradition, but internally reason had abdicated and common sense taken flight. No one suspected this dangerous shift in our common mind, unless perhaps it may have been my father, and grief so overwhelmed him that he was incapable of taking decisive action. We felt that my father had "given up," as we said, but we did not criticize him since all his children without exception knew how complete was his devotion to my mother. He reiterated again and again his desire that she should be made as happy and as comfortable as was possible, but he seemed unable to focus his attention on details.

Our first impulse was naturally to draw close together about my mother. Before Carey and Margaret went back to Bryn Mawr late Sunday afternoon a cable was sent to Grace telling her of our mother's illness and urging her to return home with her husband. No one at our end appears to have considered what the effect might be on Tom Worthington of having his studies in France cut short, and probably poor Grace in the fifth month of her first pregnancy was too much prostrated by

shock to think of possible consequences to Tom's career. They answered our cable with another saying that they would take the next steamer for New York.

My mother's faith in God's power to heal her remained unshaken. Her desire was that no change should take place in the daily routine of any member of her family. At first she had refused to countenance sending a cable to Grace, but my father and Carey persuaded her that for Grace's own sake it was better that she and Tom should come home. My mother's illness could not in justice be kept secret from her own daughter, they argued, and prolonged anxiety and uncertainty might well prove too great a strain for Grace's health. Tom had no business ties. He could continue his studies at the University in Baltimore almost as well as in Paris. Also my mother would worry about her, though this point was surely not stressed to my mother. Even if my father had believed that a sacrifice was involved for Tom, he would no doubt have felt that the situation demanded it. Grace herself would be far better off at home and could be of use in looking after my mother. Carey's duties as Dean and Professor of English at Bryn Mawr could not be neglected of course, and my mother would not listen to the suggestion that Margaret should leave college to nurse her. She needed no nursing, she declared. She would live normally and naturally, herself taking care not to overdo. Carey and Margaret could come home more often for week ends if they liked. I was to attend school as usual. Not even my father

was permitted to make the smallest change in his busy days. His religious work as well as his practice of medicine was to continue undiminished. Everything was to be the same as before.

One change, however, my mother was persuaded to accept. A new maid was added to the household to act primarily as her personal attendant, to take care of her room and her clothes, and to be always within call. My mother herself must have seen the necessity for this arrangement since she already found going up and down stairs a fatigue and the duties Katie usually performed were as much as she could manage. To add a new member to the staff of servants in so large a house as ours hardly counted as a concession to illness.

Thus the accustomed routine was maintained in the household with little change. When my mother found that attending meetings fatigued her the ladies of her committees came to the house. In this way she continued her activities. The excitement of Grace and Tom's arrival was soon over. They found a house not far from us, furnished it quickly and settled down. Tom went to work again on his interrupted thesis, while Grace spent part of every day with my mother. I attended school regularly, devoting my free time to doing what I could for my mother, and every day I sent a report of how she was to Carey and Margaret in Bryn Mawr. At first my mother continued to manage the house, but from conveying her orders to the servants I soon began to give the orders myself, relieving her of planning for the constant expansion and contraction of the family. The

Christmas holidays came and were lived through without undue fatigue for my mother. We were well on into the new year when a second catastrophe descended upon us.

My father had gradually become anxious about Harry, who was losing weight and had a persistent cough. All during the long weeks of my mother's illness Harry had sustained and helped my father in every way and now it was clear to him that Harry himself was ill. He obtained a specimen of Harry's sputum and sent it secretly to Dr. Welch for examination. By ill luck Dr. Welch's report came in the morning post. Sitting beside my father at breakfast, Harry was opening his letters for him as he often did and out of Dr. Welch's envelope fell the card containing the report. As Harry picked it up and handed it to my father he learned that he had tuberculosis in a severe form.

Though I was present on this occasion I went off to school without knowing what had happened, so quietly did both Harry and my father take the shock.

Energetic measures were essential and in a very short time Harry left for Saranac Lake to be under the care of Dr. Trudeau. The letter to Carey and Margaret in which I described his farewell to my mother still exists and reads in part as follows:

My dear Sisters—

Although Harry wrote to Carey this morning, I think you will want to hear how he got off. Poor fellow, it was very pathetic! He kissed Mother about ten times and then got up and fled, feeling

it impossible to speak. Grace and I with our usual brilliancy both wept—Grace more, I less. When we went downstairs to kiss him we found Father and him embracing each other and both crying. However the atmosphere cleared and he went off with a show of cheerfulness. Bond went with him.

Mother behaved like an angel all day, she did not cry but I think the strain has made her tired. Her back is worse today. There is an extremely sore place in her side which hurts her every time she moves. Poor Father is worn out. Cousin Lizzie Tyson is dreadfully ill. He hardly hopes she will live. . . . Mamie is coming tonight and I hope she will make Dearest go to sleep soon. She did not sleep until nearly two last night and I was awake till half past three.

Dearest sends her love. I am too sleepy to write another word.

Adieu,

H. W. T.

The letter from Harry to Carey referred to by me in the above description of his farewell to my mother contains the following passages:

"Bond, Frank and I are sitting around the dining-room fire waiting for Mother to come to breakfast. . . . Now Carey thee knows how I feel about leaving Mother and I know thee will do to me as if it were thyself who were away. Do let me hear from thee once in a while. There isn't much to say on the subject and there isn't much use in saying that. Mother has just come in and had a pretty good night in spite of Father being out

317

until four with Cousin Lizzie Tyson. Helle slept in Father's room. Mother seems very cheerful and bright and *is* perfectly lovely.

"Good-bye, dear Dean, thy brother Harry."

This letter is dated January 23, 1888.

Harry's departure left another room vacant for the visitors who were perpetually coming and going. Carey and Margaret arrived every Friday and left again on Sunday. At longer intervals Bond and his wife came for visits and John dashed on alone from Philadelphia when he could. After Mamie's new baby was born all three came together. Aunt Hannah was still in England, but my mother's brother, Uncle James Whitall, and his wife made the journey from Germantown several times to see her. My father's family were always dropping in and sometimes stopped for lunch and dinner, while Grace and Tom of course often had meals with us. Managing such a household would have been impossible for an unexperienced girl of sixteen without the help of devoted servants. I remember the general sense of responsibility, the pressure of so many visitors to be arranged for, but I fancy I did little more than keep the servants informed who was expected and when.

One afternoon, however, I looked up from my books to find Katie standing beside me in tears. The cook was leaving, she told me, had already packed her trunk so that she could go that very evening. There had been a violent quarrel between Katie and Deborah, I made out. This was a major misfortune. The quarrel had to be settled at once and I had to settle it. With beating heart,

feeling very inadequate, I went slowly down the
stairs, along the hallway, through my mother's
empty sitting room and the dining room into the
kitchen. There by the big stove stood the cook in
a calico dress, her contorted black face surmounted
by the bright bandana handkerchief that covered
her hair, a small but formidable figure. As soon as
I appeared she burst into a torrent of words. She
loved the missus, she said, nobody loved the missus
more than she did but she would take no orders
from that yaller girl Katie.

I had decided to be very humble. First I flattered
her, telling her that only she could tempt my
mother's appetite. The house could not run without her, as she well knew. My mother trusted her
to provide for my father the food he liked. He
needed it now more than ever before. I talked on
and on, and finally promised that I would myself
in future give all the orders directly to her.

Deborah's fierce expression had gradually softened and by the time I stopped speaking tears
were running down her face.

"'Tain't that I wants you always to be coming
to the kitchen, Miss Nellie," she said. "I knows you
ain't got time for that, with all you has on you's
shoulders. You just tell that Katie to speak to me
more respectful."

I went back to my room feeling weak from the
anxiety and the ensuing relief. However, I had no
time to waste. Opening my Homer again immediately at the place where I had thrust my pencil,
I began hunting in the dictionary for the word
over which I had stuck.

Spring came early. On Washington's Birthday, which was a holiday, I took a drive with my mother during the morning in my father's closed carriage, our last drive together. We went through the town to leave a note at Miss Garrett's house. Already the trees in the open square on Monument Street were thick with buds. The tall marble shaft that supported George Washington's betoga'd statue rose up gleaming into a hazy blue sky, golden sunlight lay on the reviving grass plots and gilded the bronze lions by Barrye that adorned the entrances to the square. Windows were open in the wide low houses that stood with old-fashioned Southern dignity about the open space. My mother pointed out to me these signs of spring, rejoicing in them. Our errand done, old black Horace turned up Charles Street and drove us slowly on into the park. Though it still seemed wintry there, a faint mist of color marked the red buds out from the other trees.

"Only the twenty-second of February, and the red buds are already beginning to flower!" my mother exclaimed. "What marvelous beauty there is in God's world!"

She was invariably cheerful; and often she was gay. When Carey brought home with her from Bryn Mawr the first typewriter we had ever had in the house, my mother insisted on seeing if she could use it. We stood about her, all her daughters, in a little group, while she took her seat at the table and struck the keys. In a flash she had finished. Across the big white sheet of paper Carey extracted from the machine marched sharp and

clear and correctly punctuated the sentence, "My children, you are sweet and lovely as roses and lilies!"

We laughed with pleasure, praising her skill. "It is thee, Mother, who is sweet and lovely," Carey said, and Grace voiced the old reproach that she had not handed on to us her beauty.

"You will pass in the crowd, every one of you," my mother assured us, using the very words we expected. Then having played out our little game with us, she looked fondly from one face to the other.

"The important thing is that you are all good and kind and have sufficiently good sense, I believe. Also each one of you has a particular beauty —Nellie her Titian red hair, Margaret her lovely gray eyes, Grace a smile that charms everyone, while Carey, though with her brains she does not need it, has a beautiful face." My mother's eyes moved from one to the other of us and finally rested with pride on Carey's face.

Now as always my eldest sister seemed to me paramount with my mother. Being so much younger I accepted this fact without any particular pain, nor did Margaret ever seem to be jealous of Carey. For Grace the case was different. Not only was she older than we, she had been used to the role of première daughter at home during the long periods when Carey was away. And now while Carey was forced to spend most of the week at Bryn Mawr, Grace stayed on with my mother. She shared my mother's religious faith with fervor, a bond Carey did not have. It must have been bit-

terly hard for Carey to say good-by to my mother every Sunday afternoon and perhaps she resented Grace's remaining behind in her absence. I was too young to count. Every now and then a spark of antagonism flared up between the two sisters; they seemed in a sense to be rivals for my mother's devotion. Ordinarily such slight manifestations of smoldering feelings would have passed unnoticed in a large family like ours, but our common solicitude for our mother having imposed harmony upon us, they now attracted attention. When Carey and Grace addressed each other with asperity my mother looked distressed. I wished that my sisters would control themselves in my mother's presence at least. Grace's condition occasionally made her nervous and irritable. More than once I had watched my mother soothe and cheer her. I forgave Grace, but I felt that Carey might have controlled herself better.

XXIII

ACCEPTANCE

My mother was losing strength week by week. Her appetite failed, her nights were restless, she became less and less able to hide the fact that she was in pain. In helping her upstairs I had now to push her from behind. Frank, who was stronger than I, tried to take my place in this, but he had not the necessary skill. And gradually I had to exert more and more strength until at last I too was unable to help. A chair with handles was provided so that Horace and Frank could carry her downstairs once a day for lunch. My mother so much enjoyed her meals with the family that we made every effort to put off the inevitable time when she would have to remain in her room.

Meanwhile my attendance at school had become increasingly irregular. When I had a free period I dashed up the street just to see if my mother wanted anything; I cut important classes to spend time with her; I studied only when my father or one of my sisters was with her or while she slept. Her maid, Marie, proved unable to protect her from visitors, which was not surprising, since even I found difficulty in cutting short the stay of the important ladies who came to consult her. Occasionally they would take the hint and rise to go when I entered the room and stood behind my mother's chair; more often I had to tell them as

politely as I could that their time was up, and
some of them seemed to resent my interference.
These ladies I hated for their selfishness and stupidity. How could they fail to notice the fatigue
on my mother's white face? Then Marie had little
skill in adjusting pillows. She could not make my
mother really comfortable in her easy chair or on
the couch. She was only a lady's maid. On my
mother's bad days I simply could not trust her to
Marie.

Many were the hours I spent reading aloud to
my mother while she rested, biographies of notable
Quakers, a history of the early Christian hermits
in Africa and Syria, tracts on faith cure, on mind
cure, on Christian Science. These tracts I could
hardly endure, since I felt that but for the beliefs
they expounded my mother might have sought the
help of a surgeon in time. But they gave her comfort and it was now too late, so I read on and on
in an even voice their false, deceiving words. Often
when she was safely in bed and my father had said
good night to her I read a passage from the Bible
to her, usually from the last chapters of the Gospel of John, until I could say the words with no
more than a glance at the page.

"I am the vine, ye are the branches; he that
abideth in me, and I in him, the same bringeth
forth much fruit: for without me ye can do
nothing.

"If a man abide not in me, he is cast forth as a
branch that is withered; and men gather them
and cast them into the fire, and they are burned.

"If ye abide in me, and my words abide in you,

ye shall ask what ye will, and it shall be done unto you."

"These things have I spoken unto you, that my joy might remain in you and that your joy might be full."

Or:

"And ye now therefore have sorrow: but I will see you again, and your heart shall rejoice and your joy no man taketh from you.

"And in that day ye shall ask me nothing. Verily, verily, I say unto you, Whatsoever ye shall ask the Father in my name, he will give it you.

"Hitherto ye have asked nothing in my name: ask, and ye shall receive, that your joy may be full."

Or again:

"And now, O Father, glorify thou me with thine own self with the glory which I had with thee before the world was.

"I have manifested thy name unto the men which thou gavest me out of the world: thine they were, and thou gavest them me; and they have kept thy word."

"And the glory which thou gavest me I have given them, that they may be one, even as we are one.

"I in them and thou in me, that they may be made perfect in one; and that the world may know that thou hast sent me, and hast loved them as thou hast loved me."

A look of peace, the peace that passeth understanding, gave to my mother's face unearthly beauty.

Between the braids of her bright hair her countenance shone white like the countenance of an angel. Without speaking I would adjust the screen, see that everything she might need was on her bed table, open the window, extinguish the lamp, and moving softly, leave the room.

My mother's weakness increased and I knew that she was often in pain though she made no complaint. My concentration upon her grew more and more intense. Any event not directly concerning her passed almost unnoticed by me. The birth of Grace's baby early in April was important only because it kept Grace at home and worried my mother. When Grace could come again to be with my mother that was a great relief, for she was often alone. By this time the school authorities, who had long objected to my neglecting my work, had issued an ultimatum. I must either leave school entirely, which my mother still refused to permit, or I must be regular in my attendance. This was a frightful blow. During five days of the week, between Sunday and Friday afternoons, I was in virtual charge of my mother. Her care required more skill and knowledge than I possessed but under my father's direction I managed to do what was necessary. Conscious of my inadequacy, I longed at least to devote my whole time to my mother, but I knew that my leaving school would distress her too greatly to be possible. Fortunately my first morning period was a study period and the authorities compromised by allowing me to come late, so that I might see my mother settled for the morning after her breakfast, but I was forbidden to cut

classes or to leave before the other girls. Most of my studying out of school I did on the days Carey and Margaret were at home, though even on those days I often performed little services for my mother, who had become accustomed to my ministrations. During the daytime my father was very busy with his practice. Moreover, the sight of my mother's weakness and suffering affected him so deeply that his emotion communicated itself to her. After he had been with her she was often unable to lie quiet or to sleep.

Once only in my presence did my mother lose her composure and then under the long continuance of pain. My first glance at her white face when I pulled back the curtains at her windows in the morning told me she had not slept well, and when I came back from school she still looked very pale. After her lunch she asked me to go on with the book we were reading. Perhaps the sound of my voice would help her to fall asleep, she said, and shut her eyes. But before many minutes had passed, glancing at her as I turned a page, I saw her eyes wide open and fixed on my face in a kind of desperation. Immediately I got up from my chair near the window, sat down by her couch, and took her restless hand in mine.

"Thee is suffering, Dearest. Tell me where the pain is. Shall I rub thy back for thee?" I asked her.

Paying no attention to my question my mother spoke in a low, inward voice. "God has cast me out like a branch that is withered. I have rebelled against His will. I have been selfish and self-seeking."

"Darling Mother, how can thee say such a thing!" I broke in. "Thee has always thought and planned only for other people, never sparing thyself. Who should know if not I? Please, Dearest, believe what I say."

The strain of my mother's expression relaxed a little. She even smiled at me faintly. "Thee is my dear little daughter and a great comfort to me, but thee cannot know my thoughts." Her face grew very grave again as she went on. "God sees our most secret thoughts. He searches the heart. He knows how often I felt dissatisfied and rebellious when my family duties prevented my working for Him, as I said to myself. Really I enjoyed going off to meetings and conferences with thy father and Aunt Hannah and was bitterly disappointed to be left behind. By taking me now when I have so many fewer duties to keep me at home God is showing me that I am not fit to do His work in the world."

My mother had spoken slowly with pauses between her sentences. Only when she lay silent at last did I answer her.

"Darling Mother," I said, "do not let thyself feel that God is displeased with thee for anything at all. I cannot believe that thee has committed a single real sin in thy whole life," I talked on in an effort to soothe her. "If thee had temptations now and then, thee always resisted them. Thee always stayed at home and I do not believe thee ever uttered a word of complaint. But if by chance thee really has sinned, God has long ago forgiven thee. He would not be God if He did not forgive His children's sins."

My mother had closed her eyes. "His ways are past finding out," she murmured. "For now we see through a glass darkly: but then face to face: now I know in part: but then shall I know even as also I am known."

Holding the hand she had left in mine, I sat quietly beside her for a long time, my eyes on her face and my thoughts concentrated on her, hoping to restore her peace of mind by my own certainty of her great goodness.

At last she opened her eyes. "I will sit up now," she said, and smiled at me with her own bright smile.

XXIV

JULY SECOND

ONE supreme effort of faith remained for my mother to make. Some friend of hers who had been helped by a certain religious healer, a simple New England farmer, brought this man to visit her, and he exhorted her to fasting as well as to prayer. My mother had never approved of fasting, believing like all Quakers that God does not require such outward manifestations from his servants. But now she began to question the validity of her disapproval. Had not Christ himself fasted for forty days in the desert, and had not Anna the prophetess served God with fasting and with prayer? She became convinced that it was her duty "to humble her soul with fasting," as the Psalmist had said. Though totally unconvinced, my father gave his consent. He feared the effect of even a brief fast on her strength but he could not bring himself to interfere between my mother and her conscience. Carey was in despair. Failing to persuade my mother she appealed passionately to my father, but he refused to use his authority as a physician. A three days' fast was ordained for my mother with cups of sugared water at intervals to sustain her. Every afternoon the healer came to join with her in her prayers—a little, bent, middle-aged man with a gray beard and the eye of a fanatic, who

slipped through the door of my mother's room before I had half opened it for him.

Slowly the first day of the fast went by. The second day passed. Then the third day dragged itself to an end. Weak but quiet at heart my mother waited for the miracle. When it failed, she accepted her death as God's will.

After this it was that she spoke to me of the future. I had lain down beside her on her bed in the late afternoon. The dimness of twilight prevailed in the familiar room. Out of the dimness my mother spoke.

"I have been thinking of next year, while I rested," she said. "Thy father will be very lonely and I should like thee to stay at home with him and not go to Bryn Mawr until Margaret has finished there. I hope it will not be a great disappointment to thee to wait for a year."

"I should not mind a bit," I hastened to assure her. "Of course I'll wait. I will do anything thee wants me to, Mother. I will give up going to college entirely if that would make thee happier."

My mother was silent for a moment. I could not see her face distinctly but when she spoke it was in her usual calm voice.

"No, I think it will not be necessary for thee to do that," she said. "Thy father finds thee a sympathetic companion. Thee can be a comfort to him, but in a year things will not be so difficult for him. He will have adjusted himself. When the time comes thee must decide for thyself what is right for thee to do."

"I will try very hard to do what I think thee

would want," I said. "Thee can be sure of that, Mother. I give thee my promise."

"It is a great comfort to me to know that thee will be with thy father for this next year at least. Now we might turn on the light," she said, ending the conversation.

I had not a moment for thinking until after I had said good night to my mother, but none the less through my activity I was conscious deep down in my heart of sadness greater than any I had ever felt. When I had shut the door of my little room I undressed quickly and went to bed, knowing that I must save my strength, and only after I was stretched out between the sheets did I face the despair that rose up to overwhelm me. I felt as if my mother had already died. The voice that had spoken to me so quietly had seemed the voice of her disembodied spirit.

If only it were possible to give my life in exchange for my mother's life, how gladly would I do so! I loved her enough for that and really I owed her my life in expiation. Was I not partly responsible for her death, solely responsible perhaps? I shared the conviction I had heard voiced by Carey that my mother's illness was due to the great number of children she had borne. Suckling at her breast, one after the other, we had given my mother a mortal wound. And her life, cut short by us, had been devoted year by year to caring for us. As I thought of my mother's death I compared her life with Aunt Hannah's life. Bitterly I coveted for my mother all the power and influence her sister had possessed, the fun she had and my

mother had missed. The baby who had died, Frank, and I should never have come into the world. Above all I should never have been born, never, never.

Of some such thoughts was woven the tangle of my inner torment as I lay awake in my bed. I could not call to God for help. My thoughts sheered away from Him. To deny consciously the existence of the God of justice and mercy and love in whom my mother believed would have been to separate myself in spirit from her, but in my mind and heart there was no God. When my mother died I would be utterly alone. My father loved me I knew, and in some measure relied on me, but Frank would take my mother's place for him in so far as anyone could. In Frank he would find his real consolation. There was nothing left that I could live for. Not until the faint light of dawn began to gather in the corners of the room did I fall asleep at last.

I awoke in the morning calm and composed. Things were as they were and must be endured. With the desperate concentration of overtaxed strength I gave my attention to whatever I had to do, whether caring for my mother or directing the servants or preparing for my examinations. Very rapidly now my mother's strength ebbed away. Her pain seemed assuaged as the disease extended through her body. She was calm in spirit and bore her weakness with unbroken patience. In June we took her up to the mountains; she became suddenly worse and there in the house she had built and loved she died before Harry could

333

reach her. The farewell they had said to each other five months before had been farewell indeed.

Every member of her family rejoiced in my mother's release from her weakness and the terrible threat of pain. Not even my father would have kept her with him for another day or another hour. We now rejoiced in the fast that we had tried so hard to prevent because by reducing her strength it seemed to have hastened her death. Only the servants indulged in excessive weeping.

Calm like the rest in the daytime, I was at night the victim of a terrible dream. I rode on the top of some kind of open carriage, filled with benches and crowded with people. At terrible speed this coach, swinging from side to side, dashed along a curved road, and then suddenly it overturned, hurling all the people in wide arcs through the air. The next moment I found myself standing upright alone among prostrate bodies, the only survivor. Near me lay a woman's body on its face, sprawled limp and lifeless. I bent down, turned the body over and looked in its face. It was a great doll, not a woman. It had never been alive. Shaking with terror and sobbing, I awoke. This dream recurred night after night, and night after night my horror was the same.

All emotion seemed to have gone out of the waking world. The promise I had made to my mother was the only thing that remained to me. It supplied my only motive for living, the sole incentive to action. I bothered about nothing, hoped for nothing except to be faithful to my mother. I now reacted not at all or only listlessly

to things that would formerly have sent me into a state of high excitement. My father, my brothers and sisters were each absorbed in bearing the grief of my mother's loss; all except Frank had also well-defined duties and responsibilities, and Frank, though now a boy of fifteen, hardly more than a year younger than I, was too much devoted to my father to understand the significance of what had happened to us. Small wonder that my listlessness failed to attract the attention of my family. Indeed, it tended further to divert attention from me, since I no longer stood up for myself, no longer made the lively protest that used to burst from me under provocation. In the family group I had now become, as it were, anonymous.

1416